The Professional Lives of Language Study Abroad Alumni

NEW PERSPECTIVES ON LANGUAGE AND EDUCATION
Founding Editor: Viv Edwards, *University of Reading, UK*
Series Editors: Phan Le Ha, *University of Hawaii at Manoa, USA* and Joel Windle, *Monash University, Australia.*

Two decades of research and development in language and literacy education have yielded a broad, multidisciplinary focus. Yet education systems face constant economic and technological change, with attendant issues of identity and power, community and culture. What are the implications for language education of new 'semiotic economies' and communications technologies? Of complex blendings of cultural and linguistic diversity in communities and institutions? Of new cultural, regional and national identities and practices? The New Perspectives on Language and Education series will feature critical and interpretive, disciplinary and multidisciplinary perspectives on teaching and learning, language and literacy in new times. New proposals, particularly for edited volumes, are expected to acknowledge and include perspectives from the Global South. Contributions from scholars from the Global South will be particularly sought out and welcomed, as well as those from marginalized communities within the Global North.

All books in this series are externally peer-reviewed.

Full details of all the books in this series and of all our other publications can be found on http://www.multilingual-matters.com, or by writing to Multilingual Matters, St Nicholas House, 31-34 High Street, Bristol, BS1 2AW, UK.

NEW PERSPECTIVES ON LANGUAGE AND EDUCATION: 113

The Professional Lives of Language Study Abroad Alumni

A Mixed Methods Investigation

**Celeste Kinginger and
Jingyuan Zhuang**

MULTILINGUAL MATTERS
Bristol • Jackson

DOI https://doi.org/10.21832/KINGIN2507
Library of Congress Cataloging in Publication Data
A catalog record for this book is available from the Library of Congress.
Names: Kinginger, Celeste, author. | Zhuang, Jingyuan, author.
Title: The Professional Lives of Language Study Abroad Alumni: A Mixed
   Methods Investigation/Celeste Kinginger and Jingyuan Zhuang.
Description: Bristol, UK; Jackson, TN: Multilingual Matters, 2023. |
   Series: New Perspectives on Language and Education: 113 | Includes
   bibliographical references and index. | Summary: 'This book investigates
   the impact of language learning and study abroad on the career options
   and choices of US-based alumni of all ages. International education
   experiences are shown to exert considerable influence on the aspirations
   and career paths of individuals, and the long-term benefits are clearly
   demonstrated in participant narratives' – Provided by publisher.
Identifiers: LCCN 2022054168 (print) | LCCN 2022054169 (ebook) | ISBN
   9781800412491 (paperback) | ISBN 9781800412507 (hardback) | ISBN
   9781800412521 (epub) | ISBN 9781800412514 (pdf)
Subjects: LCSH: Second language acquisition. | Language and
   languages – Study and teaching. | Language and languages – Economic
   aspects. | Foreign study. | College graduates – Employment – United
   States. | Career development.
Classification: LCC P118.2 .K533 2023 (print) | LCC P118.2 (ebook) | DDC
   410.23 – dc23/eng/20230131
LC record available at https://lccn.loc.gov/2022054168
LC ebook record available at https://lccn.loc.gov/2022054169

British Library Cataloguing in Publication Data
A catalogue entry for this book is available from the British Library.

ISBN-13: 978-1-80041-250-7 (hbk)
ISBN-13: 978-1-80041-249-1 (pbk)

Multilingual Matters
UK: St Nicholas House, 31-34 High Street, Bristol, BS1 2AW, UK.
USA: Ingram, Jackson, TN, USA.

Website: www.multilingual-matters.com
Twitter: Multi_Ling_Mat
Facebook: https://www.facebook.com/multilingualmatters
Blog: www.channelviewpublications.wordpress.com

Copyright © 2023 Celeste Kinginger and Jingyuan Zhuang.

All rights reserved. No part of this work may be reproduced in any form or by any means without permission in writing from the publisher.

The policy of Multilingual Matters/Channel View Publications is to use papers that are natural, renewable and recyclable products, made from wood grown in sustainable forests. In the manufacturing process of our books, and to further support our policy, preference is given to printers that have FSC and PEFC Chain of Custody certification. The FSC and/or PEFC logos will appear on those books where full certification has been granted to the printer concerned.

Typeset by Riverside Publishing Solutions.

Contents

Figures, Tables and Box vii
Simplified Transcription Conventions ix
Acknowledgements xi

1 Introduction and Literature Review 1
   1.1 Introduction 1
   1.2 Language Learning, Study Abroad and the Post-Sojourn Experience 4
   1.3 Key Elements in the History of US Study Abroad 15
   1.4 Conclusion 21

2 Research Design 23
   2.1 Introduction 23
   2.2 Survey Development 23
   2.3 Life History Typology Development 30
   2.4 Gathering and Analyzing Interview Data 34
   2.5 Conclusion 53

3 Using Languages at Work 54
   3.1 Introduction 54
   3.2 Using Languages at Work by the Numbers 54
   3.3 The Qualities of Language Use at Work Among Study Abroad Alumni 56
   3.4 Conclusion 86

4 Discovering a Calling 87
   4.1 Introduction 87
   4.2 Career Impact of Study Abroad by the Numbers 87
   4.3 Discovering a Calling 88
   4.4 Conclusion 100

5 Quests for Identity 102
   5.1 Introduction 102
   5.2 Motives for Language Learning and Study Abroad 103

	5.3	Quests for Identity	105
	5.4	Conclusion	122
6	Exploring Features of Study Abroad Programs		124
	6.1	Introduction	124
	6.2	Background: Contexts for Language Learning	124
	6.3	Program Duration	128
	6.4	Residence Options	134
	6.5	Returning Home	148
	6.6	Conclusion	152
7	Multilingual Dispositions and Lessons for Life		153
	7.1	Introduction	153
	7.2	Snapshots of Language Immersion Over Time During Study Abroad for Anglophone Students	153
	7.3	Becoming a Better Speaker of English as a Lingua Franca	155
	7.4	Unpredicted Benefits of Language Learning	159
	7.5	Conclusion	162
8	Conclusion		163
	8.1	Introduction	163
	8.2	Highlights	163
	8.3	Insights for Research	164
	8.4	Insights for Education	166
	8.5	Insights for Policy	168
	8.6	Insights for the Public	169
	8.7	Limitations of the Study	170
	8.8	Conclusion	171

Appendices	173
Appendix A: Full Version of the Survey	173
Appendix B: List of Project Partners	178
Appendix C: Topical Interview Guide	179
References	180
Index	189

Figures, Tables and Box

Figures

2.1	Overall flow of the survey	25
2.2	An example of a modalities map created by MCA	33
2.3	An example of an individuals map created by MCA	33
5.1	Reasons for language study as a function of age	104
5.2	Motives for study abroad	105
6.1	Contexts for language learning	125
6.2	Generational changes in contexts for language learning	126
6.3	Duration of study abroad programs by time period	130

Tables

2.1	List of the 10 most common providers of study abroad programs in the sample	27
2.2	Sources of funding for study abroad programs	27
2.3	List of the 10 most common destinations for study abroad in the sample	28
2.4	List of the 10 most common languages in the sample	28
2.5	Operationalization of SA participants' life pathways	31
2.6	Participant details and study abroad destinations	36
3.1	Study abroad and ability to use language for school or work	54
3.2	Work sectors of survey respondents	55
4.1	Descriptives for survey questions about the career impact of study abroad	87
4.2	Descriptives for survey questions about the career impact of study abroad as a function of age	88
5.1	Reasons for language study	103
6.1	Residence options during study abroad	135
6.2	Residence options during study abroad by respondents' age	135

6.3 Descriptives for survey questions about returning home
after study abroad 148

Box

2.1 Celeste Kinginger's social history and cognitive–emotional
position 45

Simplified Transcription Conventions

?	raised intonation
.	falling intonation
,	continuing intonation
(xxx)	unable to transcribe
<u>underline</u>	stress or increased volume
-	abrupt cut off with level speech
:	vowel elongation

Acknowledgements

A project of this scope and ambition would not have been possible without the support of many generous individuals and institutions.

Our sincere thanks go to the many individuals who took time from their schedules to complete our survey, and in particular to the 54 people who agreed to be interviewed for the project. Those who did not choose to remain anonymous include: Dr Bonnie Bisonnette, Valerie Buss-McNeill, Hailey Crowel, Dr Thomas Edell, Courtney Hale, Carmen Hernandez, Alexander Johnson, Dr Patrick Kelley, Mary Lambrecht, Andrea Levy, Hugh Lugg, Dr Laura McLary, Amelia Parenteau, Pamela Patterson, Anna Petrovskis, Dr Heather Rice, Peter Schmitt, Dr Kelsey Thrush, Antonia Zunarelli.

We are grateful for the contributions of Robert W. Schrauf and Kevin McManus, our colleagues in the Department of Applied Linguistics at the Pennsylvania State University. Robert W. Schrauf inspired the project's mixed-methods design and led the effort to develop the life pathways typology at its core.

American Councils for International Education, particularly Dan E. Davidson and Nadra Garas, provided invaluable assistance in the design and administration of the survey. The Forum on Education Abroad, especially Amelia Dietrich, led our survey recruitment effort with grace and aplomb. WPSU Public Television, specifically James Espy and Mindy McMahon, expertly produced our series of companion video profiles. These are housed by The Forum on Education Abroad https://forumea.org/resources/data-collection/careers-of-language-study-abroad-alumni-a-comprehensive-investigation/.

Sincere thanks also to Angela Tejada, our research assistant, and to the friends and colleagues who provided critical reviews of earlier drafts: Jeannette Bragger, Maryse Genier, Rosamond Mitchell and Rémi Adam van Compernolle. An anonymous reviewer also offered constructive and useful comments that advanced some of the arguments presented in this volume.

We are grateful to Professor Hirofumi Hosokawa for providing a clear and detailed explanation of Japanese politeness practices and to Scott McGinnis for help in recruiting through the Interagency Language Roundtable.

The project's Advisory Board included three prominent figures in international education and language learning, namely Maritheresa Frain, John Lucas and Meg Malone. We appreciate the expert guidance they provided, especially in the early stages of the project.

This research was developed under a grant from the US Department of Education. However, the contents do not necessarily represent the policy of the Department of Education, and you should not assume endorsement by the Federal government.

1 Introduction and Literature Review

1.1 Introduction

This project was inspired by a desire to defend and illustrate the value of language learning for US-based students in particular, as well as Anglophone students more generally, wherever 'linguistic myopia' may prevail (Lanvers *et al.*, 2021: 5). Early project discussions took place against a backdrop of disturbing news from the Modern Language Association of America, whose most recent report on enrollment in university-level world language courses in the US showed a downward trend, with a 15.3% overall decline since 2009 and the loss of 651 programs since 2013 (Looney & Lusin, 2019). With the onset of the Covid-19 pandemic, headlines were full of news about faculty furloughs and layoffs, mainly concentrated in humanities and social science departments (e.g. Hubler, 2020). Some glimmers of hope were emerging in the domain of policy, especially in *America's Languages*, a statement from the American Academy of Arts and Sciences (2017: viii) calling for renewed investment in language education on the grounds that the ability to use languages other than English is 'critical to success in business, research, and international relations in the twenty-first century.' Also emerging were clear and public-facing findings demonstrating the advantages of multilingualism, including enhanced literacy and academic achievement for children and protection from cognitive decline with age (Kroll & Dussias, 2017). As applied linguistics researchers, language educators and alumni of study abroad programs ourselves, we were eager to contribute our own efforts to advocacy for languages by documenting their relationship to career pathways and options (Kinginger, 2021).

Our own earlier research had also informed us of some limitations of prior scholarship to do with language learning in study abroad contexts. With some important exceptions, the vast majority of studies are small scale and short term, typically involving convenience samples. Also, in the interpretation of findings, sociocultural history is routinely ignored (Kinginger, 2019a). We know, for instance, that student sojourns have decreased in length over time (Institute of International Education, 2004, 2021a, 2021b), that increasing concerns for safety contribute to intrusive 'helicopter parenting' (Kinginger, 2008), that the evolution of technology and social networking have changed what it means to be in any particular place, and that the spread of English as a lingua franca has amplified pressure on Anglophone language learners to foreground that aspect of their identities in interactions abroad. Yet, researchers routinely assume that results from studies taking place decades ago are comparable with those of today. Finally, the post-study abroad experience had been so little investigated that it was termed a 'new frontier' (Plews, 2016). Few studies investigate the re-entry process, and even fewer look into the destinies of committed language learners after graduation, when they move on to further study or professional pursuits (but see Huensch et al., 2019; Mitchell et al., 2020). Our project attempted to address all three of these issues together. It is a mixed-methods study with a large-scale survey to generate robust quantitative evidence and a series of professional life history interviews to provide the richly representative autobiographical data that are only available through one-to-one conversations. Weaving together findings from these two sources, we can better understand both the longer-term impact of in-country language learning and the history of study abroad itself.

In the US, one prominent aspect of this history has in fact been the decoupling of language learning from study abroad. The traditional Junior Year Abroad involving language majors engaging in intensive pursuit of advanced proficiency is largely a thing of the past (although such experiences are represented in this book). Insight into this change is provided in the Institute for International Education's Open Doors Reports (Institute for International Education, 2007, 2021b). These data show that the percentage of language majors among students abroad decreased from 16.7% in 1985 to 4.9% in 2012, and from this point forward the category was merged with 'international studies' and ceased to exist as an independent measure. At present, the great majority of programs do not require or emphasize language ability, and formal assessment of proficiency is becoming less common. In 2017, according to The Forum on Education Abroad State of the Field survey, 12% of institutions and providers carried out pre- and post- language testing (Forum on Education Abroad, 2018); in the 2020 survey, that figure had been reduced to 8% (Amelia Dietrich, personal communication). Provider organizations and university offices of international education insist that language is not necessary for study abroad, where courses are offered in English and language instruction is often optional. Notably, this national trend has followed the dramatic expansion of English Medium Instruction within host institutions worldwide (Macaro et al., 2018), further eroding the perceived value of world language proficiency for US-based students while also limiting their access to academic registers and practices while they are abroad. For these reasons, we wished to defend and illustrate the specific benefits accruing to language learners in particular.

Thus, our stated aim was to explore the extent to which world language ability is valued, recognized, and cultivated across the lifespan; the extent to which this ability offers personal and professional opportunities and satisfactions; to what extent and how language ability is supported after study abroad; and the advantages and challenges that these learners experience. Because we are US-based educators, we understand 'study abroad' as 'a temporary sojourn of pre-defined duration, undertaken for educational purposes' (Kinginger, 2009: 11) within a degree program and normally involving coursework. Thus, other arrangements such as degree mobility or credit mobility following the European ERASMUS model are not treated here.

The study's sequential explanatory design (Creswell, 2015) called for an initial quantitative strand in the form of a survey, followed by a qualitative strand in the form of professional life history interviews. For the first phase, we collaborated with the American Councils for International Education for expertise in survey design and administration and The Forum on Education Abroad for recruitment. After the survey results were gathered ($N = 4899$), a typology of career/ life history pathways was developed using an exploratory statistical approach known as multiple correspondence analysis (Schrauf, 2013, 2016). This typology guided the selection of interviewees from among the 2741 individuals who had agreed to be contacted for this purpose. The typology provided a robust, structural link between the phases of the project and ensured that the sample of interviewees would be representative of the participants as a whole group. Prior to and during the onset of the pandemic, a total of 54 interviews were conducted, mainly via Zoom. During qualitative analysis, the interview materials were re-constructed from raw data as written 'meta-narratives' (Riessman, 1993) and interpreted as stories of developmental drama in the tradition of cultural–historical theory. These narratives were forwarded to participants for review and/or amendment as necessary, then corrected and written into this volume.

In this book we present our materials by major theme emerging from combined survey and interview analysis. Chapter 2 (Research Design) provides an overview of the study's research methodology as well as basic survey findings on demographics, funding sources, organizations, destinations, and languages studied. Chapter 3 (Using Languages at Work) features narratives from individuals who require language abilities to carry out their work in education, business, healthcare, government service, international development, engineering, sports and the arts. This chapter also includes survey information on employment sectors, opinions about the contribution of study abroad to work-related language ability, how many alumni use world languages on the job, and which languages they use. In Chapter 4 (Discovering a Calling) we present survey findings on the extent to which participants believe that study abroad has enhanced their competitiveness on the job market and on the relationship between study abroad and selection of employer type. These are combined with narratives of individuals who found their vocations through study abroad. In Chapter 5 (Quests for Identity) we examine survey takers' reasons for language learning and study abroad along with stories about exploration of heritage and other identities. Chapter 6 (Exploring Features of Study Abroad Programs) presents survey findings on the length and number of sojourns abroad reported in our data. Also included are statistics on residence options, the experience of campus re-entry, and contexts for language learning. For each of these themes we complement the survey findings with corresponding interviewee narratives. In Chapter 7 (Multilingual Dispositions and Lessons for Life) we consider ancillary benefits from the process and challenges of language learning for strategic thinking, learning in other domains, and intercultural skills, especially proficiency in English as a lingua franca for the internationalized, multilingual workplace. In the concluding chapter, we summarize our findings and consider their implications for policy, further research and informing the public about the value of language study abroad.

In this chapter we situate our study with respect to previous research in related areas. We provide a review of prior surveys on outcomes of international education from adjacent fields. We contextualize our project within the literature on language learning and study abroad in our own field of applied linguistics, particularly selected research on the post-study abroad experience, studies adopting a narrative or life history approach, and emerging mixed-methods approaches. Also presented is a brief overview of relevant historical information about US-based study abroad in the period under consideration, including the economics of international education from the consumer's point of view, the evolution of technology, and the spread of English.

1.2 Language Learning, Study Abroad and the Post-Sojourn Experience

Since the 1960s, researchers have devoted considerable effort to investigating study abroad as a context for language learning. This research has generally followed wider trends in the fields of second language acquisition, applied linguistics and language education. Kinginger (2009) traced the history of these efforts by documenting the emergence of various strands of inquiry, most of which have retained their relevance over time. The earliest studies employed holistic constructs such as general proficiency, fluency or skills, usually assessed via tests or other measurement instruments. After communicative competence gained ground as a model for language ability in the 1970s and 1980s, researchers began to investigate how study abroad influences separate components of that model, such as grammatical competence, lexical range, speech acts and other dimensions of pragmatics, or communication strategies. The late 1990s ushered in a new emphasis on qualitative approaches to study abroad research, with ethnographic or other case studies of instruction, residence options such as homestays, or service encounters and other informal settings. Subsequently, with the rise of research on the performance of identities in particular settings, scholars turned their attention to the kinds of interaction taking place in specific contexts such as homestay dinner tables. The research to date at the time clearly demonstrated that study abroad can be useful for the development of every domain of language competence, but particularly so for abilities that are related to experience of 'real life' social interaction. However, one constant is findings of important individual differences in outcomes traceable in part to variable qualities of sojourns as settings for learning.

Especially since the 1995 publication of Freed's *Second Language Acquisition in a Study Abroad Context*, the first thematic edited volume on this topic, scholarly interest has grown to the point where there now exists a dedicated journal (*Study Abroad Research in Second Language Acquisition and International Education*), a handbook (Sanz & Morales-Front, 2018), and a special interest group of the International Association for Applied Linguistics. Recent comprehensive reviews of the literature (Isabelli-García *et al.*, 2018; Marijuan & Sanz, 2018) indicate that while the above-listed strands are still actively pursued, study abroad researchers continually adopt new theoretical frameworks (e.g. dynamic systems theory), research designs (e.g. mixed-methods) and techniques (e.g. harvesting data from social media platforms). To properly summarize this research now would require more than one volume.

To the extent that study abroad research addresses an audience of language educators, it makes sense that it would attend mainly to questions to do with preparation or the nature of the experience itself, that is, domains over which educators might exert some control, such as pre-programmatic abilities or the effects of social contact (Taguchi & Collentine, 2018). In the meantime, however, a small but vocal group of scholars has drawn attention to the relative paucity of studies examining the afterlife of language study abroad, specifically. For Coleman (2013), funding constraints (to which we would add institutional constraints such as tenure clocks or pre-established timeframes for graduate degrees) have limited the extent to which the long-term and 'life-changing' impact of study abroad is explored: 'Humans are the longest lived of all primates, and the impact of significant life events is not restricted to the immediate aftermath, or even a post-test delayed by a few months.' Yet, the number of studies on this topic is 'woefully short' (Coleman, 2013: 27). A few years later, Plews (2016) took up this issue in a call for recognition of the post-sojourn as a new 'frontier,' articulating a set of heretofore rarely addressed questions:

> How do study abroad participants maintain sojourn-related language gains upon and after their return to the domestic environment? How do they fend off language forgetting? Which types of new cultural and intercultural knowledge developed on study abroad become mobilized in the domestic environment? How and why? Which study abroad experiences, perspectives, and identity positions stay with participants in the long term? Which aspects become renegotiated over time by their ongoing lives in the home setting? How do former study abroad participants perceive themselves in their home environment with regard to multilingualism and intercultural competence? (Plews, 2016: 3)

In a similar vein, Tullock (2018) concluded his essay on identity and study abroad with a call for more longitudinal studies and a focus on the lifelong dynamics of identity development. Only such studies can reveal, for example, 'whether short-term sojourns in which little identity development seems to have taken place are in fact the launching points for long-term transnational identities, as is often expected and hoped for by SA stakeholders and advocates of international education' (Tullock, 2018: 271).

1.2.1 Prior surveys of Anglophone study abroad alumni

In fact, outside the fields of applied linguistics and language learning it is not the case that the afterlife of study abroad has been neglected. Among international educators, there is a robust tradition of survey-based research examining an array of constructs to do with personal, intellectual, intercultural or professional development. Studies indicate increased academic focus among returning students (Hadis, 2005), enhanced intercultural competence (Rexeisen *et al.*, 2008; Salisbury *et al.*, 2013), civic engagement (DeGraaf *et al.*, 2013; Mitic, 2020), and openness to other cultures or increased tolerance of ambiguity (Bakalis & Joiner, 2004; Tracy-Ventura *et al.*, 2016). Study abroad has also been shown to prepare and orient students towards international careers (Franklin, 2010; Orahood *et al.*, 2004), with some research demonstrating that the experience abroad has a long-term impact on students' later academic achievement, career direction and intercultural and personal development (Dwyer, 2004; Geyer *et al.*, 2017; Norris & Gillespie, 2009).

The SAGE project used a mixed methods 'tracer' design alongside life story interviews to investigate study abroad impacts on global engagement (Paige *et al.*, 2009). Five dimensions of global engagement were investigated: domestic or international civic engagement, knowledge production, philanthropy, social entrepreneurship, and voluntary simplicity (e.g.

limiting consumption out of concern for the environment). A total of 6391 3-to-45-year alumni from 22 programs were surveyed. A significant proportion of this group had become globally engaged, productive members of society who were civically involved, practiced environmentally aware lifestyles, and made contributions of labor or financial resources to philanthropic causes. Study participants also pursued graduate education at a higher rate than that of the general undergraduate population. Murphy *et al.* (2014) carried out a similar project with a control group of students who had not studied abroad. Findings showed no difference between the groups for social entrepreneurship or knowledge production, generally higher levels of global engagement for the study abroad group on other dimensions, and a strikingly higher propensity for the study abroad group to be involved in internationally oriented leisure activities.

Surveys aimed at gathering information about long-term impact specifically from former language students also exist but are far fewer in number. The project perhaps most aligned with our own in goals and method is a sequence of two surveys, with associated qualitative data collection, reported in Fantini (2019). The surveys were addressed to alumni of programs organized by the Experiment in International Living (EIL) as part of an effort to refine definitions of Intercultural Communicative Competence (ICC), explore the development of ICC during sojourns abroad, and assess the impact of these sojourns in adult lives. Fantini notes the extent to which intercultural abilities are discussed, defined and assessed in Anglophone contexts without reference to the role of language, and clearly outlines why ICC cannot be achieved without investment in language learning:

> Because linguacultures configure worldview components differently, many cross-cultural differences are revealed only through the host language – not in translation, not through interpreters, and not through one's own tongue [...] educational exchange programs and intercultural constructs must address and include the fundamental role that language plays in human life and its role in accessing our own and other views of the world. (Fantini, 2019: 18)

Accordingly, the surveys designed for the project query personal characteristics, intercultural abilities, communication style and self-reported language proficiency. Following an initial effort involving member organizations and alumni in Ecuador, Switzerland and Great Britain, which served as a pilot study, in 2015–2016 the project recruited similar participants in Brazil ($N = 591$), Germany ($N = 526$), Ireland ($N = 111$), Japan ($N = 338$) and the US ($N = 384$) who had experienced intercultural sojourns in more than 22 countries. In reporting highlights from the findings, Fantini notes the commonalities across the five national origins represented in the study. These findings show a robust impact on personal and professional life and the importance of a positive disposition and attitudes. Further, the homestay, when available, is the 'most powerful component of the program,' frequently termed 'transformative' (Fantini, 2019: 226). Finally, developing proficiency in the host language is consistently identified by alumni as a significant and necessary program aspect; even if participants found certain languages challenging (e.g. Polish, Japanese) their efforts to learn were appreciated. 'It is clear that language is a fundamental ICC component and a direct pathway to gaining access to another worldview' (Fantini, 2019: 227). The survey findings also demonstrate that language learning provided long-term benefits in education, life and work.

Davidson and Lehmann (2001–2005) report on a survey of 701 alumni of programs in Russia overseen by the American Council on the Teaching of Russian from 1976 to 2000. Among other topics, the survey queried education and employment history, details about contexts for learning Russian, general employment preferences and attitudes toward language study. The findings indicated that intrinsic motives for learning Russian outweighed instrumental goals such as meeting a requirement, and that 29% of respondents had participated in more than one program. In evaluating the impact of these programs, a majority described study abroad as 'incomparably better' than US-based programs for language learning and for knowledge of Russian society, also rating this experience as highly significant in comparison to other aspects of their education. Fully 71% of these alumni were of the option that it is 'crucial' for young Americans to study languages. Although data on employment per se are not presented in this work, the authors mention a large percentage of alumni who work neither in academia nor in government jobs: 'They have a much more diverse employment profile than had been previously assumed' (Davidson & Lehmann, 2001–2005: 215).

Coleman and Chafer (2011) conducted a survey of 35 British alumni of educational work placements or teaching assignments in Senegal who had graduated from university between 1998 and 2010. The project aimed to describe features of the context and of students' experiences, and to trace the long-term impact of this experience on the attitudes, employment and life paths of the participants. Highlights among the results include significant use of French in-sojourn, with a median number of days per week using that language of 6 and anecdotal evidence suggesting that these students performed well on oral language assessments upon their return, all of which argues for the benefits of study in countries where the language under study is a lingua franca. Most respondents (81%) also claimed to have achieved some proficiency in the dominant local language, Wolof; particularly for those who stayed for a full academic year, this had a significant impact on social integration locally. The participants reported various forms of engagement with local people as well as other international students or co-workers and the expatriate community. Overall, while the participants found their sojourns to be challenging, particularly as concerns incidents related to gender and ethnicity, consensus was that the stay was highly valuable, 'often awakening an enduring love of Africa while shaping a level of understanding and empathy which are a true mark of education in its fullest sense' (Coleman & Chafer, 2011: 86). Moreover, all the respondents claimed to have used the linguistic and intercultural skills learned in Dakar in their professional lives; nearly all have pursued careers with an international dimension, and half work in non-governmental or charitable organizations.

1.2.2 The post-language study abroad experience of Anglophone learners in qualitative and multiple-methods research

Within language education, there is a sparse but growing body of qualitative and multiple-methods literature on the post-study abroad experience and on longer-term life stories of language learners. In an oft-cited paper, Alred and Byram (2002) report on interviews with British Year Abroad participants 10 years after their sojourn. They found that the Year Abroad can serve as a long-term 'reference point' (Alred & Byram, 2002: 351) in the discovery of otherness, pushing some toward enhanced international engagement and intercultural learning and others toward confirmation of belonging at home. Further, early life experiences of otherness (termed 'tertiary socialization') tend to predict subsequent development of intercultural mediation knowledge and ability. Alred and Byram point to the potential of training in techniques of ethnographic observation to democratize and enhance learning. Similarly, Jackson (e.g. 2018) has written extensively on the importance of pedagogical intervention, including ethnography (Jackson, 2006) for both sojourners and returnees as they pursue proficiency, intercultural abilities and global mindedness over the longer term.

Allen (2013) followed three US-based learners of French from their home-based classroom experiences in the US, through study abroad in Nantes in a program organized by their university, and three years later, after they had entered the job market. Her primary interest was in the maintenance of motivation and the development of self-regulatory strategies. Her findings show that participants all experienced some degree of demotivation in post-SA classrooms at home. However, during study abroad they overcame folk notions of learning by osmosis and learned the significance of agentic behavior and strategies for language learning, carrying these forward into new pursuits. One went on to teach English in Russia, developing some proficiency in Russian which he then could use, along with French, at work for an international development company. Another served in the Peace Corps in Francophone Africa, then joined a charitable organization focusing on education, a post requiring frequent travel to Haiti. The third experienced significant alienation as a candidate for a master's degree in French literature and left that field to become an editor of French and German language textbooks. Thus, all three participants' professional choices 'reflect their ongoing engagement with using FLs [foreign languages] and the varied meaningful avenues beyond academia open to advanced FL learners in the 21st century' (Allen, 2013: 69). Notably, however, these participants' goals were mainly related to spoken French rather than to advanced literacy in that language.

Some potential sources of post-study abroad classroom demotivation are illustrated in Lee and Kinginger's (2018) ethnographic study of language program reintegration by an advanced learner of Chinese at a US university (see also Winke & Gass, 2018). Enrolled in a third-year course after a semester in Shanghai, 'Kevin' at first drew the admiration of classmates who had not studied abroad for his apparent fluency, and the teacher relied on his anecdotes about China to enliven faltering discussions. Soon, however, tensions arose during small-group work as Kevin quickly completed tasks while his classmates were still attempting to understand them. He became disenchanted with the course materials, particularly mandatory China Central Television videos illustrating elevated political registers, and began to wax nostalgic about the direct, immediate applicability of the language he had learned abroad. His motive for participating in the class then further devolved, from desire to develop further proficiency to 'doing to get it done' (Lee & Kinginger, 2018: 589). For the final project, which was supposed to be a survey of Chinese and Americans on a marriage-related topic, Kevin's disenchantment was such that he prepared none of the required materials but instead presented a videorecording of himself playing the roles of interviewer and participant, and re-hashing previously voiced memories of Shanghai.

The longitudinal Languages and Social Networks Abroad project (LANGSNAP) (Mitchell *et al.*, 2017) followed 56 French or Spanish specialists enrolled in a research-intensive British university over the course of 21 months, including a compulsory year abroad in France, Mexico or Spain. Language tests, questionnaires and interviews were employed at regular intervals to yield a broad array of findings about linguistic progress and identity development. Overall, the participants made substantial progress in fluency, accuracy and lexis and retained these gains after returning home. Their motives for investment in language, unlike the instrumental goals of many L2 English learners, derived from a desire to be 'different' (Mitchell *et al.*, 2017: 327) compared to monoglot Anglophones and from positive experiences with classroom learning at an early age. Among the many significant findings of this study is an unambiguous portrayal of successful learners as those who exhibit flexibility, resilience, emotional engagement in any setting (homestay, classroom, workplace, or recreational affinity groups) and 'a clear vision of the ideal multilingual self' (Mitchell *et al.*, 2017: 247). Also notable, and in line with the findings of Allen (2013), is the participants' emphasis on spoken, interactive language proficiency at the expense of formal, academic literacy.

Data were collected for a LANGSNAP follow-up study from 33 of the original participants, three years after graduation, once they had entered the job market (Mitchell *et al.*, 2020). Participants completed the same language assessments previously used as well as a questionnaire about post-university life options and choices, interviews in English (L1) and L2, and a Language Engagement Questionnaire querying contexts and amounts of language use. As reported by Huensch *et al.* (2019), Tracy-Ventura *et al.* (2020) and McManus *et al.* (2021), most of these participants had retained their L2 proficiency, oral fluency and vocabulary. Mitchell *et al.* (2020) examine the extent to which multilingual identities are maintained in the longer term for these graduates, taking up the tripartite framework proposed by Benson *et al.* (2013) to account for L2 identity development in study abroad. The framework includes identity-related L2 proficiency (sociopragmatic or interactional competence related to successful self-presentation), linguistic self-concept (self-efficacy and status as L2 learner/user), and L2-related personal competence (independence and agency). Findings indicate that while all participants had undertaken paid employment in some form, entry into the labor market was 'not straightforward,' with many employment transitions and interruptions. Only seven were committed to career paths involving regular languages use, such as teaching, interpreting, diplomacy, or business abroad. Findings on identity-related L2 proficiency showed that the participants continued to value speaking and interactive abilities in multilingual work settings or, for those pursuing monolingual careers, leisure activities. Academic literacy remained a marginal pursuit, with English a constant alternative choice for social or professional purposes. As for linguistic self-concept, participants attributed growth in independence, self-confidence and problem-solving ability to study abroad, and many also expressed the belief that study abroad had enhanced their employability by demonstrating their personal flexibility and international stance. The participants' linguistic self-concept included their awareness of a privileged status as Anglophones and as voluntary multilinguals who could flexibly navigate multilingual settings, including the use of English as a lingua franca. The authors note significant thematic continuity across the entire longitudinal study; for example, participants who had developed emotional ties with locals during study abroad retained a commitment to bilingualism. They also suggest that downplaying academic literacy during study abroad programs can lead to subsequent decisions to pursue English-medium post-graduate training and thus to limitations on multilingual career options.

A subsequent case study emerging from this project (Güney & Tracy-Ventura, 2021) clearly demonstrates the value of longitudinal research on language learning in study abroad. 'Elizabeth' was one of the initial LANGSNAP participants whose linguistic development was limited during her first extended sojourn in Spain. Elizabeth worked as an English-language teacher in a Basque-medium school, lived in shared accommodations with other Anglophones and, overall, had very limited contact with Spanish. During a post-sojourn interview, she expressed awareness of lost language learning opportunities. Two years after graduation, Elizabeth relocated to Madrid, working as an au pair, and then as an English teacher. This time, she built an environment more propitious for learning Spanish, finding an apartment with Spanish-speaking peers, and devoting leisure time to interaction in that language. By 2019, her Spanish proficiency had outstripped the group mean in many skills. Because Elizabeth attributed her later choice to the initial experience during her university years, the authors argue that the impact of study abroad on the lives of participants may remain invisible in shorter-term studies.

1.2.3 Life histories of Anglophone language learners

Two projects have investigated the long-term impact of language learning in study abroad contexts through narrative analysis of life stories. Coffey and Street (2008) examined the accounts of two British adults who had achieved high levels of proficiency in French or German, aiming to understand how these individuals performed their 'language learning project' in narrative through discursive representation of social structures meshed with accounts of personal experience. The authors requested a written language learning autobiography, then conducted in-person semi-structured interviews. To analyze these data, they first identified elements (people, places or events) presented as salient in shaping the learning process, then described the 'overarching narrative character' (Coffey & Street, 2008: 456) or performative meta-narrative of the stories. One such meta-narrative is the tale of escape from the ordinary in which participants' life paths expand outwards, away from physically and psychologically restrictive places of origin and toward the excitement, novelty and glamor of urban or foreign locales. For example, in characterizing herself as 'an Essex girl' (Coffey & Street, 2008: 457), 'Sue' indexed her humble and conventional working-class origins which she then contrasted with the sophisticated worldliness she encountered in France and the 'Catherine Deneuve-type woman' who hosted her there. Another meta-narrative references cosmopolitanism and the privilege of the non-native speaker (Kramsch, 2003) to abandon first-language cultural conventions and the scrutiny that can accompany them. For Sue, whose pronunciation in English betrays her blue-collar background, speaking French has transformed her into a flexible, adaptable 'chameleon' (Coffey & Street, 2008: 460). In contrast, 'Paul' crafted a story of excitement transforming him from a shy and downtrodden child into an intrepid adventurer. Both participants claimed to have enjoyed their involvement in the study, and that it had prompted them to reflect on their prior actions.

In a more recent study, Menard-Warwick (2019) conducted life-history interviews with 37 US-based adults, aged early twenties to late sixties, who had learned languages other than English and had used these languages for professional purposes or volunteer work. Of these, half had studied abroad. In this work, the author explores the affordances of study abroad for the development of translingual identity, per Canagarajah (2013), the ability to 'employ an expanding repertoire of semiotic resources in the interests of meaning-making across linguistic boundaries' (Menard-Warwick, 2019: 85). In this work, study abroad is reconceptualized from a site of potential language immersion to a contact zone characterized by multiple competing language varieties; a locus of conflict but also of collaboration where socialization into translingual practice can occur. Associated with translingual identities are cosmopolitan relations, including dispositions toward alignment with diverse interlocutors and willingness to withhold judgment of others' language use. An initial thematic analysis revealed the salience of study abroad in the data, and the material related to that topic was then re-coded around types of experience believed to enhance language development, such as engagement in local communicative practices or specific program features. Finally, the author extracted narrative episodes illustrating the influence of identity, learning and local engagement. 'Bill' recounted study in Barcelona in 1966–1967, with no language-related preparation. There he found a life mentor in the Spanish tutor hired by family friends, a Tunisian 'man about town' in his thirties who ran a boutique with his French wife. Rather than merely serving as a language tutor, this man became 'a role model for the cosmopolitan masculinities that Bill now realized he could cultivate' and 'played a major role in transforming this beer drinking racist rural Texas boy into the bilingual retired Oregonian educator that he is now' (Menard-Warwick, 2019: 88). By contrast to the serendipity characterizing Bill's experience, as a Japanese major 'Shana' (study abroad context: Japan, 2011) deliberately crafted an experience to maximize her language learning, committing to joining and participating regularly in a karate club, which gave her a sense of local collective identity. The remaining two cases examine engagement in the homestay ('Vivien') and 'Marc's' sociology class which required service learning with a program serving the homeless; Marc developed relationships not only with other students but also with people living on the streets who spoke 'every type of Spanish' (Menard-Warwick, 2019: 91). Notably, in each case there is a clear link between the qualities of these experiences and later professional endeavor. Bill became a teacher of immigrant youth, Shana's Japanese proficiency later helped her to secure employment with a localization company soon after graduation, Vivien is an immigration lawyer, and Marc works for a Bolivian NGO focused on alleviating poverty.

1.2.4 The emergence of mixed-methods research

King and Mackey (2016: 210) note that 'some of the key findings and rich lines of investigation in second language research have emerged from the layering of multiple research perspectives.' By 'layering' they mean 'explicit consideration of research problems from a range of distinct epistemological perspectives.' As an example, they point to Schmidt's Noticing Hypothesis (1990), which emerged through a combination of a diary study and analysis of output during Schmidt's own learning of Portuguese in Brazil (Schmidt & Frota, 1986). It is also the case that some of the most impactful projects in study abroad research have involved both quantitative and qualitative methods (Kinginger & Schrauf, 2023). These include the well-known 'predictors' study, correlating growth in Russian language proficiency with other factors (Brecht *et al.*, 1995), and three qualitative companion studies on the effects of gender (Polanyi, 1995), folklinguistic theories (Miller & Ginsberg, 1995) and student perceptions of the value of instruction (Brecht & Robinson, 1995). Other examples include Isabelli-García's (2006) use of oral proficiency scores in combination with interviews, diaries and network contact logs during study abroad in Argentina to launch the study of social networks for language learning abroad, Kinginger's (2008) case studies of individual learners of French bolstered by quantitative measures of proficiency and language awareness, or Brown's (2013) use of discourse completion tasks in comparison to naturally-occurring conversation in the study of developing pragmatic ability in Korean.

Meanwhile, in the social sciences more broadly, scholars have been increasingly drawn to the principled integration of quantitative and qualitative data and analysis, or mixed-methods, and there now exists an extensive literature exploring possibilities for innovative and creative research design (e.g. Schrauf, 2016). A key distinction in mixed-methods studies is between sequential and concurrent designs. In a sequential design, quantitative and qualitative data (or 'strands') are collected one after the other, and the data collection and analysis from the first strand influences the data collection and analysis from the second strand. In an explanatory sequential design, quantitative data are collected first, and are then illuminated or explained by qualitative data. An exploratory sequential design begins with qualitative data, and those findings helping to shape subsequent quantitative measures. In concurrent designs, quantitative and qualitative data are collected simultaneously, and there is no mutual influence at that stage. However, and crucially in all mixed-methods projects, investigators bring together the results of analyses (i.e. statistical for quantitative; interpretive for qualitative). They do so at various 'points of interface,' which can include the overall research design itself, sampling strategies, data collection, analysis and inference.

Principled mixed-methods research in applied linguistics is, as yet, somewhat rare and potentially misunderstood. Riazi and Candlin (2014) reviewed several applied linguistics studies claiming mixed methods and found that some among these failed to achieve the systematic integration that this new paradigm requires, using one or another approach merely for 'embellishment,' usually of a primarily quantitative study (Riazi & Candlin, 2014: 155; see also Riazi, 2017). However, mixed-methods research is beginning to find its way into overviews of literature on language learning in study abroad, such as Isabelli-García *et al.* (2018: 448) who refer to it as a 'fruitful and growing approach,' or Marijuan and Sanz (2018) who view it as a desideratum. Some examples include the concurrent design of the above-described LANGSNAP project (Mitchell *et al.*, 2017), where the researchers used quantitative scores to identify learners who had made the most progress for detailed qualitative case studies, and the sophisticated exploratory sequential design in Durbidge (2020) using statistical analysis of survey results to assess the representativeness of focal cases among Japanese learners of English. As outlined in the next chapter, the current project has an explanatory sequential design with a prominent sampling point of interface, using multiple correspondence analysis (quantitative) to model survey participants within a statistically generated map of their study abroad experiences and current professional positions for the research purpose of drawing a representative sample of interesting cases for interviews (qualitative).

1.3 Key Elements in the History of US Study Abroad

At the time of data collection, our youngest participants were still enrolled in undergraduate degree programs, with only plans or dreams of careers to report, whereas some older participants had retired or were contemplating retirement. Accounts of education, study abroad and careers were all somewhat influenced by the historical period in which these events took place. The survey's cross-sectional design provides a synchronic snapshot in 2019 of study abroad alumni from the 1970s through the 2000s. Since participant age and years-since-study abroad are roughly equivalent, it is possible to consider the sociocultural and political contexts of participants' study abroad experiences. The seven age-categories in the study range from Under 25 with study abroad around 2015 (Trump, Hunger Games, iPhone 6, gas at $3.80/gallon) to Over 60 with study abroad around 1975 (Vietnam, Jaws, Apollo-Soyuz, gas at 44 cents/gallon). While in this volume it is not possible to contextualize the study fully in terms of broad sociocultural zeitgeists, here we briefly consider some elements of historical evolution in the nature of the American study abroad experience that exerted obvious influence on our data. Some of these are plainly factual, such as the economics of higher education, the spread of English as a lingua franca, and the emergence of technologies for travel and communication. In addition, we examine the role of historically rooted ideology in shaping interpretations of study abroad as an adventure or a modern-day Grand Tour. Specific policies and geopolitical events are also important and may be considered in future interpretations of our data; for now we refer the reader to Dietrich (2018) or Keller and Frain (2010) for detailed treatment of these topics.

Economists Cressey and Stubbs (2010) document a dramatic rise in the cost of study abroad and of higher education in general over the course of the 20th and early 21st centuries, with this increase far outpacing the cost of living generally. For example, with statistics from the US Department of Education (National Center for Education Statistics, 2007), they analyze average costs of tuition, room and board at public and private colleges from 1965 to 2007. The cost of attending a public university for one semester rose from $526 in 1965 to $7,102 in 2007; adjusted for inflation, the 1965 amount is the equivalent of $3,461 2007 dollars, meaning that tuition at public universities increased at a rate of double the rate of inflation generally. For private institutions, the increase was steeper (from $1,101 in 1965 to $19,200 in 2007). In examining study abroad, they conclude that costs have increased as well, though not as dramatically as the price of education in general. Whereas early study abroad programs were often faculty led and relatively simple to manage, over time and with growing awareness of safely and health issues these programs have become more complex and therefore costly, requiring for example administrative expertise, health and legal services, organized social and cultural activities, and staff development and professionalization. The authors also note that, as opposed to their parents, students in the early 2000s tended to demand constant access to technology, via a bewildering 'assortment of gadgets deemed critical for today's college experience' (Cressey & Stubbs, 2010: 280), whose functions are now largely assumed by the mobile phone. If they are studying in less developed countries, they claim, American students are not interested in local integration if that translates as overcrowded dorms without air conditioning and bad food. Maintaining their US-based standard of living can be expensive, particularly for students who rely on employment to finance their education and face loss of income while abroad. The key point here, for our purposes, is that in general higher education and study abroad were far less costly and weighed less heavily on family budgets for our older than for our younger participants.

Recent discussion of the role of technology in shaping the quality of study abroad experiences has naturally centered on the rise of digital communication and social networking platforms, which have changed the meaning of such basic phenomena as 'place' and 'reality.' Like all inventions, these technologies have both positive and negative consequences. For example, and perhaps most obviously for study abroad, ease in maintaining contact with friends and family at home both increases students' sense of security and decreases their ability to develop independent survival skills. It is easy to forget that the period represented in our study, roughly 1975 to 2015, was characterized by mass adoption of many new technologies, from the daisy wheel printer or the Walkman personal cassette player of the 1970s to Zoom and the iPhone of the 2010s. Each in turn, these technologies had their impact on language learning and study abroad. The introduction of the reel-to-reel tape player in the 1960s made it possible to present the spoken voices of expert speakers. Donatelli (2010) points out that the jumbo jet, introduced in 1970, first replaced the then-traditional transatlantic crossing on an ocean liner, and then contributed to a significant drop in the price of travel. The introduction of credit cards and reliable automatic teller machines (ATMs) in the 1990s made it possible to travel without carrying large amounts of cash or travelers' checks. In replacing the error-prone 16-millimeter film projector and the filmstrip, the VCR brought movies to the classroom. As soon as personal computers and internet connections became available, language teachers began to use them for intercultural, telecollaborative instruction (O'Dowd & Lewis, 2016). The digital natives of today now simply assume the ready online availability of any language resources they might desire, from grammar tutors to communities of learners sharing expertise. Many of these technologies are described as consequential in the stories we have gathered across generations of study abroad alumni.

Another important aspect of our study's historical background is the 'unprecedented and unparalleled' worldwide spread of English: 'no other language has ever had both the global expansion and the penetration of social strata and domains that English now has' (Seidlhofer, 2011: 3). Although the concept of a lingua franca (e.g. Latin, French or Arabic) has always existed, it was not until the post-war mid-20th century that demand emerged for practical mechanisms to serve the whole world, led for example by the expansion of United Nations member countries from 51 in 1945 to 192 by the turn of the century (Seargeant & Swann, 2012). Seargeant and Swann estimate that roughly one-third of the world's population can now communicate in English, with the ratio of native to non-native speakers at 1:4. They suggest viewing this latter proportion as a 'major shift in the center of gravity of the language' (Seargeant &

Swann, 2012: 155), where ideas about ownership of English by native speakers have become outmoded and irrelevant (Widdowson, 1994). A new approach to the study of English as a lingua franca (ELF) has thus emerged to replace the nation-state view of languages and to emphasize the creativity, flexibility and fluidity of ELF communication and the tolerant dispositions of ELF speakers (Jenkins, 2011). For our purposes, these developments have three obvious consequences. First, unless they ventured into the hinterlands and away from urban or tourist areas, all our participants were likely to encounter speakers or learners of English in informal contexts, though this likelihood no doubt increased over the period in question. Second, given the rise of English as a medium of instruction for post-secondary education worldwide, increasingly over time participants have also had access to formal courses delivered in that language. Finally, research demonstrates that native speakers of English are less effective than non-native speakers in international communication because they lack the flexibility, forbearance and accommodation strategies of fluent ELF speakers (Jenkins, 2011). ELF is a second language for everyone, and ELF fluency has become a reasonable goal for Anglophone students abroad.

In considering the history of US study abroad, we must also consider certain features of the ideologies surrounding it and the rise of efforts to counter them. To uncover the historical roots of beliefs about study abroad, Gore (2005: 23) analyzed policy and promotion documents to explore how 'a constellation of dominant beliefs has coalesced to form an episteme held by the U.S. higher education community.' The dominant discourse suggests that 'study abroad programs are perceived as attracting wealthy women to academically weak European programs established in a frivolous Grand Tour tradition' (Gore, 2005: 24). The Grand Tour tradition, inherited from the education of British gentry two centuries or more ago, ties study abroad to leisure and general cultural edification rather than to productivity or focused learning. Study abroad programs have enrolled a majority of females since their inception; this feminization of study abroad further serves to associate overseas education with lack of academic rigor and professional purpose. Gore traces the presence of this attitude to the history of women's struggle to enter the academy, and then to be admitted to programs of professional development. The purported academic weakness of study abroad is further associated with underlying prejudicial attitudes in which higher education of true quality is only available in the United States, and in which the liberal arts curriculum is disassociated from vocational goals. However, some students voice alternative views about willingness to take risks and to undergo hardships in a quest for educational experience unavailable at home, emphasizing peace and intercultural understanding or the connections between the liberal arts curriculum and the skills and knowledge needed for future careers. For these students, study abroad is conceived as an important and academically strong source of professional development *by way of the liberal curriculum*, particularly for the disenfranchised female majority.

Since the publication of Gore's work, further critical examination of popular media, policy texts and other data has indicated that both dominant and alternative discourses may be built on nefarious assumptions. Zemach-Bersin (2007), for instance, argues that discourses of 'global citizenship' mask elitist, imperialistic and nationalist projects wherein the world becomes a commodity that privileged Americans have an unquestioned right to consume. In this regard, the height of cynicism may have been reached by the feckless young protagonist of Chang-Rae Lee's *My Year Abroad* (2021):

> Everybody knew the drill. You were a privileged kid going to a privileged place to engage in privileged activities like brushing dirt from pottery shards at a faux archeological dig and touring the private art collection of a filthy rich alum and taking a sustainable food shopping class with a local chef with a bunch of walking talking privileges like yourself... (Lee, 2021: 112)

According to Zemach-Bersin, student visitors to other countries are also expected to serve as informal ambassadors, expanding soft power by correcting local attitudes and dispelling prejudice against the US, while their hosts are portrayed as existing primarily to entertain them or otherwise serve their needs, including their need for linguistic input (Kinginger, 2019b).

Furthermore, discourses of adventure and personal transformation are pervasive in study abroad marketing materials (Zemach-Bersin, 2009). This can easily be demonstrated with a Google image search for 'study abroad,' which will inevitably lead to photos of young, mostly white Americans jumping up and down in front of exotic backdrops or celebrated monuments, bungee jumping or riding exotic animals (Kinginger, 2019a). Doerr (2012) examined how these discourses function in study abroad guidebooks for US students. These materials celebrate the cognitive dissonance that can emerge from encounters with the unknown and maintain that such discovery of difference is uniquely available in study abroad (although similar revelations may be provoked by crossing race, class or regional boundaries at home). Having established the need for study abroad, they then prioritize out-of-classroom adventures, thus devaluing the host country's educational provisions and positioning the student as an unsupervised, wandering explorer who remains, nonetheless, governed by a set of learning goals (e.g. global competence) that legitimize the entire enterprise as 'study.'

Trentman and Diao (2017: 179) examined ethnographic data on the experiences of individual students in Egypt or China in the light of media and policy discourses surrounding the learning of languages deemed 'critical' in the US and concerns voiced in the literature that study abroad is 'promoting US dominance rather than a more equal cultural exchange.' In media documents, they found that non-traditional destinations such as Asia or the Middle East were associated with seriousness of purpose on the part of sojourners and, against this backdrop, students portrayed themselves as particularly adventurous and willing to move beyond the 'pretty homogenous culture' (Trentman & Diao, 2017: 183) of Europe and North America. However, in examining discrepancies between rhetoric and experience, echoes of Gore's dominant discourse prevailed: like participants in the Grand Tour tradition, these serious students traveled frequently, partied in bars, engaged in romantic encounters and lived in accommodations superior to those of their local peers.

The authors then examined how Gore's alternative discourse of peace and professional preparation played out in their data. Here again the media portrayed learners of critical languages abroad as holding loftier aspirations than those of their counterparts and as responsible for safeguarding US national interests through the achievement of intercultural understanding. In addition, there is an emphasis on the value of language learning abroad for employment, with the articles focusing on Arabic emphasizing government service and those on Chinese highlighting business. Underlying all these claims is an assumption that 'the desired world peace and global market-place will retain US dominance' (Trentman & Diao, 2017: 188). Student narratives tended to reflect these larger discourses, with an accent on marketable skills for all and on peace-making particularly among the students of Arabic. However, during their sojourns, most students resisted being positioned as representatives of the US, avoided discussions about politics or other contentious topics, and tried instead to claim distinction from their ethnocentric American classmates, without necessarily developing the empathy required to see that their Muslim or Chinese interlocutors may well be accustomed to similar positioning. The students also experienced considerable challenges with interculturality, skirting polemical issues on the grounds that local peers had been indoctrinated into limited views, complaining about everyday local practices, or reinforcing stereotypes in casual conversation. Overall, they did not develop the language proficiency or intercultural understanding necessary for participation in complex business or political negotiations. According to the authors, study abroad has become 'a 21st century *neo-Grand Tour*' (Trentman & Diao, 2017: 200, italics in the original), a way for privileged students to confirm their membership in the global elite while failing to notice the imperialist dispositions that are, at the same time, part and parcel of the US orientation toward international education and one of the main impediments to their learning.

Other contemporary commentary focuses on the spread of neo-liberal ideals and their impact on the imaginations of students and families. In a nutshell, neoliberalism is an ever-expanding, transnational form of economic rationality characterized by privatization, deregulation, and the withdrawal of governmental bodies from responsibility for civic well-being. Neoliberalism 'sees market exchange as an ethic unto itself, and it holds that the social good will be maximized by maximizing the reach and frequency of market transactions.' Furthermore, it is a 'mobile, calculated technology for governing subjects who are constituted as self-managing, autonomous, and enterprising' (Gill & Scharff, 2011: 5). In the context of study abroad, these notions lead to an emphasis on the competitiveness of the individual in the global marketplace, 'equipped with communication skills, a global mindset, and intercultural competence' (Kubota, 2016: 349). Beyond glossing over the effortful nature of language and culture learning, neoliberalism obscures fundamental, structural inequality and injustice. International educational experiences, traditionally the domain of the privileged, are not available to all students regardless of how enterprising or self-managing they may be. According to Kubota (2016: 355), study abroad in fact 'reflects and reinforces gender, race, ethnic, geographical and socioeconomic inequalities.' While efforts to diversify the profiles of study abroad participants in terms of race and ethnicity, socioeconomic status, gender and disability were characteristic of the late 20th and early 21st centuries (Stallman *et al.*, 2010) much work remains ahead, not only in increasing the numbers of participants from under-represented groups but also in honoring their specific intellectual strengths as they relate to desired outcomes (e.g. Hartman *et al.*, 2020).

In our study, often with considerable hindsight, the participants interpret the meaning of study abroad as a 'reference point' (Alred & Byram, 2002: 351) in the context of their professional life stories thus far. Thus, whether or not their original understanding echoed Gore's dominant discourses, neoliberalism or efforts to join the global elite, it is possible to appreciate the varieties of meaning and value that they have come to attribute to study abroad in the longer term.

1.4 Conclusion

In this chapter we have offered a rationale for the research reported in this book along with a basic description of the project's design. Prior surveys of various scope have documented the power of study abroad to influence career direction and promote such attributes as civic and global engagement, academic achievement and intercultural communicative competence. Qualitative and multiple-methods research has illustrated frequent links between international educational experiences and career choices in specific cases. However, this research has also shown that entry into the job market for language specialists can be complex, and that Anglophone learners infrequently desire and develop the advanced literacy skills that could maximize their options for international work. In addition, we have provided a brief outline of contemporary mixed-methods research and the potential of data integration to enhance understanding of social and educational phenomena such as study abroad. Lastly, we considered some historical changes that have affected the qualities of study abroad as a language learning environment for US-based learners; these include a trend toward greater financial demand on students and families, evolution in travel and communications technology, the dominance of English as a lingua mundi, and the rootedness of study abroad both in long-standing ideologies related to power and privilege and in more recent neoliberal views of the individual as a self-governing entity struggling to acquire marketable skills. Chapter 2 provides a more complete and detailed description of the study's methodology, including planning, data collection and approaches to analysis.

2 Research Design

2.1 Introduction

This chapter is devoted to detailed description of the study's mixed methodology, beginning with the development, field testing and administration of the survey. Here we also include basic information from the survey on demographics, provider organizations, destinations and languages learned as background knowledge for the study as a whole. There follows an account of the approach used to select interviewees from among 2741 volunteers from the survey results by creating a life history typology. The process of collecting and analyzing professional life history interview data is then described. Since the beginning, we have aspired to integrate quantitative and qualitative methods in a principled manner, as is characteristic of mixed-methods studies, and this integration is most visible in the planning, sampling and interpretation phases of the work.

2.2 Survey Development

As befits the initial phase of a sequential explanatory mixed-methods study, our first step was to design and administer a large-scale survey designed to elicit facts and opinions from language study abroad alumni that could then be explored further in the qualitative stage of the study. Developed specifically for this project, the survey's overall aim was to examine the influence of language study abroad on the professional lives of these alumni. Accordingly, the survey elicited information in five categories:

- perceived impact on language skills, job-related skills, career choices and employment;
- contexts for language learning;
- features of study abroad experiences;
- current status, including education and employment;
- demographics.

In this book, we will present significant portions of the survey data, but will not attempt to cover every detail or to exhaust the possibilities for analysis of these data. Instead, we will select and present survey data that can be coherently illuminated by our qualitative findings. In this section, we describe the process for developing this survey. A full version of the survey is available in Appendix A.

Our original intent was to attempt an emic dimension for the survey by gathering focus groups of language study abroad alumni in various professions and asking them to recount memories of the experience as well as any influences of international education on their career trajectories. We intended to use these comments to craft our survey questions, and, in the pre-Zoom era, we attempted to do this in an in-person format. However, the great majority of study abroad alumni living in our rural university town are involved in education rather than other professions. Ultimately, we were able to recruit a small group of diversely employed alumni attending invited or other events on our campus. However, these efforts did not yield the desired results, as the alumni participants in question were among those whose memories of study abroad were imprecise and for whom the experience had little evident impact. In a second attempt to achieve this aim, a corpus of study abroad online alumni testimonials was collected from the websites of university study abroad programs (see Section 2.4 below for more information). Although this corpus was primarily used to inform the qualitative analysis, it provided some guidance in designing the survey.

As noted in Chapter 1, the survey was created and administered in collaboration with the Research Center within the American Councils for International Education. We relied on their expertise and extensive previous experience in survey research among alumni of language programs; particularly valuable were their recommendations for design to maximize both the appeal of the instrument and the likelihood that participants would not find it overly time-consuming. An initial meeting in fall 2017 yielded a topical outline as well as a timeline for a completed draft and pilot testing. Subsequently, the survey was revised to enhance clarity, ease of completion, and a proper balance of fixed-choice and open-ended questions (see Dörnyei & Taguchi, 2010). The visual presentation of the survey was streamlined and made accessible on Survey Monkey to a variety of electronic devices. Pilot testing took place in December 2018 and involved a small sample of alumni within the American Councils organization; no further revisions were required. The survey was opened in February 2019 and closed in June of that year. Figure 2.1 presents the overall flow of the survey.

2.2.1 Survey administration and recruitment

Recruitment for the survey took place in collaboration with The Forum on Education Abroad, an association of approximately 800 member institutions and organizations who provide study abroad programs and services to about 95% of all US-based students. The Forum has a history of regular data collection efforts yielding high

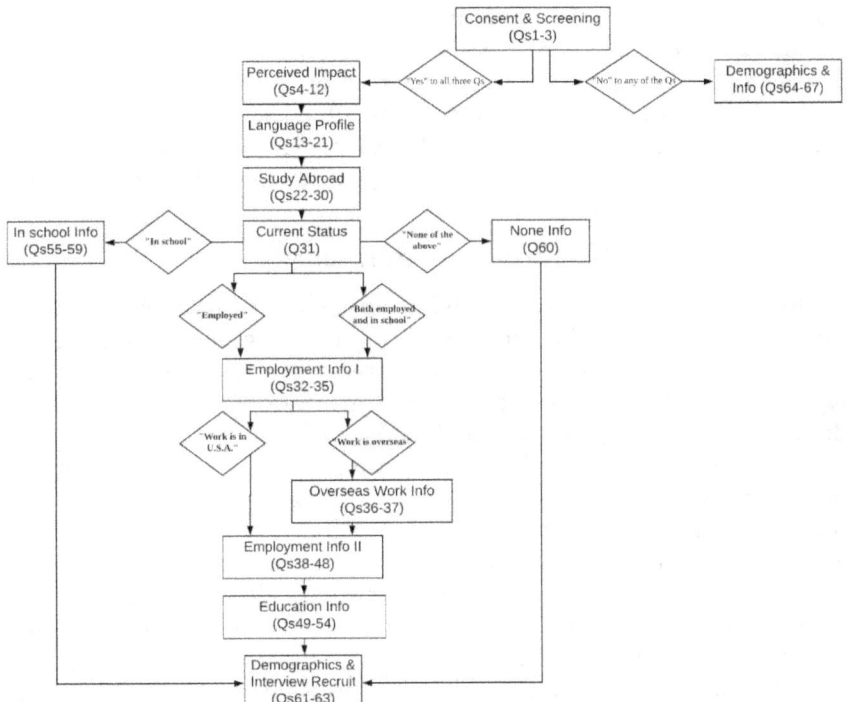

Figure 2.1 Overall flow of the survey

rates of participation and a database of more than 9000 contacts in the international education profession. In advance of the survey launch in February 2019, The Forum contacted all its member organizations with information about the aims of the survey, a timeline for data collection, and an invitation to contribute to the recruitment effort by contacting their study abroad alumni to complete the survey. For organizations that agreed to participate (see Appendix B for a full list), the Forum created an outreach kit that included sample text to be sent to alumni, sample posts for social media, recommendations for where to post (e.g. the study abroad office social media account), and a sample short text for use on websites, blogs and newsletters. Partnering organizations agreed to promote the survey to their alumni at regular intervals over the data collection period (February 2019 – June 2019). The Forum additionally provided links to complete the survey via their weekly Forum newsletter, social media posts by the Forum, and targeted emails to all contacts in the Forum's database.

While these methods led by the Forum represented the main recruitment effort, to complement this approach additional invitations to complete the survey were posted to the Interagency Language

Roundtable listserv (for government employees) and to American Associations of language teachers (e.g. American Association of Teachers of French, American Association of Teachers of Spanish and Portuguese). The project director also attended the Forum's annual meeting to recruit in person. When the survey closed in June 2019, more than 11,000 initial responses were received, of which 4899 were complete.

2.2.2 Basic information from the survey sample

In this section, we provide basic information from the survey about the demographics of the survey sample, including gender and age. In support of an overall understanding of the survey sample, here we also report information about provider organizations, funding sources, destinations, languages learned and levels of education.

A majority of respondents identified as female (77%), with just under one-quarter of respondents identifying as male (22%; 'prefer not to say' and 'other' each represented in less than 1% of the sample). These figures reflect the historical tendency toward greater participation of female than male students in study abroad as reported by the Institute of International Education with data from 2001 through 2020 (Institute of International Education, 2021c). In terms of the ages of the respondents, the survey included representation across the adult life span. Almost one-third of respondents identified as aged 25–30 (31.7%), which represented the largest single group of respondents. The proportions of the other age brackets were as follows: under 25 (15.4%), 31–35 (14.6%), 36–40 (11.7%), 41–50 (12.7%), 51–60 (7.3%) and over 60 (6.6%).

Respondents were asked about the organizations that provided and organized their programs. For this question, they were able to select more than one provider such that the total number of selections made was 8139. Table 2.1 displays the counts for the 10 most frequent providers of programs abroad. The data show that the most common provider of programs in the sample was the home university, as either a full or part sponsor of the program. In addition, a number of private and non-profit organizations were also major providers of experiences abroad in our sample: 17%, $n = 1366$. These include ISA (International Studies Abroad), ISEP (International Student Exchange Programs), IES Abroad (Institute for the International Education of Students), CIEE (Council on International Educational Exchange) and CEA (Cultural Experiences Abroad). Programs associated with high schools were also relatively common in our sample, with 7% of the study abroad experiences ($n = 571$) taking place during respondents' high school years.

In terms of the funding mechanisms to finance study abroad participation, as shown in Table 2.2, the most frequent categories included self-financing as well as school or university scholarships. This

Table 2.1 List of the 10 most common providers of study abroad programs in the sample

	Provider	n	%
1	University-sponsored study abroad	2519	30.9
2	Academic high school program	372	4.6
3	ISA	334	4.1
4	ISEP	329	4.0
5	IES Abroad	245	3.0
6	CIEE	235	2.9
7	CEA Study Abroad	223	2.7
8	Summer high school program	199	2.4
9	Foreign Language and Area Studies (FLAS)	104	1.3
10	Fulbright English Teaching Assistant	103	1.3

Note. In Table 2.1 the denominator used in percentage calculation was the total number of selections made on providers, i.e. 8139 (each respondent could indicate information for more than one study abroad experience).

finding suggests that the ability to finance study abroad by oneself is likely a key factor in deciding whether to invest in study abroad or not. This finding also supports the previously reported result that universities are a major supporter of experiences abroad.

Our sample included nearly 120 different destinations. Among these, the 10 most common are presented in Table 2.3, showing an overwhelming tendency for participants to choose non-English speaking countries in Europe. France and Spain are the most visited nations in our sample, likely reflecting the status of French and Spanish as commonly taught languages offered in post-secondary institutions in the US since the 1970s.

To appreciate what languages participants learned after their first language, respondents were asked to list up to five languages that they have learned or are currently learning. Since most respondents in our sample listed English as a first language ($n = 4510$), English as an additional language was excluded from our analysis. The most

Table 2.2 Sources of funding for study abroad programs

Funding source	n	%
Self-financing	3407	69.5
School or university scholarship	2363	48.2
Covered in tuition	1668	34.0
Loans	1542	31.5
Government scholarship	677	13.8
Other	312	6.4

Note. In Table 2.2 the denominator used in percentage calculation was the total number of survey respondents, i.e. 4899. Each respondent could select more than one funding source.

Table 2.3 List of the 10 most common destinations for study abroad in the sample

	Country	n	%
1	France	1205	18.96
2	Spain	958	15.07
3	Germany	661	10.40
4	Italy	367	5.77
5	Mexico	231	3.63
6	United Kingdom	225	3.54
7	Japan	188	2.96
8	Costa Rica	167	2.63
9	China	150	2.36
10	Russia	117	1.84

Note. In Table 2.3 the denominator used in percentage calculation was the total number of selections made on destinations, i.e. 6356 (each respondent could indicate information for more than one study abroad experience).

commonly learned languages in our sample were Spanish, followed by French and German (see Table 2.4), the most commonly taught languages in the US. These general trends are also found across the age groupings, although with small variations over time. For example, a smaller percentage of older participants reported knowledge of Spanish than did younger participants: 75% for 25 or younger, 73% for 31–35, and 57% for 60 or older. In contrast, higher percentages for French and German were found for older participants than for younger participants: For French, 32% for 25 or younger, 49% for 31–35, and 82% for 60 or older; for German, 15% for 25 or younger, 26% for 31–35, and 45% for 60 or older. As a result, there is some evidence to suggest that while the

Table 2.4 List of the 10 most common languages in the sample

	Language	n	%
1	Spanish	3148	69.80
2	French	2182	48.38
3	German	1194	26.47
4	Italian	811	17.98
5	Portuguese	436	9.67
6	Chinese	392	8.69
7	Japanese	355	7.87
8	Russian	322	7.14
9	Arabic	315	6.98
10	Korean	163	3.61

Note. In Table 2.4 the denominator used in percentage calculation was the total number of survey respondents who listed English as a first language, i.e. 4510. Each respondent could select more than one language.

main languages learned have remained relatively constant, there appears to be some movement away from French and German and towards Spanish in recent years. There is also some evidence of greater study/knowledge of critical languages (or less commonly taught languages) among younger participants. For example, 7% of 25 and younger and 10% of 31–35-year-olds reported knowledge of Chinese, compared to 5% of respondents aged 60 and older. In addition, only one respondent aged 60 and older (Mark, whose case is treated in Chapter 3) reported knowledge of Korean, compared to 6% and 5% of respondents aged 25 and younger and 31–35, respectively. These data thus indicate new and emerging trends in language study in the US.

In addition to the languages learned, we also examined how many languages participants reported that they had learned or were currently learning. Overall, these results indicate remarkable multilingualism in our sample, with 29% of participants indicating knowledge of one additional language, 32% of participants indicating knowledge of two additional languages, and 20% of participants indicating knowledge of three additional languages. In addition, the data tentatively indicate some evidence that younger study abroad alumni are less multilingual than older generations. For example, of participants aged 60 or over, 17% reported knowledge of one additional language only, whereas this percentage was higher at 26% among 31–35-year-olds and 40% among participants aged 25 or younger. Indeed, the largest proportion of respondents with knowledge of one additional language only is those aged 25 and younger. For knowledge of three additional languages, the percentage was highest among participants aged 41–50 (25%) and lowest among participants aged 25 or younger (16%). Taken together, while all groups demonstrate knowledge of multiple languages, older generations in our sample indicate more knowledge of a greater number of languages. This, of course, is likely related to the under-25 category of participants being less experienced in life (i.e. older participants have lived for longer and have had more opportunities to learn languages).

Finally, to gauge levels of education in our sample, respondents who are currently employed were asked about their highest degree. For almost half the sample, the highest degree received was a bachelor's degree (43.6%) and just over one-third of respondents had received a master's degree (38.8%). A small proportion of respondents had received a Doctor of Philosophy (PhD: 8.6%), a Juris Doctor (JD: 3.3%) or a medical doctorate degree (MD: 1.2%). In terms of survey respondents currently in college, the majority were enrolled in a bachelor's degree program (62.1%), followed by a master's degree program (18.8%), and a PhD program (8.2%).

In summary, our survey sample appears to represent individuals among the general educated public who choose to study languages and to go abroad during their student years. Females are in the majority, programs are most often self-funded, and the destinations chosen tend to correspond to commonly taught languages.

2.3 Life History Typology Development

As noted in Chapter 1, the principled integration of quantitative and qualitative data and analyses, which lies at the heart of mixed-methods research (Bazeley, 2018; Creswell, 2015; Tashakkori & Teddlie, 2010), is as yet somewhat rare in applied linguistics (Hashemi, 2019; Hashemi & Babaii, 2013; Riazi & Candlin, 2014). In our sequential explanatory mixed-method project, one critical point of interface between the quantitative and qualitative methods was the development of a sample of interview candidates for the second phase qualitative interviews drawn from the much larger sample of survey respondents in the first phase quantitative survey. In short, we developed a participant typology from the survey with multiple correspondence analysis (MCA; Greenacre & Blasius, 2006), and we used that typology to inform the selection of a representative sample of participants for the interviews. In this section, we first explain how we operationalized study abroad participants' life pathways in the design of the survey, then we give a brief introduction to MCA as an exploratory method, and finally we explain how we used MCA to develop the typology.

2.3.1 Operationalizing SA pathways

The purpose of the qualitative interviews was, in part, to capture two phenomena: (1) the lived reality of each interviewee's experience of study abroad and second language learning (a focus on the remembered past) and (2) their current position in life (a focus on current language use and employment), for the mixed-methods purpose of relating their narrations to the survey itself. That is, the qualitative interviews were to illuminate, illustrate, exemplify, comment on and explain the results of the quantitative survey, which is of course the logic of a sequential explanatory research design. For this reason, we wanted to interview as wide and representative range of survey participants as possible.

To operationalize the participants' *past tense study abroad* and their *present tense life position*, we chose items from the survey that fell within the purview of each category (see Table 2.5). First, regarding participants' *past tense experience of study abroad*, we selected two sets of questions from the survey: their number one reason for studying abroad (selected from a list provided in the survey) and the duration of their first program (allowing for the fact that some individuals participated in more than one program). Second, regarding participants' *current life positions*, we selected three sets of questions from the survey: (1) their current L2 language use (with an item about types of activities

Table 2.5 Operationalization of SA participants' life pathways

Construct	Aspect	Variable (survey question number)	Number of response options
Participants' *present* (MCA I)	L2 use	Number of L2 activity types (Q17)	5
		Number of L2 interlocutor types (Q19)	6
	Employment	Type of organization (Q38)	11
		Work sector (Q40)	19
		Position (Q39)	7
	Cultural capital	Undergraduate institution's admission rate (Q49, Q56)	10
		Highest degree (Q50, Q57)	6
Participants' *past* (MCA II)	SA experience	Top reason for SA (Q22)	11
		Duration of first SA program (Q23)	4

in which they used their L2, and an item about categories of people with whom they spoke their L2); (2) their current employment (with items about the type of organization where they worked, the more general work sector within which that organization fit, and finally their position at work); and (3) their cultural capital (with items about the admission rate of their undergraduate institution, and the highest degree that participants attained). In effect, we operationalized past experience of SA with 2 items and present life experience with 7 items.

Importantly, we analyzed these two constructs separately for each age group (rather than for the entire sample as a whole), for two reasons. First, we expected age-cohort differences because participants made their study abroad programs at very different historical and cultural periods (those of the 1970s occurred in a different 'world' than those of the early 2000s). Second, in the present (i.e. at the time of data collection), we expected generational differences in the world of employment (being 30 years of age versus 50 years of age in the current labor market/professional world is associated with different experiences, opportunities and futures).

2.3.2 Multiple correspondence analysis as an exploratory method

Since most of our survey items generated categorical (instead of continuous) data, we chose multiple correspondence analysis to scrutinize our survey data (MCA; Greenacre, 1992, 1994, 2017; Greenacre & Blasius, 2006). MCA is a multivariate exploratory statistical technique that analyzes the pattern of relationships among several categorical variables based on associational frequency. It is worth noting from the start that MCAs 'describe, rather than analyze, the data' (Greenacre, 1994: 3): that is, MCA is not designed to test hypotheses and makes fewer assumptions about the data such as linearity or normality (Greenacre & Blasius, 2006). As noted in Schrauf (2013: 28), it assumes 'multiple, many-to-many and bi-directional influences,' unlike 'a regression-based model that privileges the unidirectional influence of many variables on one outcome.'

MCA derives from much simpler tests of association – like the chi-squared statistic – between very few variables, but crucially it adds to that analysis a mapped visualization of the associations between variables in two-dimensional space. In such maps, the variables are represented as points, and the degree of their association is represented by Euclidean or chi-square distance measures. The proximity of points represents higher association between them: that is, where each point on the map represents a variable, shorter distances between points reflect closer relations between the corresponding variables, while larger distances represent less association. A second contrast between chi-square and MCA is that the latter allows us to analyze the complex and overlapping associations between a potentially *large* number of variables, which proves invaluable for analyzing the results of surveys with many items. Usually, of course, the meanings assigned to the x- and y-axes of two-dimensional graphs help interpret the relations or associations between points. However, as the number of dimensions increases with the number of variables mapped, the task of assigning simple meanings to the x- and y-axes becomes more difficult. Fortunately, because our aim was to locate participants relative to identifiable study abroad pathways and to identifiable employment patterns, working out the meaning of the axes was less important than discovering groupings of individuals associated with our variables of interest (see below).

2.3.3 Applying MCA to the project survey

In this project, we used MCA maps as a descriptive tool to identify different groups of participants (see Purhonen & Wright, 2013). Again, respecting age-cohorts and generational differences, we conducted two MCAs within each of the seven age groups (i.e. under 25, 25–30, 31–35, 36–40, 41–50, 51–60, over 60), with the first MCA capturing participants' *present*, and the second MCA capturing their *past*.

There are two steps in the MCA process that we followed. First, sets of variables were cross tabulated with one another (e.g. L2 use, employment, cultural capital) in large contingency tables from which MCA is used to construct two related maps: a *modalities* map, which shows the associations between variables, and an *individuals* map, which shows associations between participants (based on their relations to the variables). Second, by overlapping the modalities map with the individuals map, it becomes possible to identify different groups of participants and construct a typology.

Research Design   33

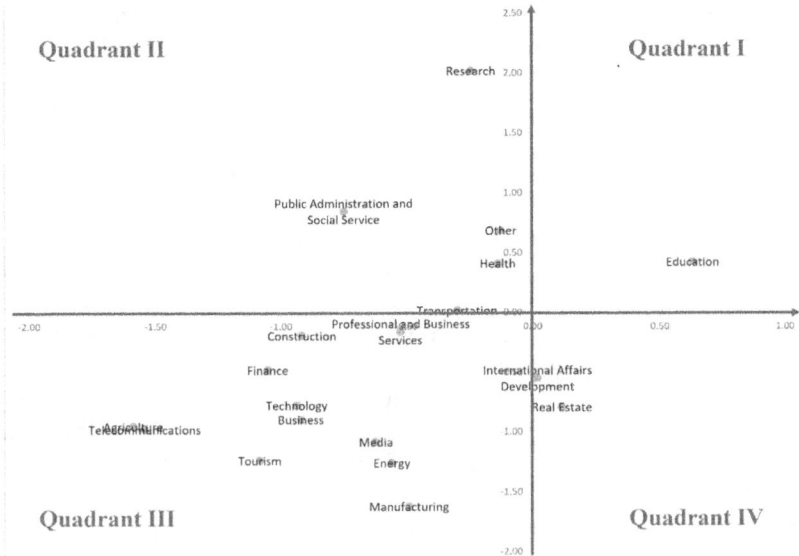

Figure 2.2 An example of a modalities map created by MCA

As an example, Figure 2.2 is a modalities map created from MCA that shows the various work sectors, with public administration, health and research in Quadrant II, the majority of for-profit businesses in Quadrant III, and education in Quadrant I. The corresponding individuals map in Figure 2.3 shows the survey respondents mapped

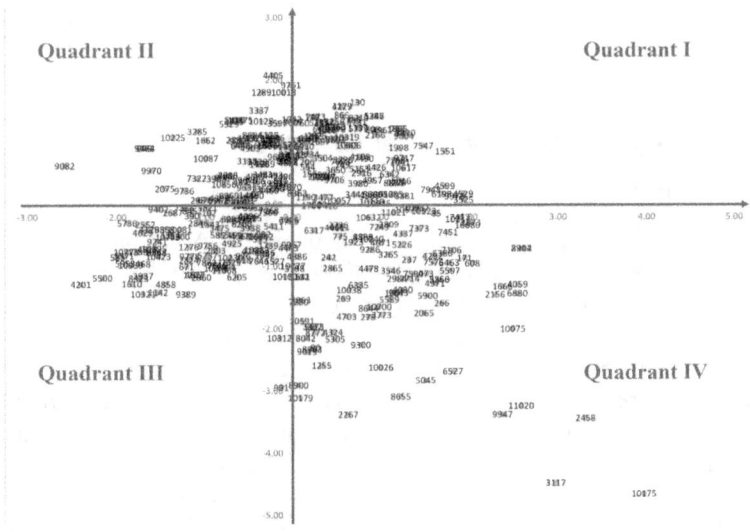

Figure 2.3 An example of an individuals map created by MCA

onto the same four quadrants as represented in this modalities map. Note, for instance, the relatively large number of individuals engaged in education (Quadrant I), which reflects that there were proportionally more participants employed in education than other employment sectors in our data.

Once we had conducted the two MCAs in SPSS separately for each age group, we then randomly sampled participants from each quadrant of the combined MCA map, with 7 participants in total for each of the seven age groups. By design, we envisioned an interview sample of 60 individuals, with 49 drawn from the typology and allowing for opportune identification of 11 'intriguing cases.' Also, although it is common practice in sampling from age groups to weight the age-related subsamples by the size of the age group (i.e. larger age-groups contribute more participants), we decided to draw the same number of individuals from each age-group (in the event, 7 from each). We did this because the survey sample had a higher proportion of young versus older respondents, and we wanted to preserve the number of older participants (whose more extensive professional experience may be related to study abroad). As specific steps, we first identified individuals who appeared in the same quadrants for each of the two MCAs within age groups, then generated a random number for each individual, and finally chose the planned number of individuals as candidates for interviews according to the order of random numbers.

As will be shown from the interview data in the following sections, this typology enabled a systematic sampling that maximized between-subject variability among the 54 interviewees selected from the 2741 survey respondents who had agreed to be contacted for interview. Importantly, the sampling design takes age-cohort and generational differences into account.

2.4 Gathering and Analyzing Interview Data

2.4.1 Recruitment

As noted above, a key feature of this project is principled integration of quantitative and qualitative methods at the sampling stage. Through systematic querying of the survey results, we were able to select interviewees who were representative of the study as a whole. Once a pool of interviewees had been identified (see Section 2.3), email invitations were sent to the addresses listed on the survey in batches of approximately 6–10 per 10-day period from September 2019 through June 2020. Each invitation was personalized using information provided by the participants about their study abroad destinations, languages learned or other commentary from open-ended survey responses. A total of 109 such invitations was sent; of these, 54 resulted in an interview, for 46 there was no reply, and 5 accepted but then could not schedule the interview or did not appear at the appointed time. Four individuals turned down the request for various reasons to do with privacy and/or the sensitivity of their professional identity. Potential interviewees who did not reply were sent a second invitation but this effort yielded no results. The first 46 participants were recruited using the typology. At that point, in examining the group of interviews as a whole in comparison to the statistics on employment field in the survey, it became clear that business and health care were poorly represented, and an effort was made to recruit from those career areas. Also, to date our efforts to recruit members of under-represented minorities had been marginally successful, either because these individuals did not respond to our invitations, or because they were in highly visible, therefore sensitive professional roles and did not wish to share potentially identifying information about their work lives. We began to deliberately seek interviewees who were graduates of historically black colleges and universities or who had referred to these identities in open-ended survey responses.

Participants who had agreed to be interviewed were asked to complete an online Human Subjects Consent Form in which they specified potential uses of their data (for this project, for future projects, and/or for public presentations), indicated possible times for the interview and whether they were comfortable with Zoom. It was suggested that they forward a photograph of a memorable event in their careers if they chose to do so. They were also asked either to grant permission to use their own name, to select a pseudonym on their own, or to direct the research team to provide this pseudonym. Table 2.6 lists the names or pseudonyms, age groups, languages and professions of the 54 interview participants. Languages are listed in the order in which they appear in the participant's life history narrative. Professions are similarly listed in chronological order, with concurrent occupations separated by a comma. Due to privacy concerns, one participant (Catherine) withdrew permission for the use of her entire narrative later in the process, allowing selected reference to certain events only.

Table 2.6 also provides information on the participants' study abroad destinations, the duration of their sojourns, and the residence options either chosen or required by their programs. Once again, if the interviewees described more than one program in high school (HS) or university, these are listed in chronological order, with academic year programs designated as 'AY.'

2.4.2 Interview procedure

In *The Science of Qualitative Research* (2018) Packer cautions against a view of qualitative methods as involving the extraction of

Table 2.6 Participant details and study abroad destinations

Number	Name/ *Pseudonym	Age group	Language(s)	Profession	Study abroad experience(s)		
					Destination(s)	Duration	Residence
1	Tim*	25–30	French	Ocean engineering	France	AY	On-campus, then shared apartment
2	Jo*	36–40	Japanese	Study abroad administration	Japan	AY	Homestay in HS
3	Courtney	Under 25	Navajo Korean Japanese	Secondary education, graduate student	Japan Korea	Summer Summer	Hostels
4	Steven*	51–60	French Italian Spanish Catalan Romanian German	Higher education: History	France	AY	Homestay
5	Maryse*	Over 60	French Italian Spanish	Management consulting	France	Summer AY	On campus
6	Mark*	Over 60	French German Korean Japanese Chinese	Peace Corps Foreign Service (retired)	Nigeria	Summer	School building under construction
7	Amelia	25–30	French	Literary translation, arts journalism, creative writing	France	AY	Cité Universitaire Internationale
8	Grace*	41–50	Spanish	Chemical engineering	Venezuela	AY	Homestay
9	Heather	41–50	Russian	Higher education: Russian	Russia	AY	Homestay
10	Hailey	31–35	Japanese	Market strategy	Japan	Semester	Homestay
11	Catherine*	51–60	Russian Others	Foreign Service (withdrew partially from the project)	UK	Summer	(Partially withdrew from project)

(Continued)

Table 2.6 Continued

Number	Name/ *Pseudonym	Age group	Language(s)	Profession		Study abroad experience(s)	
12	James*	36–40	French	Higher education: Sociology	HS: France France	Summer AY	On campus Homestay
13	Valerie	51–60	French Russian	Government service: Commerce	France	Semester	On campus
14	Alexander	Under 25	Spanish	Sports management	Dominican Republic	Semester	Homestay
15	Jessica*	36–40	Spanish	Law, Founder of a charitable non-profit organization	Mexico	Summer Semester	Homestay On campus
16	Florence*	41–50	Spanish German Catalan	Higher education: Cultural studies, Department Head	HS: Venezuela HS: Spain Spain	6 weeks 6 weeks Semester	Homestay Homestay On campus
17	Leonora*	31–35	Arabic	Secondary education: English	Morocco	Summer	On campus
18	Freida*	41–50	Spanish	Higher education: Spanish	Chile	Semester	Homestay
19	Rose*	41–50	French	Secondary education: French and ESL	France	Summer AY	Homestay Homestay
20	Bonnie	51–60	French	Foreign Service International education	HS: France Ireland	Summer AY	Homestay On campus
21	Emma*	31–35	Spanish Chinese Russian	Technology development	HS: Mexico China	Summer AY	Homestay Homestay
22	Felicity*	31–35	Spanish	Higher education: Graduate program admissions	UK Spain	3 weeks 2 months	On campus On campus
23	Blair*	Under 25	Spanish	Aspiring attorney	Spain	Semester	Homestay
24	Slug Cactus*	Under 25	Korean Spanish Thai	Accountancy	Korea	Semester	On campus

(Continued)

Table 2.6 Continued

Number	Name/ *Pseudonym	Age group	Language(s)	Profession		Study abroad experience(s)	
25	Laura	51-60	German	Higher education administration: Provost	Austria	AY	Urban residence hall
26	Max*	36-40	Spanish	Psycholinguistics Systems engineering	Spain	Semester	Homestay
27	Anton*	51-60	French Arabic	International development	France	AY	Homestay
28	Antonia	51-60	Italian	Hospitality and catering	Italy	Summer Summer AY	Shared apartment with American roommates Family friends Shared apartment with American roommates
29	Erik*	41-50	Japanese	Business and entrepreneurship	Japan	AY	Homestay
30	Mary	31-35	Spanish Somali	Secondary education: Aspiring high school principal	Spain	Summer	Homestay
31	Pamela	51-60	French	Law	France	Semester	Residence hall in a remote location
32	Gloria*	Over 60	Spanish Chinese	Business	Spain	AY	Homestay
33	Hugh	Under 25	Korean	Aspiring Foreign Service Officer	Korea	Semester	On campus
34	Beverly*	31-35	French Italian Spanish	Study abroad administration Accountancy	France	AY	Homestay
35	Lily*	25-30	French Italian Hindi	Academic advising Seeking a career in international education	France India	Gap Year Semester	Homestay Homestay
36	Vera*	Over 60	French	Manufacturing management (retired)	France	AY	Homestay

(Continued)

Table 2.6 Continued

Number	Name/ *Pseudonym	Age group	Language(s)	Profession		Study abroad experience(s)	
37	Miranda*	25–30	Spanish	Marine biology	Ecuador	Summer	Homestay
38	Andrea	51–60	French Spanish	Government service: Commerce Mental health	France	AY	Shared apartment with American roommates
39	Kelsey	31–35	Spanish	Health care: Obstetrics and gynecology	Spain	Semester	Homestay
40	Astrid*	36–40	Chinese	Affordable housing finance	Thailand Sweden	Semester Semester	Residence hall Residence hall
41	Helen*	31–35	Spanish	Health care: Pediatric occupational therapy	Guatemala Mexico Ecuador	Summer Summer Semester	Hostel (solo trip) Homestay Homestay
42	Anna	25–30	Latvian French Wolof	Health care: Nursing and public health	Senegal	Semester	Homestays (urban and rural)
43	Eleanor*	31–35	French Spanish Italian	Online language education	France	Semester	Homestay
44	Patrick	31–35	Spanish	Family medicine	Spain	Semester	Homestay
45	Clementine*	41–50	Russian Chinese	Health care: Acupuncture and herbal medicine	Russia	AY	Residence hall
46	IU Sigma Girl*	41–50	Italian	Commercial real estate	Italy	AY	Shared apartment with American roommates
47	Victoria*	36–40	French Spanish Hausa Zarma Tamil Sestswana	Health care: International public health	Niger	Semester	Residence hall, one week homestay

(Continued)

Table 2.6 Continued

Number	Name/ *Pseudonym	Age group	Language(s)	Profession	Study abroad experience(s)		
48	Afrika*	Under 25	Korean isiZulu	Music, Online language teaching	South Africa	Summer	Hostels
49	Moira*	25–30	Spanish	Mechanical engineering	Argentina	Semester	Homestay
50	Frances*	36–40	French Fante/Twi Lingala	International education and creative writing	Ghana	Semester	Homestays (urban and rural)
51	Carmen	36–40	Spanish	Study abroad administrator	Italy	Semester	Shared apartment with other female students
			Italian		Chile	Semester	Homestay
52	Peter	31–35	German	Renewable energy	Germany	AY	Residence hall
53	Owen*	25–30	Spanish	International insurance	Hungary	Semester	Residence hall
54	Thomas	Over 60	French	Health care: Anesthesiology, pain medicine	France	Summer	Residence hall

knowledge from participants by researchers in a position of detached neutrality. This posture, Packer argues, may be routinely equated with objectivity and genuine knowledge, but it also contributes to attitudes of domination:

> This kind of research promotes a way of knowing other people that leaves them feeling misunderstood and treated as objects and fails to recognize either the political and ethical dimensions of understanding or its own transformative power. When we understand another person, we don't merely find answers to our questions about them (let alone test our theories about them) but are challenged by our encounter with them. We learn, we are changed, we mature. (Packer, 2018: 5)

In his critique of the semi-structured interview as a conversation with a purpose, Packer observes the many ways in which these speech events differ from ordinary conversation. They are scheduled rather than spontaneous, usually involve strangers, and are about the past or the future rather than the here-and-now. They are conducted for a third party, represented by the recording device. The participants are not social equals, because the aim is to obtain accounts of subjective experience delivered in one direction only, with the interviewer attempting to enhance rapport while maintaining a certain skepticism toward the ongoing comments. Semi-structured interviews, Packer concludes, employ discursive flexibility in the service of asymmetrical power relations. Further, reporting most often omits any reference to their qualities as interactions between two or more human beings, even when participants' identities have a clear influence on the outcomes.

Packer also rejects the notion of qualitative research as 'the objective study of subjectivity' (Packer, 2018: 8), because true objectivity is impossible and the subjective is ultimately unknowable. Rather, he argues, the goal of social science research should be the achievement of intersubjectivity, wherein participants and interviewees work toward mutual understanding. This position is echoed in recent debates in the field of applied linguistics where, for example, Talmy (2011) has argued against viewing interviews as research instruments and for recognition of the interview as social practice. As research instruments, interviews have traditionally been framed as tools for the 'excavation' (Talmy, 2011: 28) of truths, facts or attitudes, with data analyzed thematically in a decontextualized manner. To recognize interviews as social practice requires acknowledgement that data are produced collaboratively and that the voices of all parties, including the interviewer, are discursively constructed and situationally contingent. Other scholars such as McGregor and Fernández (2019) and Prior (2011) have taken up conversation analysis and systematic introspection to demonstrate how researcher identities are inevitably invoked during data collection and come to influence the fundamental nature of these encounters.

The qualitative data collection for this project involved standard semi-structured interviews conducted by Kinginger accompanied by Zhuang for thematic note-taking and technical assistance. Our insistence on carrying out all the interviews with one interlocutor stemmed from awareness of the identity-related influence noted by Packer. It seemed important that each participant craft their responses in relation to the same primary interlocutor with some comparable life experiences.

Eight of the interviews were conducted by telephone or using audio only, because the participants were either unfamiliar with Zoom or unable or unwilling to use it. All the others took place on Zoom with video and audio recording. Telephone interviews were recorded either with a separate digital recording device or by running Zoom in the background. Interviews ranged in length from 31 minutes (Pamela) to 2 hours (Thomas) but were typically one hour long. In each case, the first question elicited the story of the participant's career to date. Subsequently, if these topics had not been visited, we inquired about college study abroad experiences and the return to campus following a sojourn away, influences in youth that had inspired interest in language or international education, and the role of study abroad in professional choices. We then asked about current use of languages studied, activities for maintaining proficiency, learning of additional languages, and the joys and frustrations of language learning. Finally, we addressed the participant's aspirations for the future. Two topics originally planned (views on the value of language study abroad on the job market, and forces that help or hinder language learning) were eventually discontinued because they seemed difficult for the interviewees. After several participants spoke about their enhanced ability to function in English-medium professional settings, a new topic – English as a lingua franca – was introduced. The topical interview guide appears in Appendix C. Following the interviews, Zoom-generated transcripts were downloaded and corrected for clarity and comprehensibility.

2.4.3 Theoretical framework: Vygotskian approaches to experience and development

The basic approach to qualitative inquiry taken up in this project is derived from contemporary Vygotskian cultural-historical theory (CHT). In essence, CHT is a theory of consciousness in which language and other historically derived cultural and semiotic means play a defining role. At every level, the theory rests on dialectics, or the study of internal contradictions as the driving force of change, and an attempt to expand 'our notion of anything to include, as an aspect of what it is, both the process by which it has become that and the broader interactive context in which it is found' (Ollman, 2003: 13). The theory posits that in the development of human higher mental functions the social and the biological operate in dialectic unity and that human action, thinking and speaking are mediated by psychological tools analogous to physical tools (Kozulin, 1998). Through engagement with artifacts and others, humans gradually internalize repertoires for thinking and speaking that are provided by, and dependent upon, their historically derived environments. The sociogenetic nature of the theory is expressed in Vygotsky's General Genetic Law of Cultural Development claiming that any function in the child's cultural development appears twice: first between people as an inter-psychological category, and then within the individual as an intra-psychological category (Vygotsky, 1978).

Development is thus viewed as a dynamic, historical process. In *The Dialectics of Nature* (1940), Engels argued that while nature plays a role in human development, this development also influences nature, thereby creating novel developmental conditions. To pursue this dialectical approach in the psychology of higher mental processes, Vygotsky believed it necessary to trace the history of these processes over time in the development of the species, the formation of human cultures, the lives of individuals, and in moment-by-moment psychological changes (Lantolf & Swain, 2020). He therefore proposed a process ontology, observing the genesis, or history, of development at four interconnected levels: phylogenesis (history of the species), sociocultural history (evolution of human cultures), ontogenesis (life history), and microgenesis (history of particular psychological functions over short periods of time).

Per Veresov and Mok (2018), Vygotsky's early work, and the concepts most influential to date among applied linguists, focused on aspects of cognition such as sign meaning, the process of mediation and the dynamics of internalization. The latter years of his career, however, witnessed a shift toward holistic accounts of consciousness as a dynamic, constantly reorganized system including cognition but also, and crucially, personal and emotional dimensions. Vygotsky understood psychological systems as unities of function, not comparable to machines or reducible to their component parts, just as the function of water in extinguishing a fire cannot be studied by separating hydrogen from oxygen (Vygotsky, 1987). This shift, in turn, yielded a new concept and unit of analysis to study the role of the environment and to explain what drives development: 'perezhivanie' ('emotional' or 'lived' experience). As a concept, perezhivanie represents the dialectical unity and inseparable nature of cognition and emotion: 'perezhivanie is not merely an emotional experience but a complex psychological phenomenon, a unity and nexus of different psychological processes such as awareness and interpretation, among others' (Vygotsky, 1994: 343).

As a unit of analysis, perezhivanie also captures the dialectical relationship between the person and the environment, permitting understanding of the *social situation of development*. This term does not refer to the objective external conditions being experienced but, rather, to the unique ways in which these conditions both shape and are shaped by the *individuals* living through them, as refracted through their perezhivanie. In other words, the individual is not a passive recipient of environmental influences but instead plays an active role in constituting the environment. According to Lantolf and Swain (2020):

> the social situation of development is itself a dialectic process in which the environment shapes the individual, but at the same time that individual brings particular features of his or her own psychology to the environment and that in turn shapes the social environment and influences how it will be refracted by the person. (Lantolf & Swain, 2020: 85)

In this way, Vygotsky explained why environmental effects are not deterministic but are relative to the lived, cognitive–emotional experiences of concrete individuals. An environment that appears to be objectively the same but is experienced by two different individuals, or the same individual at different ages, will yield different outcomes. Individuals are part of their environmental ecology and so produce different relations with the various conditions present within it.

Veresov (2017) reunites the concept of perezhivanie with the General Genetic Law of Cultural Development, noting that while higher mental functions are transformed from social relations to inter-mental functions through internalization, not every social relation has the capacity to provoke change. Qualitative reorganization, thus development, occurs through drama, that is, the resolution of contradictions that arise in social situations: 'only those social relations that are "dramatic"; that is, those relations that have an impact on an individual's emotions which arise in the contradictions that occur in the dialectical relations taking place in the social environments inhabited by individuals, qualify as sources of development' (Lantolf & Swain, 2020: 59). Notably, an event need not be momentous to serve as a source of development: some dramatic relations, such as minor errors in speech during language learning, can even seem trivial on the surface but can still provoke searing embarrassment and thus remain relevant in memory (Mok, 2015). Citing Blunden's (2016) explication of the term, Lantolf and Swain note that, as derived from the verb *perezhivat*, the noun perezhivanie 'implies that someone has survived a painful circumstance or experience but only after having relived the experience and worked through it many times' (Lantolf & Swain, 2020: 82), although dramatic experiences can also be joyful. The term therefore refers not only to the experience itself but also to subsequent, cathartic resolution of the contradictions inherent in the experience and thus to development.

Veresov and Mok (2018) propose that observation and various forms of self-report, including interviews and elicited narrative, are appropriate for the study of perezhivanie in which the researcher can seek to explain which features of environments and personal characteristics affect development. In the case of self-report, however, validity issues arise in the disjuncture between the experience itself and the expression of that experience, and these are confounded in several ways. Participants can only recount those aspects of their own history of which they are aware; they may not have grasped every element of their experiences or their developmental consequences, or indeed they may still be working to resolve the inchoate contradictions they have experienced. The nature of self-report is dependent on the speaker's language ability and skill at narration. Further, participants may not be willing to reveal every aspect of their emotional life to a researcher whom they do not know. Also, it is important to be aware, as Packer (2018) and others (McGregor & Fernández, 2019; Prior, 2011; Talmy, 2011) also emphasize, that interviews are social interactions: the materials they produce are co-constructed in dialogue and do not necessarily reflect reality. Analysis of textual content is meaningfully supplemented with attention to 'text reality' (Pavlenko, 2007: 169): that is, formal features such as rhetorical organization, or ways of building coherence, and those themes that might have been invoked but remain absent. Further disjuncture will inevitably exist between the participant's report and the researcher's interpretation. In common with many commentators on contemporary qualitative research, to address this issue Veresov and Mok (2018) advocate that researchers reflect on their own perezhivanie, as it informs their project and influences their analysis (see the Box 2.1 below). Overall, the research project may be conceived as a dialectic unity of the researcher's values, interests or dispositions and the object of the research. 'It is through the sublation and synthesis – that is, qualitative reorganization – of these oppositions and contradictions to higher levels of conceptualization that new insights and knowledge are produced' (Veresov & Mok, 2018: 97).

Box 2.1 Celeste Kinginger's social history and cognitive–emotional position

> Given the recent general emphasis on reflexivity in qualitative research, and its importance for the study of perezhivanie, Kinginger here reveals some particular features of her own social history and cognitive-emotional position in the interview process.
>
> I am a white, female, middle-class American academic. I grew up in the prosperous post-war 1960s and 1970s as the daughter of an engineer and an artist who moved their modular furniture set back and forth across the US four times during my childhood, chasing better jobs before settling in Pennsylvania, and exposing me to the concept and daily reality of mobility. My father had been raised in modest circumstances and was among the veterans of World War Two who benefitted from an education

benefit, the 'GI-bill,' to earn an otherwise inaccessible college degree. My mother was the third child of farm managers in the south. Her struggles to correct her pronunciation and the prejudice and assumptions of ignorance she encountered due to her marked speech in various locations, especially California, inspired my early interest in the power of language. Both my parents experienced hardship and strife in their youth, though my mother drew considerable support from a large and cohesive family – until she embarked on her journey of upward mobility with my father, my sister and me. Personal stories of escape from poverty and expansion of possibility through educational and physical mobility were woven into the fabric of my childhood, as were the tensions engendered when these changes compromise family unity and draw resources away from communities of origin (Morton, 2019).

From 1976 to 1980 I attended Antioch College largely at my parents' expense and graduated as one of two French majors in my class, after very consequential study abroad experiences in France. These included a summer as a farmhand in the Tarn, a semester at Paul Valéry in Montpellier, Professor Anna Otten's Paris Seminar in the spring, including face-to-face meetings with such luminaries as Eugene Ionesco, Nathalie Sarraute, and Roland Barthes, and work during the following summer for a beach-front ice cream concern in St Tropez. While at Antioch I also carried out a co-operative work assignment at the Newberry Library's Center for Family and Community History; there, I discovered scholarship involving the collection of oral history narratives and read Studs Terkel's (1974) *Working*, thus developing a fascination for the stories of regular folk that remained mostly latent in my own work until this project began.

I then gradually made my way into an academic career, with an MA degree in French literature followed by a stint as a contractor to the Foreign Service Institute where I taught French quite unsuccessfully using the required method. I pursued a PhD in the SLATE program (Second Language Acquisition and Teacher Education) at the University of Illinois and took up a series of academic posts in language departments within the US, oddly enough, moving my own small family's own modular furniture back and forth across the country before settling in Pennsylvania. At Penn State, I was a member of the core faculty group that established the Department of Applied Linguistics. When this project began, I had accumulated a degree of professional gravitas in a career devoted to language teaching, learning and research. I had also lived for two decades in an isolated land grant university town where my access to adults in professions other than academia was severely limited.

I therefore brought to the interviews a lifelong investment in language education and its potential for expanding the horizons of Americans, coupled with a sense of the ethical cost of educational mobility. I also had long-term memories of study abroad, sincere interest in the working lives of others, and genuine naïveté regarding the career paths and daily lives of non-academics. While I was also aware of the little that could be done to improve the basic structure of the interview, and while it is clear that manipulation can characterize any interaction, I was not interested in enhancing the extraction of knowledge from our participants though strategic building of fake rapport. I wanted to learn, be changed and mature, just as Packer suggests. For all these reasons, I expressly abandoned any pretense of detached neutrality in favor of honesty about the various aims of the study and active involvement in exchange around peripheral topics when the occasion arose, such as the discovery of common experiences or professional goals, and opportunities for the sharing of information pertinent to either party. All participants were informed that while research was the primary purpose of the study, another goal was to provide material for advocacy of language learning and international education. It must be acknowledged that I also brought my own culturally derived preference for stories of redemption with 'happy endings' (see below) and that this predilection most likely contributed to the qualities of the narratives presented in this book.

2.4.4 Analytic method: Narrative analysis

The method for qualitative analysis for this study was influenced by views on lived experience and development from CHT and by Packer's writing on methods for qualitative science. As explicated by Van Compernolle (2019), Packer's views on qualitative research as the study of historical ontology and of how forms of life are constituted are fully consistent with CHT while adding both a thorough grounding in the history of Western philosophical inquiry and specific recommendations for methods freed from the constraints of logical positivism. Packer argues that, in its attempts to emulate positivist approaches in the natural sciences, qualitative research in the social sciences systematically destroys the unities of function that are present in their objects of study. Instead of attempting to apprehend the whole phenomenon, how it came to be, and how it functions in context, parts of the phenomenon are extracted and measured independently.

A prime example of this process is the widespread use of coding in data analysis, grounded in the conduit metaphor for language (Reddy, 1979) in which ideas are conceived as objects which are packed into containers (e.g. words) then sent to their recipient who unpacks them, presumably intact. There is a contradiction, according to Packer, between contemporary views of language use as activity involving negotiation, repair and other forms of collaboration to achieve intersubjectivity, and the notion that meanings independent of the interaction are simply delivered to an audience in the same way that that the postal service might deliver a box of consumer products. Furthermore, meaning does not reside within words but depends on the identities of speakers, the manner of delivery, and contexts such as the entirety of a research encounter or the nature of the interactive scene. The meaning of words is not fixed, but indeterminate and subject to interpretation. Vygotsky (1987) famously established a distinction between the conventional and the personal meanings of words: znachenyie ('meaning') refers to the generalized denotational definition of a word such as might be found in a dictionary, and smysl ('sense') describes the individual's idiosyncratic constellation of word representations built up through concrete experiences. Coding may provide access to generalized 'meaning' but does not capture the semantic domains that are significant for individuals. Nevertheless, in attempting to enhance the appearance of objectivity, qualitative researchers routinely rely on coding which erases context, favors commonality over diversity, imposes one specific interpretation usually guided by what the researcher already knows about the topic, and is fundamentally a form of nominal measurement, thus a quantitative technique.

What, then, would be an appropriate alternative? As noted above, Packer believes that qualitative researchers should abandon both stances of detached neutrality and positivist methods that enforce piecemeal rather than holistic study. Instead, they should pursue understanding of historical ontology: that is, how forms of life are constituted over time, how the cultural becomes individual and vice-versa. Such research must acknowledge the fundamental value and meaning of interpretation as well as its particularity. Citing Gadamer's hermeneutics, for example, Packer argues that freedom from preconceptions is a mirage: 'every reader encounters a text within a specific horizon, a place in history, and expectations that cannot be eliminated and [...] shouldn't be' (Packer, 2018: 97). Understanding is always interested, not detached, and involves application to the current situation. Furthermore, no text has a single, correct interpretation: the meaning of a text is an effect of reading it and varies depending on who the reader is, what preconceptions they harbor, and the situation. In this case, and in alignment with Packer's call for emancipatory research, an important goal is to advocate for the future of study abroad and language learning.

To understand how cognitive–emotional experiences of study abroad are constituted in the long term, in this aspect of the project our main method is narrative analysis or using story telling as an analytic strategy and means of presenting findings (Barkhuizen et al., 2014). In this book we focus mainly on the participants' professional life stories, which were re-told in written form as 'meta-narratives' (Riessman,

1993), mainly from the perspective of one researcher (Kinginger), then sent to interviewees for comment and correction. We took this approach in full acknowledgement of the fact that narrative research involves interpretation at every level: in the participants' original perception of the storied events, in the participants' and interviewer's choices of focus during the interview, in the writing and negotiation of content, and in the reception by an audience of readers (Riessman, 1993). In this process we attempt to preserve a holistic sense of each unique story and the diversity of experience represented in our materials as well as, where relevant, the context in which the data were gathered.

In further support of our method, we propose that narrative is much more than mere self-report (Veresov & Mok, 2018) but is, rather, as famously portrayed by Bruner (1986), an essential form of thought that is particularly well suited to the study of dramatic events in life experience and to providing an alternative to positivist research. Bruner famously argued for the existence of two main modes of thought, each of which provides distinctive ways of ordering experience. The paradigmatic, or logico-scientific mode attempts to fulfill the ideal of a formal, mathematical system of description and explanation, dealing in causes and procedures to test for empirical truth. The narrative mode, on the other hand:

> … leads instead to good stories, gripping drama, believable (though not necessarily 'true') historical accounts. It deals in human and human-like intention and action and the vicissitudes and consequences that mark their course. It strives to put its timeless miracles into the particulars of experience, and to locate the experience in time and place. (Bruner, 1986: 13)

Moreover, for Bruner, life stories in particular have ontological significance as they are in a two-way relation of mimesis with life itself. Since they are drawn from the array of cultural resources that a person encounters over time in particular settings, they reflect the range of possible lives within one's culture (Bruner, 1987). Over time, the culturally shaped cognitive and linguistic resources that shape the telling of lives gain the 'power to structure perceptual experience, to organize memory, to segment and purpose-build the very "events" of a life. In the end, we *become* the autobiographical narratives by which we "tell about" our lives' (Bruner, 1987: 15, italics in the original).

Here, although our focus is mainly on the content of life stories generated from the interaction of researcher and participant rather than on the form of the original telling, the stories we have gathered do present some formal features (or 'text realities') worthy of discussion. In a study involving narratives of professional choice among white middle-class Americans, Linde (1993) focused on how these stories enable the creation of coherence. For Linde, narratives are made coherent by temporal continuity, in which the past is made relevant to the present, by a vision of the singularity of individual lives, by the reportability of (possibly unexpected) events, and by reflexivity, in which a narrator separated from the protagonist may edit, adjust or correct the narrated events and thereby establish the moral value of the self. The most basic moral proposition, contained in most forms of first-person narrative, is 'I am a good person' (Linde, 1993: 123) who does what any good person would do in these circumstances, or when confronting obstacles. Coherence is also established through adequate causality, neither too thin (life is random) nor too thick (fatalism). In Linde's data, the most important form of adequate reason for career choices is personal character or talent. Remarkably, there were no references to economic constraints or class limits on professional opportunities, neither were gender, race or ethnicity invoked by these white participants: 'The belief that one is not subject to external limits of opportunity imposed by gender, social class, race, or ethnicity appears to be common to middle-class Americans of the postwar generation' (Linde, 1993: 132). Linde goes on to link these findings with the notion of common sense, or beliefs that everyone is assumed to share, and from there to declare positive thinking to be the 'unnoticed religion of America' (Linde, 1993: 199). As reflected in the quasi-religious tone of self-help literature on success, positive thinking reinforces the notion that the individual is in control of their destiny.

With the passage of time and the inclusion of a more racially and socioeconomically diverse group of participants, thanks in part to our typology, in our data some such external limits are relatively visible, yet the narratives we have gathered remain in many cases tied to the fundamental vision of the agentive individual that Linde describes and that has since taken on more intensive significance with the rise of neoliberalism. Moreover, our narratives are also shaped by a cousin of positive thinking, namely a story arc that inevitably leads to redemption, as described by the personality psychologist McAdams (2006). For McAdams, personality is built on three levels: (1) dispositional traits such as extraversion or openness; (2) characteristic adaptations to situations; and (3) integrative life stories, or 'those internalized and evolving self-narratives that people construct to make sense of their lives in time.' Like Bruner and Linde, McAdams argues that these narratives are drawn from an array of available cultural resources and that 'we live in and through our stories' (McAdams, 2006: 16). McAdams' research has revealed a strong tendency toward life stories of redemption among psychologically healthy, generative Americans – that is, caring and productive people who invest in their own communities and commit to the well-being of future generations. In these stories, the protagonist is inevitably delivered from suffering or dire straits to emerge in an enhanced state. Deeply rooted in the Judeo-Christian tradition, these narratives echo the spiritual journeys recounted by 17th-century Puritans, rags-to-riches Horatio Alger stories from the 19th century, and, as noted by Linde, contemporary popular self-help literature.

> From the Puritans to Emerson to Oprah, the redemptive self has morphed into many different storied forms in the past 300 years as Americans have sought to narrate their lives as redemptive tales of atonement, emancipation, recovery, self-fulfillment, and upward social mobility. (McAdams, 2006: 17)

We are aware, of course, that accounts of life stories given by Linde and McAdams may be rightfully critiqued as essentialist in that they link nationality with identity in an apparently straightforward way, and without detailed consideration of variation. Also, Linde's claims about an entire generation of post-war Americans, based on the life stories of white people only, would surely raise eyebrows today. Nonetheless, we believe that these accounts help us to understand the basic coherence and plot structure, that is, some aspects of 'text reality' (Pavlenko, 2007) in our narratives emerging from negotiation with participants, of which many, though not all, do involve the redemption of individuals exerting independent control of their lives.

As described by Doerr (2012) and outlined in Chapter 1, the form that this redemption takes in both formal and informal tales of US-based study abroad often presents a special character. Study abroad marketing and ancillary materials such as guidebooks present the experience as one of personal transformation through adventure, where the protagonist voluntarily opts to face and conquer unknown vicissitudes, ultimately emerging with new wisdom. Accordingly, many alumni do craft stories mainly focused more on their own heroic quests and less on their interactions with or effects on local hosts or ecologies abroad, thus potentially echoing colonialist perspectives where the focus is on extraction of benefits for the visiting student. These ideological forces have no doubt influenced many of the 'text realities' presented in this volume, particularly in Chapters 4 and 5 where the emphasis is in fact on professional or personal transformation. In addition, the pressure to present a well-formed story of successful transformation may force certain intractable problems related to gendered, racial or other identities, out of the limelight if they cannot be overcome. On this latter point, Carmen's narrative (Chapter 5) presents a compelling example of an alumna's struggle to juxtapose accounts of prejudicial ill treatment with the elements of a canonical study abroad success story.

As noted above, the analysis of qualitative data in this project was also primed, in part, by the collection and review of online autobiographical texts and testimonials of language study alumni published on the webpages of post-secondary language departments. A corpus of 89 such personal statements was assembled and organized according to the degree of competitiveness for entry to the institutions advertising their programs in this way. The original purpose of this exercise was adding an emic dimension to the survey, and this succeeded only to a minor degree due to concerns about survey brevity. However, reading these texts did prepare us for encountering a broad range of professions as well as many themes that would later appear in the interviews. These include, for example, the contributions of language study to compassion and empathy for healthcare professionals, to efficiency in learning technical jargon or programming languages, to perceived changes in personality, or to general articulateness, skill in using English as a lingua franca, and ability to work in international contexts. Moreover, there were differences between the testimonials given by graduates of more, as opposed to less, selective universities and colleges, with the former better equipped to describe the specific professional benefits of language learning and the latter emphasizing discovery of their ability to take risks and strike out on their own, all of which suggested a social-class related dimension to the experience of study abroad.

On a practical level, the process of arriving at the narrative texts included here involved several steps. First, as is typical in the analysis of qualitative data, we watched and listened carefully to each interview while refining the transcripts automatically generated by Zoom, since Zoom's transcripts included incomprehensible sequences, particularly, it seemed, when the speaker was not a white male from the Midwestern section of the country or when a proper or non-English noun was used (for instance, Jingyuan Zhuang's first name was rendered as Chang One, Jane When, Genuine, Gentlemen, King Man and Stephen). We then continued to listen and read the transcripts until we had a sense of the overall story, which we outlined, then drafted, then reviewed to add detail, including carefully transcribed, illustrative excerpts of the actual interview data. In an effort at member checking, these drafts were sent to the participants with a request for correction of inaccuracies and a message to the effect that any suggestions for editing would be welcome. We did not receive replies to all these messages, and when we did the suggested corrections were usually minor issues of exact chronology or the like. However, since most of our participants are not familiar with discourse or conversation analysis and had never seen their own speech portrayed in this way, in the beginning of this process some concerns did arise over the transcribed excerpts: for instance, Clementine found it 'jarring' to observe that she does not always speak in complete sentences. Since our main concern was to collaborate with our participants as much as possible in creating a mutually acceptable version of each narrative, our compromise position is a transcription system that preserves some elements of the spoken medium while avoiding features that could appear unflattering to a layperson (see Simplified Transcription

Conventions in the prelims). Thus, with the exception of the quotative 'like,' extensively used discourses markers (e.g. you know) and other indications of dysfluency were edited out to avoid offense. Complete professional life stories appear in Chapter 3 on language use at work, Chapter 4 on discovering a vocation, and Chapter 5 on exploring identities. Shorter stories relevant to unpredicted benefits of language learning and program features are included in Chapters 6 and 7.

2.5 Conclusion

In this chapter we have provided an overview of the project's design. This includes a description of the process by which the survey was developed and administered, with significant contributions from our partner organizations, the American Councils for International Education and The Forum on Education Abroad. We then explained how we generated a life history typology to guide selection of interview participants from among 2741 volunteers and to support a principled, mixed-methods design at the sampling stage. There followed details about the process of recruiting participants for interviews, our orientation to the practice of qualitative interviewing, and the theoretical and methodological foundations of our cultural–historical approach to narrative inquiry. Subsequent chapters of this book are devoted to our findings, with each chapter drawing from both quantitative and qualitative sources.

3 Using Languages at Work

3.1 Introduction

The focus of this chapter is the direct applicability of language competence in the workplace for the participants in our study. We first present some quantitative data from the survey to show how participants evaluated the role of study abroad in enhancing their language abilities for practical purposes. We then examine the sectors where our survey takers were employed and what percentage claimed to use additional languages at work, as well as which languages are used and for what purposes. To illuminate these data, we offer intact professional life history narratives of individuals who require language abilities to perform their duties in various sectors including education, business, healthcare, government service, engineering, sports management and the arts.

3.2 Using Languages at Work by the Numbers

To begin our discussion of this topic we will first consider a question included in the survey about the long-term impact of study abroad. Specifically, the participants were asked to rate on a scale from 0 (not at all) to 10 (to a great extent) how much study abroad had influenced their ability to use a language other than English for school or work. For this question, the mean score was 7.48 ($SD = 3.09$) and the median was 9, meaning that respondents recognized a strong influence of this experience on their professional language ability. Furthermore, if we scrutinize responses to this question across the age ranges represented in the survey (Table 3.1), we find little variation and even a slightly stronger positive opinion among the older participants.

This suggests that the perceived benefits of study abroad for this purpose are not ephemeral but are retained in long-term memory. The qualitative data presented in this chapter illustrate in rich detail how cognitive emotional drama in language learning contexts abroad makes these experiences memorable.

Table 3.1 Study abroad and ability to use language for school or work

	Under 25	25–30	31–35	36–40	41–50	51–60	Over 60
Mean	7.46	7.12	7.34	7.81	7.69	8.09	7.77
SD	3.00	3.16	3.15	2.88	3.12	2.94	3.25

Next, to understand language use at work, we must first establish the nature of this work, that is, the employment sectors claimed by our participants. Among the 4899 respondents in our survey sample, most respondents (77%, $n = 3786$) indicated that they were employed at the time of the survey while 16% were in college and 7% were neither in college nor employed, perhaps retired. Among the employed participants, a significant percentage worked in education (42.9%) and other recognizable groups worked in healthcare (8.8%), technology (4.8%) and professional and business services (4.5%). Table 3.2 displays all the work sectors of survey respondents as well as the estimated number of interviewees in each sector.

Table 3.2 illustrates the variety of career paths that have been open to language study abroad alumni over the past several decades. It also suggests that while our typology was not intended specifically to seek out interview participants from particular employment sectors, it nevertheless led to the representation of most areas of pursuit represented in the survey. The numbers in the rightmost column are estimated only, due to the complex information we gathered about actual life paths. For example, the participant working in construction was

Table 3.2 Work sectors of survey respondents

Work sector	n	%	Estimated number of Interviewees
Agriculture	31	0.8	0
Business	145	3.8	4
Construction	31	0.8	1
Education	1626	42.9	15
Energy	30	0.8	1
Finance	158	4.2	1
Healthcare	335	8.8	7
International Affairs/Development	135	3.6	7
Manufacturing	69	1.8	1
Media	80	2.1	0
Real Estate	23	0.6	1
Technology	180	4.8	3
Telecommunications	24	0.6	0
Transportation	28	0.7	0
Tourism (including Leisure & Hospitality)	65	1.7	0
Professional and Business Services	171	4.5	1
Other	644	17.0	12
No response	11	0.3	0

Note. In Table 3.2 the denominator used in percentage calculation was the total number of employed respondents, i.e. 3786. Each respondent could select one sector at most.

earning and saving money in preparation for law school, another who is now a mental health professional moved in mid-life from a career in international affairs, and a third who is currently in business services first worked for several years in study abroad administration. Should we classify the participant who works on language learning apps as belonging to technology or education? Our qualitative analysis gives us space to explore these kinds of transitions and vagaries as well as the meaning of work for our participants and the ways in which labeled work sectors actually represent a wide variety of activities.

One of the most remarkable findings from the survey is that fully 65% (n = 2429) of respondents claimed to have used their additional languages for professional purposes. This proportion increases with age such that 48% of participants aged under 25 have used a world language at work, while the figures are higher among 36–40, 41–50, and 51–60 age groups (66%, 74%, and 79%, respectively), a finding that may be explained by the simple fact that older respondents have more experience. Our main finding, of course, also signals that overall 35% of participants do not have experience of additional language use at work, although as we argue in Chapters 4 and 5, subsequent non-use of languages learned abroad in no way detracts from the professional significance of these experiences.

Our survey also yielded data on the particular languages in question: the ten most common languages used at work were Spanish (accounting for 40% of reported languages), French (22%), German (9%), Italian (4%), Chinese (3%), Japanese (3%), Portuguese (3%), Russian (3%), Arabic (2%) and Dutch (1%). When asked how additional languages are used in the workplace, the most common responses included work meetings (accounting for 16% of language uses), client outreach (15%), and researching/working with sources in other languages (14%). Other work-based tasks included presenting work at conferences (9%), negotiating (9%), and working with non-English-speaking colleagues (9%). These figures indicate that study abroad alumni use their languages in a variety of different contexts to achieve a variety of work-related objectives.

3.3 The Qualities of Language Use at Work Among Study Abroad Alumni

If 65% of our participants have used an additional language in their jobs, how exactly does this take place? Made possible by the life pathways typology based on the survey findings, systematic selection of interviewees resulted in the inclusion of people in a wide variety of professions, yet roughly matching the distribution of organization types represented in the quantitative data (non-profit educational, for-profit companies, government, and international organizations). This section will highlight the careers of individuals whose jobs require regular use of additional language abilities for various purposes, focusing on direct, practical applications of language proficiency rather than related skills or other ancillary benefits as described in Chapter 7. We recruited participants who currently use their languages, or have done so in the past, in a range of employment fields. The largest group included in this section is involved in education, of course, but within our qualitative data there are also multiple representations of business, healthcare, and government service/international development, as well as one case each in engineering, theater arts, and sports.

3.3.1 Education

In the survey, as in the qualitative data for this project, the largest number of participants are employed by educational institutions, mainly non-profit. However, even a cursory glance at the qualitative profiles of individuals will reveal that 'education' in our data is anything but a monolithic category. Of the 7 educators highlighted in this chapter, 4 identify primarily as teachers or professors, but they are not all language teachers, nor do they work in similar institutions. These include Rose, who teaches French at the secondary level; Freida, an instructor of Spanish at a private college; Steven, a professor of history at a small public college; and James, a professor of sociology at a public university in France. One of our participants is involved in the design and marketing of materials for language instruction at work in a for-profit tech company (Eleanor) and another is involved in the oversight of study abroad programs (Jo). Another has been promoted from the ranks of her faculty to an administrative post as associate dean and then provost (Laura).

3.3.1.1 Teaching
Rose: Secondary school language teaching

As further described in Chapter 6, for Rose (age group 41–50) the homestay component of her year abroad in France involved deeply significant cognitive–emotional development. Her hosts extended a generous welcome, included her as if she were a member of the family and helped her to secure an internship in a local elementary school, no doubt influencing her decision to become a teacher. Rose had grown up in a North Atlantic semi-rural area, with modest circumstances and relatives who deliberately limited their own horizons: for example, by harboring suspicions about 'socialist' countries like France. While in school herself, she encountered favoritism toward her wealthier classmates, particularly in French class, and was somewhat overshadowed by her sister's local fame as a star athlete: 'Nobody knew who I was. Nobody took the time to get to know me.' She attended a small liberal arts college in that same area and, after completing her teaching certificate and an ill-fated experiment with jobs in inner-city schools, returned there to establish her career as a high school French teacher and raise a family. Rose claims that, in retrospect, she discovered her identity while abroad ('one of the most pivotal moments in my life,' 'that's when I realized who I am as a person'). Altogether Rose's history has made of her a fiercely egalitarian and devoted teacher, committed to engaging, creative instruction and attentive to the general well-being of every student who crosses her path. 'Concerned about the whole student,' she often works with the same cohorts over periods of years and can recognize and signal social or psychological problems that others do not notice. Beyond this, another overarching goal is to help students in her region to see beyond entrenched provincialism and narrow world views:

> I have a student that's studying at the American University of Paris, and she came home because her grandma's having surgery, she was my intern last year, and for me it was a really fun moment because she started French with me in eighth grade, she took five years of French with me, she traveled to Europe with me. she's my first student out of 13 to ever [...] get accepted to American University of Paris, and she tested out. she doesn't take any French classes, so everything is entirely in French, and I was sitting there listening to her today, and that's why I do what I do.

(Note: all quotations and extracts in the narrative sections of the book come directly from transcripts of the interviews and are in the participants' own words.)

As the only French teacher in her district, Rose can feel isolated at times. On the other hand, since her subject is not regulated by high-stakes standard achievement tests, she is free to design her curriculum as she pleases. She tries to emphasize the literacy skills that will equip her students to excel at the university level. To encourage her students' investment in French courses, she also takes up a content-oriented approach, challenging students to nominate topics for exploration in class, such as the meaning of Armistice Day or the contributions to science of French inventors. Although these impromptu lessons can occasionally occupy her weekend time with planning, this does not dampen her enthusiasm: 'If my students are engaged, and they want to come to class, I'm doing something right.' Because it is crucial for her work, Rose actively strives to maintain and enhance her French language proficiency through social and other media, and by hosting a conversation group for diverse local adults wishing to practice together. She also regularly accompanies groups of students on summer study tours in France, occasions that allow her to visit and nurture an ongoing relationship with her original host family. In recent years, she has expanded her teaching repertoire to include English as a

Second Language and night classes for adults preparing a high-school equivalency diploma. She has also taken up the study of Spanish, in part to hold up her own incompetence in that language to demonstrate empathy with her ESL students. In the future, she hopes to continue travelling and learning languages.

Freida: University language teaching

Like many of our participants, especially those who discovered their vocation during study abroad (see Chapter 4), Freida (age group 41–50) attributes the arc of her career path to a semester in Chile during her junior year in college. Having previously focused her studies on English literature, with only a few prior introductory courses in Spanish, which she found difficult, at the start of her sojourn she struggled with the language, fortunately receiving highly valuable tutelage from the school-aged children of her host parents in Valparaiso. During the final six weeks of the program, participants were invited to carry out an independent project on a topic of their choice, traveling alone to the research site and sustaining themselves on their own. Freida intended to study folklore on a small island in Patagonia, living in a tent within the boundaries of a national park. However, upon arrival she found the location deserted because of flooding. She traveled instead to a local town where she investigated sustainable traditions in agriculture and fishing. These experiences awakened in Freida a passion for teaching language and culture; she 'wanted to get out and do something that mattered.'

Upon returning to campus for her senior year, Freida was disenchanted with the study of English literature at which she had previously excelled, yet she found a topic for her thesis in travel narratives. After graduation she found employment with a non-governmental organization and taught English as a Second Language in a remote Costa Rican village for a year, then remained there for an additional year to work with small communities hoping to develop ecotourism. This, she says, 'was literally the most rewarding experience of my life [...] their lives were changed, literally.' During the following year, she continued to work for the same organization, this time in the Yucatan Peninsula training volunteer teachers. Then, after three years abroad, she returned to the US and worked as a volunteer ESL teacher herself while studying for a master's degree in Spanish, to prove that she could teach Spanish. She was then hired as a Spanish teacher at the small women's liberal arts college where she has been working since.

Freida's approach to teaching Spanish is highly influenced by the nature of her immersion experiences, teaching herself grammar by reading, writing and seeking patterns, and watching native speaker friends argue over her queries about colloquial versus proper usage. She insists on the practical value of world language proficiency, and on a communicative approach that values formal accuracy and the ability to negotiate meaning equally. In addition to teaching language, she has developed interdisciplinary honors courses on migrant farmworkers, with guest lectures from local farmers and labor advocates. Most importantly, however, she has developed considerable expertise in the design and overseeing of some of her institution's study abroad programs. Beginning with a language-focused summer program in Costa Rica that now operates every other year, she has also accompanied students on a service-learning sojourn in Ghana and directed a community-based interdisciplinary course on culture in a small town in Italy. She particularly enjoys opportunities to train faculty for international education, and, at the time of our interview, was working on materials to develop students' intercultural competencies for study abroad at her college.

Steven: European history

In childhood Steven (age group 51–60) was an avid reader whose parents encouraged the expansion of his horizons through books. Like Rose, he also harbors cherished memories of dramatic development in a homestay experience during his year in Paris. As a history major, he was delighted to be living with an older couple who were Holocaust survivors and former settlers in North Africa (known as 'pieds noirs'), and who had been eyewitnesses to many of the events he had to date learned about mainly in the library (see Chapter 6). After graduation from a small liberal arts college in the South, he chose to attend a PhD program in history at an elite, private university on the East Coast, having expanded his interests to include Italian history. Unfortunately, the only professor who might have supervised research on that topic moved to a position elsewhere, requiring Steven to find another solution. After seeking permission to apply, he brushed up his Italian language skills and was granted the one fellowship awarded yearly to foreigners at the Scuola Normale Superiore in Pisa. This arrangement allowed him to concentrate on Italian history during a 3-year stay in Italy.

After completing his PhD Steven initially accepted a post at a public university in New York City. However, the tragedy of 9/11 abruptly and permanently changed his orientation to the city. He had been raised in a small town nearby as the son of a blue-collar family with strong connections to the city's service sector: 'Most everybody was police or fire department. That was how you made it.' When his schedule became overcrowded with funerals or memorial services, life in the city became too difficult. Steven then relocated to a small, public university located in a rural area of the North Atlantic region where he has worked since. He specializes in modern European history, and for this reason eventually became a polyglot: He possesses general proficiency in French, Italian, Spanish, Portuguese, Romanian and Catalan, and he can read texts written in German. Steven makes it quite clear that languages are crucial to his work because 'history didn't happen in English, it happened in many languages.' To maintain and improve his language ability he makes 'an effort every day,' infusing his history lessons with language-related insights, seeking world-language mediated interaction with students and colleagues, participating in more formal conversation groups, or reading both popular and scholarly materials. He is 'a big advocate' for language study at his institution, and routinely encourages students to study abroad.

James: Sociology

As outlined in Chapter 6, for James (age group 36–40) the homestay component of his year-long sojourn in southwestern France revealed itself to be highly consequential in the long term, but not for the same reasons cited by Rose or Stephen, that is, because of a warm welcome or an enduring friendship. For James the homestay experience was alienating and confusing, but in a way that led to the discovery of his vocation. At the time, his program tended to select host families from among the local elite, and James was placed in the home of a wealthy, traditionalist, bourgeois Catholic family very different from his progressive, middle-class family of origin. To sum up this experience, he said: 'They were very conservative, and I'm gay.' At first, he was ill at ease in the extreme, and considered requesting a different family. However, over time he began to expand his social circle outside the home through contacts in the local gay community, involvement in Pride interventions, and an internship with an HIV-prevention organization, making any reliance on the host family peripheral to his social integration. Looking back, James declares that despite the difficult adjustment, this homestay arrangement awakened his 'sociological imagination' precisely due to the culture and class-related shock he experienced as an 'outsider within' a microcosm of a society previously quite unknown.

After returning to the small liberal arts college where he completed his degree, with a major in French, James' sole ambition was to live in France again by whatever means he could find. He obtained a one-year position as an assistant in the office of the program he had recently attended himself and enrolled as a student in a local university. He sustained himself for two years by teaching English. Then, to maintain his legal status, he completed a master's degree in American Studies. At that point he had exhausted all possibilities short of taking up studies at the doctoral level. His advisor, who happened to be American, counselled him to consider PhD studies in the US to secure maximum flexibility for the future: a French PhD would not be recognized in the US whereas an American degree 'might not be a problem' in France. Thus, and although he had recently met the man who would become his husband, James returned to the US to join a prestigious sociology program on the West Coast. Over time, through professional contacts and 'institutional workarounds,' he arranged to complete a dual degree with an even more prominent institution in Paris and finished the degree in seven years.

James is now an early-career professor at a university in France where he teaches courses in Anglophone studies, coordinates the gender studies program, and carries out research on the uses of expertise to inform debate in different societies. In his dissertation he examined how same-sex marriage in France is viewed though the lenses of psychoanalysis and philosophy whereas in the US economic interpretations tend to prevail among lawmakers. Currently he is working on a project to untangle features of so-called 'hard debates,' such as climate change, which is assumed to require technical expertise, versus 'soft debates,' such as same-sex marriage, where no such abilities are presumed necessary. In his teaching, writing for publication, interactions with colleagues and everyday life communication, he operates in both French and English.

As a university faculty member abroad, James must live up to expectations that he present very high levels of literacy and spoken presentation skill in his adopted language, and for this reason his case is somewhat unique in our materials. By his own admission, even in the fourth year of his employment, and after more than a decade of involvement in French higher education, mastery of academic writing is an ongoing project; when in doubt he still requests advice from colleagues or editors, and he reads the French language publications of others with an eye to their style. He remains uncertain that his email communications always convey the desired tone, and his formal writing is sometimes accused of coming across as too 'American,' that is, excessively assertive. At the same time, James has begun to manifest some of the same ambivalence toward local norms previously documented among high-achieving language learners living or studying abroad when those norms require a departure from a cherished identity (e.g. Brown, 2013; Siegal, 1996; Wieland, 1990). Specifically, having been trained in the US to value prose that is clear, 'crisp,' and explicit about causal relations, he resists precisely those strategies that French academic writers employ to avoid the appearance of assertiveness: abundant hedging ('potentially, we might suppose that…') and use of the passive voice. Moreover, many French academics in his field rigorously avoid the use of the first person singular ('I') in favor of the first-person plural ('we'), a practice that James finds 'awkward' and 'weird.' Consequently, even though he is well aware of these conventions, they do not match his desired identity as a scholar, and he does not always observe them. At this stage in his career, given his many accomplishments, he can afford to be slightly unorthodox: 'If I get dinged for it,' he says, 'so what?'

3.3.1.2 Materials design and development
Eleanor: Online language education

In college, Eleanor (age group 31–35) majored in French and neuroscience, with a term abroad in Brittany, a thesis on Creole in Martinique, and another thesis on dragonfly visual neurons. After graduation she spent a year teaching English in a rural primary school in France, 'a really good chance to work on my French.' Having developed a strong interest in helping people to learn languages, she then took up PhD-level study of neuro- and psycholinguistics at a prestigious university on the East Coast, followed by a post-doctoral position in a Canadian laboratory focused on cognition related to language acquisition. Since this research was sponsored by a research industry brand, she worked half-time in a university lab, and half-time for an animation studio that was developing educational apps for language and literacy. 'It was good to branch out a little bit and [...] get an idea of how language learning could be applied in the real world.' Following her post-doc years she returned to the US, started a family, and eventually landed her current job.

Eleanor is a professional linguist, working for a company that designs and implements learning apps for more than 70 languages: 'I got amazingly lucky in that I found this job where I'm just surrounded by languages, all the time, and by people who really love languages. [...] so I realize the privilege that I'm in, being a linguist who actually has a career as a linguist.' Eleanor's job involves working with language teachers to develop new content for the app as well as editing lessons based on user feedback. She is engaged in a project to make the app more friendly to instructors by creating ancillary materials suitable for classroom use and by working to align its pedagogical objectives with the guidelines and standards that schools must respect. Within the team of three linguists employed by her company, one of her specific roles is to ensure that the product's characteristics are informed by research on language acquisition and to carry out original research initiatives to test the product's effectiveness.

3.3.1.3 Administration
Laura: Provost

Growing up in a 'homogenous' mid-Western town as the child of parents who had also been raised in a notably insular community, Laura (age group 51–60) nevertheless cultivated openness and respect toward other cultures and a strong desire to explore the wider world. Prior to study abroad, she caught glimpses of otherness through 'little windows.' Her father worked as a corporate lawyer in a position requiring international travel and would return home with gifts from Asia and Eastern Europe. Her mother earned an undergraduate degree in social work while Laura was in grade school and encouraged her daughter's appetite for reading with such authors as Chaim Potok and James Baldwin. In a classic example of an apparently banal event serving as a dramatic source of development, she retains a vivid memory of her high school language teacher's having brought a German magazine to class in the pre-internet era: 'I just looked at this, there's this <u>entire</u> magazine in German, I mean it was just, this is <u>amazing</u>.'

During her first year-long sojourn abroad, Laura lived in Austria for a year in a dormitory with other international students and local students at a well-known music conservatory. She found it difficult to establish friendships with Austrians and built a social network with peers from South Africa, Italy and Poland who shared her circumstances. She then returned to Austria for a second year, this time as a graduate student with much improved language skills and an Austrian boyfriend who introduced her to friends and family. For Laura, the German language is 'evocative and beautiful,' and her love of German literature, particularly poetry, is tied to the study abroad experience where 'you become so connected to the place in way that is different from where you grew up, it's an adopted love.'

As a professor of German at a comprehensive university on the West Coast, Laura concentrated her scholarship on the literature, music and art of early 20th century Austria. She also worked to strengthen the language curriculum through a carefully articulated path toward advanced literacy and she mentored many students as they prepared grant applications for study or research abroad after graduation. Several years prior to our conversation, she had taken up an administrative role as associate dean of her college, helping faculty to seek funding for their research, co-organizing a student–faculty research initiative on the history of women's suffrage and leading a collaborative effort for international studies and global outreach. Later, she was appointed interim dean, and guided her college through the challenges of the COVID-19 pandemic. More recently, she has taken up the role of provost at a small liberal arts college. She has received prestigious local and national awards for teaching and faculty leadership. In her own words, 'the excitement about learning a second language and being able to study abroad was something that I wanted to be able to pass on to others.'

3.3.1.4 Study abroad
Jo Kapusta: Study abroad administration

Jo Kapusta (age group 36–40) was raised in a small town in the Northeastern region with family roots in Poland. Her family took many trips together when she was growing up, including excursions to Florida and across the country to San Francisco. These activities planted the seeds of pursuing international education in her mind:

> I think it was just the fact that they showed me that all these places you see on TV or read about in books, in newspapers. they're <u>real</u>, and you can go there. it's not just something that you see on a page. there's stuff happening, there're people who look a lot like you but they might talk funny or they might talk a little differently from you. and I think that really opened me up to want to travel more.

In high school, Jo went to Europe for a summer month with a choral group and realized that 'wow, I really can do this, I can go somewhere other than Canada.' Subsequently, she opted for a Rotary Youth Exchange for a full year in Japan. Although France was her number one choice, she was also interested in Japanese popular culture. Her first several months in Japan were challenging. However, through her persistence in trying to adjust and her continued work on the language, by the end of her stay, she had a wide social circle and basic mastery of Japanese. She was particularly grateful to her Japanese host father: she remains in contact with him and visits whenever she can (see Chapter 6).

Jo highlighted how comic books in Japanese were a 'brilliant learning tool' to her, because they align kanji (adopted Chinese logographic characters) and the two syllabic alphabets used in writing. With the support of the alphabets, she is better able to decipher the kanji. She said: 'It was even better for the fact that it's all dialogue.' She appreciated the opportunity to study conversation in this way, and 'all the slang, all the different onomatopoeias that they have for like drip, drip, drip, they have a whole slew of them. And this just blew my mind because I had no idea that there was such an enormous library of just words for sounds.' She enjoyed reading comic books so much that after the year ended, she shipped her clothing home and packed her suitcases with these books.

Jo then attended a liberal arts college in New England, during which time she continued to study Japanese and secured a summer internship in Japan. Following graduation, she was accepted into the JET (Japan Exchange Teaching) Program and taught English in Japan for five years. When she returned to the US, her ideas about the future were unformed, although she knew that she was interested in education and wanted to return to Japan. In the interim, she took a job at a bank, her first real job within the United States, and 'that's when the culture shock really hit' because 'the work dynamics were completely different.' After a few unsuccessful applications to study abroad jobs, she decided to enroll in a master's program in international education at an institute well known for the quality of its programs in that domain. After graduation, she successfully secured her 'dream job' – working for a Japanese company at its Boston branch to help support Japanese students who want to study abroad in the US, as well as American students who want to find internships or jobs in Japan:

> I think they like the fact, not only that I spoke Japanese, even if it wasn't perfect, but especially that I had a good idea of what the experience of studying abroad is like, also the educational system in Japan because I had gone through it as a high school student, which is the general demographic that we're looking to bring to the United States.

When we spoke, Jo had recently supported her first group of Japanese students as a program coordinator. Going through a guided tour of Boston, she was able to talk with students and get to know them, seeing what they were looking forward to or what they were worried about, and trying to help them set goals or understand what can be challenging and how that can be overcome. It is meaningful for her to 'have an opportunity to work with students and help them develop their goals and help them be successful in their futures.'

3.3.2 Business and management

In this section, we focus on the stories provided to our project by three individuals who have made careers in for-profit business and management and who also offered specific information about their use of language ability at work. Only one of these participants – Erik, who is relatively younger – deliberately set out to make a career in business by specializing in that domain while in college. We note that, historically, post-secondary business curricula became more common and visible for his generation than they had been for his parents. The other two are retired women in the over 60 age group whose stories, each in their own way, reflect the youthful insouciance toward career-related striving that characterize their generation's attitude. Maryse became an accidental specialist in management consulting for an international bank. And Vera, in order to be reunited with her future husband, in early adulthood threw caution to the wind and moved to France with no job prospects, but eventually settled into a business-related career much enhanced by her language skill. These stories help to illuminate further the variety of ways in which study abroad alumni use their languages in work-related contexts.

Erik: Business and entrepreneurship

For Erik (age group 41–50), one of the major insights of study abroad was the realization that language study could be taken very seriously. At home, classmates in the Japanese program of his large, public university were minimally invested in developing advanced proficiency in that language. In Japan, however, he encountered a rigorous, demanding program and a cohort of classmates determined to excel. Rising to the occasion, during his year-long program in Osaka, he attended classes from 8:00 a.m. to 5:00 p.m. on each weekday and undertook an arduous commute to and from his homestay, where he was again put to work on household chores (see Chapter 6). Despite these hardships, he refers to that time as 'the best year of my life.' In addition to gaining functional proficiency in Japanese and an insider's view of Japanese culture, he made lifelong friends, all of which proved essential for his later success in business.

After graduation, for a time Erik struggled to find relevant work, in part, he believes, because of the general economic picture at the time, and in part because when he was in college, business majors at his university were required to choose between study abroad and an internship. With no such experience or connections, he was at a disadvantage compared to his classmates. After nine months of searching, during which he contemplated with despair such options as running a Blockbuster Video store or a fast-food outlet in his provincial hometown, he was hired by a Japanese printing company. Employment with that company allowed him to relocate to New York and Hong Kong, and he enjoyed some aspects of the work, such as localizing and bringing to market the Japanese anime he had loved as a child.

He moved on to an entry-level position with a major US retailer, and then was recruited to a major national office supply company with an offer of a beginning management position. Within the first week of his employment at that company, he was sent to Japan along with senior members of the company, to resolve a conflict with a supplier of pens. Seemingly intractable, the problem had been simmering for months with no prospect of a solution and extreme frustration on both sides. However, listening to commentary in Japanese during the meetings, Erik was able to discern immediately that the issue was to do with politeness. Specifically, as he pointed out in the interview, his American colleagues had not appreciated the distinction, in Japanese, between 建前 'tatemae' and 本音 'hon'ne.' In Kanji 建 tate, refers to 'construction,' and 前 mae, refers to 'front,' thus 'tatemae' refers to what is said in public, when hiding one's true thoughts. By contrast, 本 hon, refers to 'true,' and 音 ne (or 'oto') refers to 'sound,' and 'hon'ne' is the expression of one's honest, unfiltered opinion. First, Erik's company had violated a tacit norm regarding the establishment of trust over the long term by repeatedly cancelling orders. Then, the American side had expected a clear and direct explanation of the problem, which was not forthcoming. No one among Erik's colleagues in the US had understood that, in Japanese business communication, a veneer of positive outlook, tact and politeness concealed the actual nature of problems, and that Japanese professionals would avoid direct self-expression on conflictual topics whenever possible. After the meetings, Erik escorted his senior managers on a most enjoyable tour of Tokyo nightlife. Then they all returned to the US, where Erik again saved the day, finding an error in the ordering process, and solving it by requesting new packaging. The Japanese company accepted the entire order and the pens went on to become the most profitable product line in company history. As Erik expressed it, 'they thought I was a miracle worker.' At this company, Erik was promoted from manager to senior manager and then to acting director, all in the span of 18 months. After he completed an MBA, he was asked to return to the company as vice president.

> both sides were fighting for almost a year, just arguing on the phone, back and forth, and no one could understand either side's stance or

the real root of the problem. however, for me, having understood the Japanese culture and understood the language, it was rudimentary how to fix this problem. there were a lot of analytics and a substantial amount of math involved, but in the end I utilized my cultural understanding of both sides and utilized my language skills working directly with the Japanese senior management to ultimately come up with a win-win solution. in the end both sides were extremely happy. [...] this whole experience understandably also did wonders for my career, as it propelled me from just 3 years earlier sitting in an entry level position to in the end becoming the youngest senior manager in their company's history. I very much credit much of this success to what I learned in my study-abroad and university language program studies.

The happy ending to Erik's story might have stopped here, but there is an unusual plot twist. As a child, he had cultivated a deep love of Japanese video games, anime and toys; he had often wondered why the range of these products available in the US was so limited. On departure for Japan, to cover living expenses without credit cards, he had borrowed $20,000 from his father and had deposited that money in a Japanese bank. Communication paths having crossed, he then discovered that he would be the beneficiary of a scholarship from the Japanese government that would provide a generous stipend. At the end of the year, due to favorable interest and exchange rates, his account showed a balance of $28,000. Erik's father, no doubt highly pleased to recover his own funds, insisted that he keep these profits. While he was still at the printing company, Erik invested this money in a line of popular Japanese toys that were not distributed in the US and sold them for $16,000 – considerably more than he could earn in months at his regular job. Over time, as he continued to buy and sell these toys, his company became the largest e-commerce website for such products. These achievements by his early forties have allowed him to leave the corporate world and focus on his own entrepreneurship, and to travel to Asia frequently to consult with suppliers. Ultimately, in his words, he was 'able to pair his passion and love of languages and other cultures with a career that brought him both success and the freedom to live as [he] chooses.'

Maryse: Management consulting

Maryse (age group over 60) was born and raised in small-town Kansas, an environment she describes as thoroughly Midwestern and monolingual. During her childhood, her family did not travel, and there were few readily visible signs of internationalization in her community. She attended her local state university and majored in French, with a 9-week summer immersion program in France after her first year, and a full year in Bordeaux when she was a senior. She then went on to graduate study, completing a master's degree and then a PhD in French literature, with a specialization in contemporary women's writing.

During this time, she spent one summer working in Paris as the assistant director of the program she had attended herself, received a year-long Fulbright grant for her research, also in Paris, and then spent another year in that city accompanying her husband during his Fulbright-supported time abroad. During most of her graduate years, she taught language: French in the US and English in France. Altogether she was in France for four years.

Throughout that time, Maryse fully intended to pursue a standard career in academia, working as a professor and continuing her research. However, after following her husband to Chicago, where he had found an academic job, her own search yielded 'one opening in French for a tenure-track position in the greater Chicago area.' She interviewed for that job and felt confident in her performance, but then the job itself was defunded, becoming a contingent position with neither long-term security nor support for research. It had become, in her terms, 'a junk job.' She took up a post in program development for 'humanistic studies' in a medical school, carrying out administrative duties while teaching courses on medicine and literature intended to educate future doctors about the human condition.

In this position, she became involved in networking with other professional women, particularly in a collective effort to identity women who could be nominated for high-level positions in higher education administration:

> we had the idea that women if we're relatively happy in the jobs we're in are less inclined than men to go out always looking for the bigger, better job. so we were kind of pumping one another up to apply for jobs.

Through this connection, she was offered a seat on the Illinois Planning Committee. There she met a former dean who had also accompanied her husband to Chicago and who had found a position with a multinational bank. Eventually Maryse received a phone call from this new friend, saying that the bank was looking for someone with proficiency in Romance languages and asking her to schedule an interview. Initially, Maryse found this proposal slightly outrageous: 'I never wanted to be a <u>banker</u>!' However, after a delightful interview conducted entirely in French, which Maryse did not quite take seriously, the offer arrived:

> and I thought, what is wrong with this picture? I didn't really plan to leave higher education, but this is something I can't just say, nah. so I took the job and [...] the man who was my boss [...] said the wonderful thing that I've quoted many times. he said, I've spent thousands of dollars teaching MBAs language and culture. I'm willing to spend thousands of dollars teaching you business. and he <u>did</u>, so I had a mini-course of accounting and a mini-course of finance, in a variety of

things of that kind and loved the learning curve. I went in with French and Italian and then he sent me to private classes for Spanish, and so I thrived. it was a group of smart people that I worked with. [...] well, this was charming. one of the guys who turned out to be a boss, a couple of levels away, said, well, we know you're smart because you have a PhD, does anybody ever say that in higher education?

Maryse had been concerned that she might find the work dull and uninspiring but she soon discovered that she enjoyed 'global treasury management' consulting. Considerable international travel was involved, as was the discovery of business cultures she found intriguing 'in an anthropological way.' In addition to her newfound quantitative abilities, she brought an astute and sensitive approach to observing and navigating these cultures, and a facility in writing that was not always characteristic of her colleagues who had studied business administration in college. In addition, her language abilities were 'immensely valuable to our business because so many U.S. consultant groups would just come in and assume everything would be done in English, so they felt valued, they felt surprised.' All this took place during the 1980s, concurrent with the creation of the European Union, and Maryse was frequently invited to address US corporate treasury personnel on that topic. She remained at the bank for 12 years and, through promotions, to a management position and then to a vice-presidency, until it became clear that the institution was 'going down' and would be acquired by another concern. Subsequently, she worked as vice-president of a non-profit education consortium until she lost that job when a new president arrived wishing to install her own leadership team. For a time, she affiliated herself with a fund-raising consulting group in order to learn that skill, and hoping to help the group expand their management and international focus. Eventually she found the courage to establish her own, independent consulting practice and has spent the past 20 years working with non-profit organizations such as 'fragile colleges,' human service organizations, or childhood education groups.

Maryse never learned the source of the funding ($600 on a program fee of $750, in 1964) that made her first trip to France possible, but now she is on the International Affairs Advisory Board for the state university she attended and promotes study abroad as a life-changing experience. She and her husband have endowed a study abroad scholarship. She says, 'I feel as though paying back is pretty important.'

Vera: Manufacturing management

Vera (age group over 60) is a descendant of Jewish immigrants from Poland who arrived in the American mid-west at the turn of the 20th century. Her father's early career in Hollywood film production came to an end on his return from a stint in the military during the Second World

War, and he chose to join his father-in-law in the oil business. When Vera was 2, the family moved to a small town in the South to be near the centers of oil production. Growing up, Vera enjoyed 'a nice upper-middle class life,' with parents who maintained high expectations for their children; but, with her progressive views, she 'just felt like something was wrong' and that she 'needed to get the hell out of there.' She added: 'I didn't even go to integrated schools.' When it came time to consider colleges, she applied only to institutions within the contiguous US but at a maximum distance from her hometown. Offered a choice, she opted for a small liberal arts college for women on the West Coast where she majored in French and spent a full year in Paris.

Among Vera's many adventures while in France, one became by far the most consequential. She was hitchhiking to visit the Mont-Saint-Michel with two American friends, a woman and a man. 'Everybody was out on the road hitchhiking. And there were nuns hitchhiking and priests hitchhiking, so we hitchhiked.' After waiting quite a while for a ride, the friends hid the man behind some bushes until a driver finally offered to pick them up. That driver became Vera's lifelong partner.

Vera's career presents another example of the nonchalance and sense of freedom that characterized her generation's youthful attitude toward work. She graduated with academic honors and toyed with the idea of respecting her parents' wishes, taking up graduate study to become a professor. However, she realized that 'I didn't want to do that. I just didn't.' Instead, she packed her bags and informed her parents that she was moving back to France to be with her boyfriend and would just find whatever job she could. Her parents 'thought it was awful' that their 'nice little Jewish girl' would plan her life in such a haphazard way, and especially that she would decide to live with a man out of wedlock.

In the first job she found, Vera worked as a bilingual receptionist for a hotel chain, an experience that proved her ability to work well with people. Since the commute to that job was long and involved driving on tortuous roads at night, she visited the employment office of the small town where she lived and was immediately offered a position at a private hospital. This job did not require English, but the ability to use that language occasionally proved useful. After five years, with her parents growing older and pleading with her to come home, she and her husband decided to marry and relocate to the US, 'without a plan in the world.' Her husband's engineering background qualified him to work for a French manufacturing company with plants in South Carolina. During a chance encounter with a Francophone group at a theater, Vera secured a position with a French-owned-and-operated textile company, where she used her French language ability every day, either during calls to the parent company or in translating documents. She was promoted to management and worked there for 25 years, until the textile industry moved to parts of the world with less expensive labor and the factory closed. In the final chapter of her work life, with two children in college, she managed the office of a renovation franchise based in Montreal, where once again she used her French regularly in communication with the main office there. Thus, even though she lived in the US during most of her working years, French was always a key asset, contributing much to her success by allowing her to build good relationships with parent companies in France and Canada.

3.3.3 Healthcare

Another group of active language users among our interviewees work in various healthcare fields. Spanish is the most obviously useful language for those who are employed in the US, as is the case for Patrick's practice of family medicine. However, two of our participants in this category have also used French for communication in healthcare settings, as a coincidence, in both instances in the Democratic Republic of Congo (DRC). For Thomas, whose full profile appears in Chapter 5, French is not particularly relevant to his work as an anesthesiologist/pain medicine specialist in the US and applies mainly to his personal life. However, Thomas has also volunteered to join Doctors Without Borders in a war-torn region of the DRC where the ability to communicate in French is crucial. Victoria, a global medical officer with an international development agency of the US federal government, often works in the DRC as well, and currently finds French to be the most routinely necessary of the seven European, East Asian and African languages she has tried to learn. Finally, we include in this section the unique profile of Clementine, a former Russian and fine arts major who, in adulthood, became a specialist in acupuncture and a student of classical medical Chinese.

Patrick: Family medicine

When we interviewed him, Patrick (age group 31–35) was in his second year of residency in family medicine. He studied Spanish almost continuously from the age of 12 until his third year in college, when he embarked on a semester-long sojourn in Grenada. Like Thomas, he graduated with determination to become a doctor, but felt that he needed some experience of the world before committing to medical school. Unlike Thomas, and more in keeping with the focus on career typical of his generation, he found a series of positions related to his ambitions for the in-between years, working in a sports concussion lab on his home campus, then transitioning to a post in Alzheimer's disease and memory research in a major New England city. Three years into the research post, he was accepted to medical school at an Ivy League university. When that degree was complete, he moved to another Northeastern city where he had found an excellent program in his specialty.

Apart from his sojourn in Spain, Patrick has taken up many opportunities to enhance his language abilities and awareness of Hispanophone cultures. As an undergraduate, he traveled to Mexico twice to volunteer in clinics. As a medical student he interacted in Spanish regularly with patients and participated in a travel exchange program with the Dominican Republic. More recently, he has traveled to Honduras with one of the attending physicians in his program who is involved with an infrastructure building program. There is a large population of Spanish-speaking residents in the area where he now works, many of whom emigrated from Puerto Rico following the Hurricane Maria disaster. According to Patrick, opportunities to use Spanish are 'everywhere,' in the clinic, the hospital or the emergency room.

Of course, Patrick also works with speakers of many other languages and he insists that language per se should never influence the essential quality of the care that he provides. However, he recognizes a therapeutic effect in the rapport he can build with Spanish-speaking patients, noting for example experiences in a pediatric emergency room where families seemed 'relieved' that he could interact with them in their own language. Beyond this, in his travels and volunteer experiences abroad he has learned a great deal about folk medical practices. For example, the Mayan population in the rural area of Mexico hold beliefs about the heating or cooling properties of plants, and so 'if a girl had an abscessed tooth, they would put a leaf over it because that's a cooling presence.' These experiences have taught him to avoid quick judgment, to be humble and remain open to appreciating 'different ways of seeing things.' In turn, these stances are helpful 'every day with the kinds of stuff I deal with [...] like people who think the flu shot gives you flu. There's always stuff like that no matter where you are.' He has also encountered racist attitudes among colleagues who issue negative generalizations about Latinx patients and he finds that his experiences of diverse healthcare practices and attitudes help him to keep these kinds of commentary in a broad and critical perspective.

In the future, Patrick aspires to work in one of the Federally Qualified Health Centers situated in resource-poor areas. He has carried out such work as part of his residency and found that he enjoys the 'dynamic' and the 'mission sense of the people.' In such a center, where many patients' lives are affected by socioeconomic determinants of health or refugee status, he feels that he can contribute to addressing the root causes of illness. He wishes to continue using Spanish in his interactions with patients. In addition, he is looking forward to broader opportunities for clinical teaching, already a part of his work as he helps to instruct medical students during his residency. He feels it is important for doctors to reflect on 'the right way to use their language ability, depending on what their level is, and using it appropriately, being humble about when they need help and need an interpreter [...] so I want to be, I think, a good mentor.'

Victoria: Global public health

because we don't do anything domestically, most Americans wouldn't have encountered us, and especially if you go to developed countries when you go overseas you again would not have encountered us. but anybody who spent time in a developing country or a war-torn area, or any place where there's a famine, they've seen our stickers.

Victoria (age group 36–40) is a global medical officer working for an international development agency of the US federal government. Her primary foci are tuberculosis and HIV, which often go hand in hand. In ordinary times she travels during approximately half a typical year, mostly to Africa, in order to support US-government-funded local teams, in following 'the latest and greatest thing is in terms of the science, and also in terms of the implementation.' Victoria has extensive experience of language learning, having developed functional proficiency in French and Spanish, and having also tried to learn Hausa and Zarma in Niger, Tamil in India, and Setswana in Botswana. Each of these experiences has conveyed wisdom that is valuable for her international career, and currently it is the French language that plays the most visible role for her work in the Francophone DRC:

in the last few years I was supporting not just the HIV effort but was also asked to help support partly the Ebola response, again not clinically, but going to meetings, interacting with the other funders, deciding who was going to fund what, getting information for daily updates and such. so I would go to the daily briefing and take notes. again, obviously, it's all in French. and then reading documents in French and such and just having conversation.

Victoria was raised in an expatriate community in the South, the daughter of an Irish nurse and a South African doctor. She attended an elite college on the East Coast, and although she had already confirmed her own interest in medicine, she majored in history with a minor in French, to be sure that there were no other tempting paths. Her semester abroad took place in Niger, where she intended to improve her French while examining global health issues. During this 'eye-opening' sojourn, she learned what it is like to live in a country with a non-functional government. The university where she might have taken courses was closed and there was no public health system:

the main thing that I learned from that experience is that it wasn't going to be enough just to get a medical degree if I wanted to work in global health. I had to do a public health degree as well, because I shadowed a doctor at the hospital and I spent one night in the ER and there was a meningitis outbreak and they had no equipment whatsoever. you can be the greatest doctor in the world, but if you have no equipment, there's nothing you can do.

The Niger program was the 'first domino' in a career path marked by multiple sojourns abroad. After college, Victoria selected a combined medical and global health program at a private university in the South, spending a year in India as part of her studies. For her residency in internal medicine and pediatrics, she attended an Ivy League university offering an opportunity to work in the Dominican Republic. For two-and-a-half years afterwards, she worked as an adult and pediatric tuberculosis specialist in Botswana before taking up her current post. At this point her daily routine involves very little clinical practice, but from memory she cites the same phenomena mentioned by Patrick, namely the sense of security for patients, and the reduction of interpersonal distance allowed by her use of their language in clinical settings. Moreover, she appreciates the movement in Western medicine toward non-judgmental approaches to cultural variation in healthcare. Drawing simultaneously on her medical, public health and language training gives her great satisfaction and helps her to feel as though she is capturing her full potential as a professional.

Clementine: Acupuncture and herbal medicine

Now in the age group 41–50, Clementine is one of the few adults among our participants who is actively learning a new language for professional purposes, although without external constraints such as those faced, for example, by members of the Foreign Service. Clementine practices acupuncture and traditional Chinese herbal medicine in the rural North Atlantic farming community where she grew up. Having found inspiration for language study in high school French classes, she attended a local liberal arts college and discovered a love for Russian, which she combined with fine arts. She spent a full academic year abroad in St Petersburg, 'an extremely positive experience' during which she was 'dropped somewhere else to wake up.'

After graduation, however, she struggled to find relevant employment: 'the Peace Corps didn't even want me,' because 'fine arts with Russian wasn't a tremendously useful combination.' Nevertheless, her knowledge of art and her language skills helped her to secure a position as an administrative assistant at the Museum of Natural History in New York City where she worked for a 'difficult' supervisor and then for a manager who was profoundly deaf and appreciated her clear enunciation for the purposes of lip reading. Subsequently, she worked for a publisher of Russian reference materials in translation, where she learned to program database applications for page layout, a skill she then applied for several years as a programmer. During this time, Clementine was exposed to Chinese medicine for personal reasons, and decided to change careers. For training in acupuncture and herbal remedies, she attended a well-known school in New England and obtained a master's degree. She then returned to her hometown to begin her practice.

Before the Covid crisis, Clementine had been learning modern Chinese as an auditor in a local university classroom, but her real passion is for classical medical Chinese. In graduate school she had opted to learn the names of medicinal herbs in pinyin rather than Latin, because

> that's the universal language of Chinese medicine. If you know that an herb is called danggui (当归), everyone calls it danggui, and if you have a formula, it's called shaoyaosan (芍药散), everyone for thousands of years has called it shaoyaosan, whereas when you buy herbs in the United States, somebody may call it, you know, free and easy wander or rambling powder or something like that. but you can look at the bottle and go, oh, this is just their marketing name for shaoyaosan.

At the time of our interview, Clementine had been studying for about a year with a translator of ancient Chinese herbal texts who offers a correspondence course for acupuncturists, working on classical grammar and vocabulary. Given her art background, she finds great satisfaction in learning new characters, practicing her calligraphy, and seeing the subtle ways in which these characters combine visual and professional meaning:

> I just learned one of the characters in an herb that is *gegen* (葛根) and it's kudzu, which is [...] an herb that you can use when someone has a certain presentation, which includes thirst. and it's interesting because one tiny component in that character is also a tiny component in the word thirst. and that just makes my brain go crazy. I just get so excited about that.

Although initially she was concerned that her specialization might not enjoy wide appeal in her hometown, Clementine's practice is now well established and so busy that she cannot accept new patients. Still, she remains devoted to continued learning and hopes to grow her language ability to the point where she can 'really enjoy' not only the technical but also the philosophical aspects of the texts she is studying.

3.3.4 Government service and international development abroad

As is the case for the survey, a number of our interview participants have made careers wholly or partially in international service to the US federal government. Mark retired from the Foreign Service following a distinguished career learning and using Asian languages, Bonnie was also a Foreign Service Officer in various Francophone locales until moving on to international education, and Valerie works for the

Department of Commerce and was posted to Russia for two years early on in her working life. As government employees working abroad, they all received extensive language training to prepare them for their duties, and were required to achieve specific, documented levels of proficiency. Anton has also worked abroad throughout his career, using French and Arabic, but he has been employed by agencies and organizations other than the US government. Notably, and although we also interviewed one younger person who aspires to join the Foreign Service (Hugh, age group under 25), all these participants are over 50 years of age, and all of them describe feeling relatively free, in their youth, to explore activities, disciplines and places without regard for their career-enhancing potential.

Mark: Foreign Service

Mark (age group over 60) grew up in the Finger Lakes region of New York State. In high school he learned French, and then German using the 'revolutionary' audiolingual method referenced in Chapter 6. He then chose an elite university in the South because it was far from home and at the time charged no tuition, majoring in philosophy and studying Russian. His study abroad experience was a summer service-learning trip to Nigeria to help build a school as well as goodwill among young people from various regions in the build up to a civil war over the successionist state of Biafra.

As was typical for his generation, in college Mark 'was not thinking about jobs and all of that' until his senior year when he realized that a career as a philosopher would be an unlikely prospect for him. Upon graduation, he became eligible to be drafted for the Vietnam War but, to his relief, received a high lottery number making it possible to avoid that fate. After he 'rattled around a little bit' he remembered the Peace Corps volunteer who had facilitated his stay in Nigeria and he decided to apply himself. As part of that process, he took a language aptitude examination in which he was asked to classify words according to their parts of speech. Upon receiving his score of 77, he was convinced that he had received an average grade of 'C' but in fact there was a total of 80 points possible. As a representative of the 'cream of the crop' he was eligible to learn Korean, one of the languages classified as most difficult for Anglophone learners, along with Japanese, Mandarin Chinese and Arabic.

Now enrolled in the Peace Corps, Mark studied Korean for three months in a rural location within the US surrounded by 'language jocks' who were 'duking with each other to see who could do more.' He then joined the second ever cohort of Peace Corps volunteers in Korea, assigned to teach English in an isolated rural area, and lived there for two years in 'the absolute ideal immersion situation' (see Chapter 7). At the end of his assignment, he was not yet ready to leave Korea, and negotiated an additional year of teaching in Seoul, where he learned about the Foreign Service. After an additional stint with the Peace Corps, this time as a trainer in Honolulu, he found himself unemployed with little more than 'prospects' to sustain him. He remained in Hawaii and worked for a detective agency, to 'keep the wolves from the door,' during the three years it took him to conquer the Foreign Service examination.

When notification of his posting finally arrived, it was as an assistant to the science counselor at the US Embassy in Tokyo, and Mark spent two years learning Japanese. Next, he volunteered for two 3-year tours in Korea. He spent the first year back in language training to become the first American certified as a Korean–English interpreter for diplomatic encounters. Though that year was a lonely time for Mark, his success was 'unprecedented' as no previous Foreign Service Officer had achieved this feat. After a stint at the Korea desk in Washington, he decided that he had 'one more of these hard languages in me,' and volunteered for China. Following language training, he served for two years in Shanghai then for another two in Beijing, where he met his Chinese wife and 'things got really complicated.' Upon announcing his engagement, he was recalled to Washington and lost the security clearance that made him placeable in the Foreign Service, due to rules banning fraternization. He was, however, able to keep his salary while working in the international program of the National Science Foundation. Eventually his clearance was restored and, at the same time, he was promoted.

In a new, post-retirement career, Mark once again lives in the US and serves as a freelance or volunteer translator and interpreter helping speakers of Chinese and Korean to navigate medical exams, including their interactions with all the people they encounter: doctors, physical therapists, dietitians, receptionists and nurses. He also translates business, legal or technical documents from Chinese or Korean into English.

Bonnie: Foreign Service and international education

Bonnie (age group 51–60) was born into a working-class, blue-collar family in the upper Midwest and grew up with very little exposure to the world outside her community. The family took one vacation away from Minnesota, to visit family in Colorado. Everything changed in her perspective, however, when she participated in a week-long high school exchange program in France, organized by her French teacher and in connection with a sister city arrangement and her father's job running the copy room at a local manufacturing company. In this early homestay experience she learned, among many other things, that her host family took showers only once a week, as was typical in more remote settings at the time (Ross, 1995). This discovery was so dramatic for her that she became determined to find an international dimension in her career (see Chapter 6).

As a first-generation university student, Bonnie went to college 'because just everybody seemed to be going to college.' She continued to study French and spent a full academic year in western Ireland. After college she still wanted her work to involve travel and be international in some way, so she accepted a scholarship for a master's degree in international affairs in Washington, DC. At this point, she had never heard of the Foreign Service, but her transition to that career was a great deal easier than Mark's: one morning she and some friends casually took the Foreign Service examination to have something to do before going out to lunch, and, to her astonishment, she passed. She presented this information to her long-term boyfriend, another Minnesotan whose travel had to date been limited to fishing trips to Canada, noting that the two of them would need to marry if he wanted to accompany her abroad. He agreed and they moved to London, where Bonnie worked the visa line, occasionally encountering Francophone applicants. She then received 6 months of intensive training back in Washington, DC to upgrade her proficiency in French, and was posted first to Mauritius and then to Madagascar. She recalls this time in her life as full of 'amazing adventures,' including one occasion where she was called to duty following the crash of an Ethiopian airplane that had been hijacked by 'guys with fire extinguishers.' The survivors, including several Britons and Americans, were rushed to a hospital in Reunion, a French protectorate where English was not spoken, and for two weeks Bonnie was responsible for translating the doctors' information to the hijacking victims: 'so that was probably the highlight of my language usage in my career, to be honest. I mean, when you use it in an emergency, you realize how critical it is.'

Following several more tours of duty and the births of their three children, and because their parents were aging, Bonnie and her husband decided that it was time to return to the US. She accepted an administrative role in a community college located in a small and insular Wisconsin town. She quickly realized that her job would not be about encouraging local students to study abroad but, rather, about bringing the world there so that they could learn in an environment where they felt safe. As a prime example of success in this endeavor, she recalls convincing a local Jewish family to host an Israeli Arab student for a week. Based on television coverage of the conflict in Palestine, the family needed reassurance, and Bonnie agreed to take over the hosting should any issues arise. On the contrary, as it turned out, the family's college-aged son visited his former guest in Israel, majored in Middle Eastern studies, and became a city official advocating for diversity and inclusion.

Ten years later, Bonnie was ready to move into a larger professional arena. She worked with a career counselor and opted to return to school for an EdD degree in higher education administration. In the interim she had become active in a major professional association for international education, eventually rising to roles as vice-president and member of the board of directors. Through those connections she found her current job in a major East Coast city, helping professional graduate students to devise international experiences relevant to their careers. Should her work change in the future, she would like to be more involved in policy, but would also like to 'maintain close ties to students and young people – that's what really gets me excited.'

Anton: International development

In childhood, Anton (age group 51–60) and his brothers identified as 'faculty brats,' that is, as children of a professor living in a small Midwestern college town. The family traveled often and spent a sabbatical year living in France, where the children were directly enrolled in local schools. Anton went on to major in French literature at a prestigious liberal arts college and to spend a full academic year in Paris attending courses at the Sorbonne and living with a host family. After college, he opted to teach English in Cairo for a program supporting local scholars who wished to take advantage of financial support for studies in the US. By his own admission, he was not well trained to teach, and the program did not fill his time, leaving plenty of opportunities to explore the city and develop a fascination for the country and its language. His next step, therefore, was to find a way to remain in Egypt, and he took up an opportunity to volunteer for a village development program that offered a near-total Arabic immersion experience:

> when I went down to this village project [...] taking public transport, finding my way across the city to the (place) where you took the felucca to cross the Nile to get to this little village, I learned a dozen words just to get there. so we were living [...] in this sort of ashram-style compound and we used to have meetings at meals. somebody would be translating, which was perfect for me to listen and learn, and soon enough I was one of the translators. I was single, and so I was probably immersed 75% of the time in Arabic.

At this point in his life, Anton can claim nearly 40 years of international development experience. He spent seven years in villages, witnessing the dire effects of mechanization, corruption and other issues, then received a Fulbright grant for masters-level formal study in his field. According to him, this work can involve various actors, from governments to community groups, and a range of foci, including for example humanitarian assistance, reducing poverty, or giving voice to the disabled or to other disadvantaged groups. On some occasions the work calls for developing services that a government might decide to adopt; on others it means working directly with governments, schools, or hospitals to influence the way they deliver services. The basic idea, though, is 'trying to build up the capacity of actors to manage their own development.'

With degree in hand, Anton returned to the Middle East to pursue freelance opportunities. Subsequently, he was 'drafted' by a major humanitarian organization that was pursuing a competitive funding opportunity to establish a non-governmental service center in Egypt. He joined a special project intended to empower citizen groups in their communication with the government, then moved to the Republic of Georgia for another project with a similar purpose. Five years later, he went back to Egypt as the head of the organization's country office, directing efforts to improve health education, child protection and poor family livelihoods in rural areas, and to address issues such as infant mortality and illiteracy. Twenty years later, and just prior to the Covid crisis, he decided to resume freelance activities while continuing to maintain his language abilities.

Anton is careful to specify that his proficiency in Arabic is concentrated in abilities to speak, read, and listen, and that he would not be confident in professional writing. His speaking ability, however, is such that when he is teaching, he can switch from colloquial usage to Modern Standard Arabic for occasions requiring extra 'gravitas.' For Anton, French and Arabic have been instrumental in his career, both because his ability to secure contracts has been greatly facilitated by this skill and because language abilities are in fact crucial to effective work in the field.

Valerie: Department of Commerce

'There's really no such thing as international business. It's all international business.' So says Valerie (age group 51–60) in the context of a conversation about her career with the United States Department of Commerce. Equipped with an undergraduate degree in finance from a flagship state university in the North Atlantic area, Valerie first found employment with a major domestic manufacturing company. She then relocated to the Washington, DC area to pursue a master's in business administration, followed by a paid internship with the Department of Commerce, where she has worked since. Her job has involved various duties, such as working at a US Export Assistance Center helping companies, manufacturers or service providers who wish to export and find overseas partners, or, more recently, in a chief-of-staff position managing the flow of trade-related information for the Secretary of Commerce. The highlight of her career came when she passed the Foreign Commercial Service examination with a high score and then was sent to Russia as a diplomat after intensive language study.

According to Valerie, her stint in Moscow corresponded with a sea change in Russian business practices, with the arrival of commercialization and a 'wide-eyed kind of excitement for the Russian people to be exposed to things that were otherwise inaccessible in the past.' At the same time there were 'different types of norms in that new business culture,' including illegal bribery and government involvement in privatized companies, that needed to be navigated by the concerns she served. Valerie's role in that position basically called for working with the US government in dialogue with the Russian government to facilitate agreements between their respective companies. Her responsibility for the transportation and aerospace sectors was the most memorable; one of her successes involved a meeting between major airplane manufacturers and the Russian Ministry of Trade to reduce prohibitive tariffs on the Russian side and enable a purchase agreement.

Valerie was raised in a small town in the same state where she obtained her undergraduate degree, in a family with roots in Eastern Europe. Like many of our other participants, she mentioned study abroad as the first relevant episode in her professional life. However, her decision to study in France was something of a serendipitous affair rather than a deliberate step. In her words, she 'just happened upon a study abroad program' in an obscure corner of campus where 'by chance' she found a brochure describing a semester-length business-related offering. Until then she had no particular interest in French, but she duly enrolled in the language classes required for admission to the program. This experience became the highlight of her student years and the context in which she formed the most durable, life-long friendships with other Americans enrolled in the program. Although during the school week they also interacted with French students in the local dormitory cafeteria, because these American students could rely upon each other for company, these encounters were somewhat limited. At that age, she says, she 'wouldn't have wanted to be so alone' in attempting to avoid her compatriots. Together, Valerie and her American companions would use their Eurail passes to visit another country every weekend. The experience was largely about having 'freedom to travel and see' and she saw every European country during that semester. Upon returning to campus, Valerie continued to study French, adding that minor to her degree program.

Even though language learning was not the focus of her time in France, Valerie believes that entry into her career was very much facilitated by her interest in languages and the proficiency in French that she was able to demonstrate. Furthermore, candidates for positions in the Department of Commerce are at a distinct advantage if they present a history of study abroad and language learning:

> that absolutely kind of puts them into a higher level that we might want to hire them over somebody who's not studied any language. because we're working with international trade policy. so just having another language or especially having lived abroad absolutely puts you in a higher understanding of what we do.

3.3.5 Other careers, other uses of language

In this section we include three cases illustrating some of the more unusual career paths we discovered in our interviews. These include a French-speaking ocean engineer from New England, an aspiring sports professional who learned Spanish to work with Latin American baseball players, and a Francophone specialist in theater arts management and journalism who is also a playwright.

Tim: Ocean engineering

Tim (age group 25–30) is a recent graduate of a state university's 5-year program in which students double major in engineering and a world language, in his case ocean engineering and French. The program design calls for three years of domestic study, a fourth year abroad with the first semester in a local university and the second in a paid internship, and a final year back on campus to complete all degree requirements. While on campus Tim enrolled in French courses varying in focus from business to 17th-century literature. During his first semester abroad, he attended a technology-oriented university north of Paris, studying the language at the C1 (advanced) level as well as engineering, journalism and the history of the European Union. At a university-sponsored job fair he found his first internship with a construction company in Dunkirk that was building a prototype for a floating wind turbine. When that project was delayed, his manager found another opportunity for him in Marseilles, working on a new highway. Throughout his time in France, he lived in rented apartments shared with French students, which he sometimes found 'taxing,' if ultimately very beneficial for his language proficiency.

After completing a master's degree, Tim found his current position working as a support engineer for a French company that designs underwater positioning and navigation systems. The position calls for frequent travel to customer sites for demonstrations, installations and troubleshooting as well as to company headquarters for training and other meetings. For Tim, language proficiency was not necessarily the main criterion that made his candidacy appealing to his employer. However, once he was on the job, the ability to use French for both conversational and specific engineering-related purposes allowed him to 'grow by leaps and bounds.' Although many of his colleagues do speak English, French allows him to 'get another level of connection with a lot of the employees, because they can only talk so far outside of a technical conversation.'

Alex: Sports management

Alex (age group under 25) recently graduated from a large, Midwestern public university with a major in sports management and minors in Spanish and leadership. Given his lifelong enthusiasm for team sports, an instructor in high school had encouraged him to consider these areas of study. He entered college 'on this general sports track' and, at the end of freshman year, he 'started to really get passionate about working my path to get involved with MLB [major league baseball].' To tailor a study abroad experience to these interests, for his destination he chose the Dominican Republic, 'the hotspot' where Major League teams scout for international prospects and have established training facilities. To his delight, while abroad he was offered an opportunity to work as a cultural education intern at the Developmental Academy of the Kansas City Royals. There he assisted in English language teaching and US cultural preparation for Latin American players seeking to climb the ranks of the professional baseball system. For Alex, the semester abroad was a very positive experience that promoted his language, personal and professional development.

One of the important lessons that Alex took away from his experience abroad was the realization that attaining additional language proficiency requires a sustained, long-term effort. He had been studying the language continuously since the age of 12 and, like many other US-based learners, had overestimated his abilities before they were tested in contact with a Hispanophone community. 'Taking a one-hour Spanish class at school, maybe two three four times a week, is not going to let you learn a language,' he said. 'If I had known that sooner, I would have done whatever I could to get abroad sooner and be in a fully immersed experience.' Nonetheless, he began to find real satisfaction in learning Spanish while abroad and at the beginning of his career:

> knowing how much I know about baseball and the whole influx of Spanish in baseball, I've really enjoyed being able to understand that. I follow the Spanish versions of the Major League accounts on social media [...] so I can receive baseball content in another language, and I can understand that. and that's enjoyable for me.

After graduation, Alex became a brand partnership intern with a professional baseball team based in the Midwest, working to ensure business-to-business relationships with their organizational partners, including in-game promotions and partner events. Subsequently he entered a second, year-long internship with the same team, housed alongside the players and once again involved with efforts to enhance cultural understanding, literacy and English language competence. During the Covid-19 crisis, he has remained active in his teaching work. As for the future, he has his 'full passions geared toward getting a position within international operations, within player development off field, where I'm working with players on their English acquisition, on their cultural assimilation, something hands on, but also within the realm of how baseball is adapting to this influx of external labor force from outside of the borders of the US.' More recently, he has secured a full-time, permanent position with a Midwestern Major League baseball team.

Amelia: Journalism and theater arts

Amelia (age group 25–30) cannot remember a time when theater was not important to her. At the age of 8 she enlisted the help of a teacher and budding playwright to form a drama club at school. Throughout high school and into her college years she participated in theatrical events, although early on she decided against a career as an actor and began searching for other ways to be involved. She studied abroad for a year in Paris, living in the American House of the Cité Internationale (see Chapter 6), including a course on the history of French theater and another in which students were asked to document the contemporary Parisian theater scene. She translated a play, with the blessings of the author, and volunteered at Shakespeare And Company, a celebrated bookstore where she then was employed for the summer. Returning to her home in Connecticut, Amelia was inconsolable (see Chapter 6). However, the experience of independent living had empowered her to take her senior year 'by the horns.' She secured an internship in theater communications in New York City by demonstrating that she could discuss contemporary French theater with a 'fresh off the plane vibe' that 'shifted the balance of things in the room' and, in retrospect, sent her on a path to her current work life. She served as a research assistant to her favorite French professor. And she produced the play that she had translated in Paris.

Following graduation, Amelia worked for a play development center in New York City, then spent another year in Paris working for the program in which she had participated. She then took a job as a programming coordinator for the French Institute (Alliance Française) in New York, where she stayed for two years, facilitating the visits of French artists to the United States while building her professional network. Her next step was to go freelance with a variety of pursuits: arts journalism, translation and interpretation, film subtitling, assistant directorships, and company management for French theater troupes on tour in the United States. She is hired for these tasks because of her

> ability to be translating between the two languages, which means not only translating the text of a play, but also helping with networking, organizing a tour, communicating with theaters, and being the go-between person, because I can shift between those two languages and cultures.

Recently, as part of a team, she has completed the translation of a book about a famous French theater. She has also seen the production of a play that she herself had authored in English and that she describes as 'a step left of realism through a feminist lens.' She has begun to explore equity, diversity and inclusion consulting as yet another activity she can embrace to further her goals. Amelia's long-term dream for the future is to find and nurture community in a residential theater collective, offering classes and contact with visiting artists while promoting a social justice agenda.

3.4 Conclusion

This chapter opened with a selection of survey findings related to employment. Among the highlights in these data is the finding that 65% of language learners in the general educated population use their languages at work, and that this proportion is stable across age ranges. The survey also revealed that while language study abroad alumni work in a broad variety of fields and sectors, a majority is involved in education, and notable groups work in for-profit organizations or in government service. Because the selection of interviewees was based on the survey findings in a systematic way, our qualitative data generally reflect these proportions of language use and field of endeavor.

In this chapter, we focused on participants who were able to articulate precisely how and why they find language ability useful in their careers. Overall, our participants value their language ability for reasons that may seem self-evident, but also in less immediately obvious ways. Individuals working in international government service or development simply must possess the ability to function in local languages; and in other fields, such as the theater arts and sports management described in this chapter, language can be an invaluable resource for getting things done. However, we have also found, for example, that language educators clearly need language skill, but so do educators in other fields such as history and intercultural sociology. In business and management, language abilities have direct, practical applications for problem solving in international contexts, but also contribute considerably to the quality of relationships that undergird success. For healthcare providers, similarly, the ability to interact with patients in their own language can have a therapeutic effect, but the experience of learning a language and exploring other health-related worldviews lends empathy, humility and wisdom in encounters with otherness, whether at home or abroad.

4 Discovering a Calling

4.1 Introduction

In this chapter we consider in detail how study abroad influences and sometimes drastically changes professional aspirations. Our survey participants strongly believe that their experiences abroad influenced their career choices and their ability to present professional skills on the job market. But what does that mean, exactly? Here, we illustrate these beliefs with the stories of individuals who discovered a vocation or specific aspirations through international education and language study. We include both professional life histories from the 65% of survey takers who claimed language use at work, and from the 35% who did not.

4.2 Career Impact of Study Abroad by the Numbers

In the survey, participants were asked to evaluate the impact of study abroad on the following: selection of employer type, selection of employment field, interest in working overseas, interest in working for a multinational organization in the US, and acquisition of skills informing career choice and leading to employment. For each statement, participants selected a value on a scale from 10 (to a great extent) to 0 (not at all). In these ways, the survey gauged participants' perceptions about the general impact of study abroad on their careers. Table 4.1 presents group descriptives for each of these statements, which indicate a remarkably positive evaluation of the perceived contribution of international education to career choices.

If we examine these evaluations as a function of age (Table 4.2) it once again becomes apparent that there are few meaningful differences across the groups, suggesting that despite changes in program design

Table 4.1 Descriptives for survey questions about the career impact of study abroad

Statement	Mean	Median	SD
Selection of type of employer	6.39	7	3.30
Selection of field of employment	6.68	8	3.27
Interest in getting a job overseas	7.52	9	2.95
Interest in working for a multinational organization in the US	6.49	7	3.28
Acquisition of skills that helped you get a job	7.32	8	2.79
Acquisition of skills that informed your career choice	6.91	8	3.04

Table 4.2 Descriptives for survey questions about the career impact of study abroad as a function of age

	<25	25–30	31–35	36–40	41–50	51–60	>60
	Mean (SD)	Mean (SD)	Mean (SD)	Mean (SD)	Mean (SD)	Mean (SD)	Mean (SD)
Selection of type of employer	5.72 (3.13)	6.19 (3.23)	6.30 (3.30)	6.87 (3.24)	7.06 (3.25)	7.09 (3.44)	6.83 (3.64)
Selection of field of employment	6.03 (3.12)	6.49 (3.21)	6.55 (3.30)	7.23 (3.22)	7.34 (3.24)	7.26 (3.35)	6.93 (3.63)
Interest in getting a job overseas	7.99 (2.55)	7.74 (2.74)	7.58 (2.77)	7.63 (2.92)	7.13 (3.24)	7.11 (3.34)	5.81 (3.78)
Interest in working for a multinational organization in US	7.10 (2.97)	6.79 (3.15)	6.40 (3.17)	6.63 (3.21)	6.04 (3.38)	5.82 (3.69)	5.03 (3.77)
Acquisition of skills that helped you get a job	6.80 (2.80)	7.10 (2.73)	7.28 (2.79)	7.66 (2.67)	7.95 (2.61)	8.03 (2.69)	7.53 (3.25)
Acquisition of skills that informed your career choice	6.29 (2.99)	6.70 (2.94)	6.82 (3.04)	7.41 (2.97)	7.49 (3.06)	7.65 (2.89)	7.19 (3.47)

(see Chapter 6) study abroad has been consistently viewed as influential for career options and choices since the 1970s. The role of study abroad in sparking interest in overseas or internationally oriented employment is particularly visible here. We also see that participants value skills obtained abroad both for orienting to employment and for securing it.

These findings are particularly important when we consider that the perceived benefits of study abroad undertaken during our twenties might lessen with age. On the contrary, here we see for instance that in evaluating 'Acquisition of skills that helped you get a job' and no doubt considering this question in retrospect, participants in the 51–60 age group rated this item at 8.03, somewhat higher than the rating given by the youngest respondents (6.80). Thus, our results indicate that study abroad tends to have long-lasting career-related benefits.

4.3 Discovering a Calling

Given the high ratings, consistent across age groups, assigned by survey participants to various perceived impacts of study abroad on career choices and abilities, in this chapter we present intact professional life histories illustrating how this occurred for particular individuals, regardless of whether they continue to use their additional languages on a routine basis. A number of our participants crafted the general coherence of their professional life stories around dramatic cognitive–emotional events or experiences during study abroad that in retrospect involved the discovery of a calling, whether or not that vocation requires continued investment in language or an international focus. For several of these participants such realizations prompted a radical change in direction. Such was the case for Peter, whose decision to pursue a career in renewable energy was inspired by the discovery of eco-conscious lifestyles in Freiburg, for Miranda, a marine biologist whose travels convinced her to make a vocation of her hobby, for Anna, who attributes her interest in nursing to a sojourn in rural Senegal, and for Hailey, who was an English major intending to become a journalist when a sojourn in Japan piqued her curiosity about advertising, leading to a career in market strategy. For others, the experience altered their perception of career paths upon which they had already begun to embark. Owen intended to pursue a career in business but it was only after study abroad in Budapest that he fully understood his desire to work internationally, and the need to become multilingual to reach that goal. Max was interested in psychology before studying in Spain but it was this experience that inspired him to link that field with linguistics and make a career in language acquisition research. Antonia's first taste of a zucchini flower indexes her discovery of specific farm-to-table practices and the general richness of international culinary traditions that would go on to enhance her work in the hospitality industry.

Peter: Renewable energy

Peter's (age group 31–35) family of origin emigrated from Germany to the American Midwest just after the First World War, entering a society where their language had become taboo (Pavlenko, 2003). His decision to study German in middle school was therefore somewhat informed by considerations of heritage, although he also cites the excellent reputation of the local program. Subsequently, he continued to invest in German and found many opportunities to enhance his proficiency and tie it to other interests. While still in high school he was hired to serve as a counselor at a well-known summer language immersion program in his home state; he continued to work there for the next ten years and retains his connections to the program to this day. As a German major at his local state university, he spent a full academic year in Freiburg, the 'solar capital' of Germany, where he lived in a bike- and public transit-friendly neighborhood and was exposed both to the latest green technological innovations and to the very notion of an entire, cohesive eco-community. Witnessing these phenomena through the prism of his cognitive–emotional lived experience (perezhivanie) prompted a change in life direction.

On returning to campus, Peter had fulfilled most of the requirements for his major and became involved in designing a sequence of university courses highlighting the environmental movement in German culture and combining those with language instruction. While at the time he was uncertain about next steps, ultimately the Freiburg experience had so inspired him that, even though this would mean beginning his studies anew to fulfill requirements, he decided to pursue a second degree in environmental science focusing on policy, planning, law and society. After graduation, the summer immersion program where he had been teaching German through environmental content connected him to the Fulbright program; he spent two years teaching English in Austria, learning a new dialect of German and competing in international matches with the local Ultimate Frisbee team.

After his years in Austria, Peter's goal was to live in an urban setting but to have a positive impact on the environment. To follow this passion, and to earn a living, he enrolled in a dual Master of Business Administration/Public Policy program. To satisfy an internship requirement for that degree, he also spent one summer researching recycling and compost policy best practices for a small Austrian town, then presenting a series of recommendations to the city which were subsequently taken up. In the second year of his graduate program, he used funds from business plan competitions and other resources available to students to co-found a compost processing company with his German-speaking wife, a soil and water engineer. When the composting company ran afoul of antiquated urban industrial zoning laws, the couple was forced to close it.

Peter then became the sixth employee of the 30-person solar energy start-up company where he continues to work to date. He develops community solar projects that feed power into the utility grid, with local customers receiving credits on their electricity bills in exchange for supporting this community asset. Working out of his Midwestern home city, he negotiates leases with rural landowners and contracts with local utility companies while also seeing to every aspect of due diligence required for construction. German is not essential to his daily work, but he does occasionally find himself in conversation with a German-speaking farmer. He also continues to teach from time to time, including courses on culture, dialects and solar energy for the local German American Institute. He and his wife also have participated in events as part of a state-organized exchange program involving cities of various sizes in his home state and in Germany focusing on renewable energy and climate change challenges at the local level. While he sees himself remaining in private-sector renewables for the foreseeable future, he would also be interested in expanding this work to an international scale, perhaps in partnership with European or African governments.

Miranda: Marine biology

When we spoke with Miranda (age group 25–30) she had recently moved from Paraguay to Australia to pursue PhD-level research on juvenile sharks in the waters around the Galapagos Islands. Growing up in a small town near the Great Lakes, she resisted the local tendency to remain sedentary in thought and deed, watched innumerable nature documentaries filmed in 'exotic places,' and dreamed of her own travels. She took up the study of Spanish in middle and high school and continued to learn that language at the Midwestern state university where she enrolled in a pre-medical curriculum. Determined that she would eagerly accept the first chance she saw to leave the US, she seized an opportunity in the first term of her first year in college to volunteer for a conservation project in South Africa. This trip was particularly inspiring to her because she was 'obsessed with Shark Week,' and there are many sharks in the waters off South Africa. In retrospect, she believes that this experience 'probably started steering me in this direction without me realizing it.' While still in college, she visited some 20 countries and participated in a 2-month summer program at a university in Ecuador. Finally, in her third year, the contradiction between her planned career in medicine and the satisfaction that she found in worldwide experiences of nature prompted the dramatic realization that she should make a vocation of her hobby. She switched her major from medicine to fisheries and wildlife, although the change would demand an extra year of study.

After graduation, Miranda was required to accept low-level employment, partially because there just were not 'a ton of jobs for women in fisheries with bachelor's degrees.' A year later, she decided to obtain a master's degree in fisheries at another Midwestern state university. Then she worked as a research supervisor at a conservation NGO in Paraguay for a year, and from there she was accepted into her current PhD position based at an Australian university.

As for Spanish, Miranda admits that she 'was never super good at it,' but she also has no doubt that the experience of language learning and study abroad have had a significant impact on her career path. Without Spanish, she would not have had the opportunity to work in Paraguay, neither would she have had the confidence to apply for such a position. Without the job in Paraguay, she believes that she would not have been a competitive applicant for her PhD program. She also shared her broad reflections on how, despite challenges, language learning has enhanced her confidence and influenced her approach to collaborative work (see also Chapter 7):

> the main thing for me is how beneficial it is to a career in science, which doesn't necessarily always seem like a related thing. but the skills you learn from learning a second language, not least of which is just learning how to be bad at something and feeling embarrassed, I think it's something that can translate into really any part of your life. they help you build confidence, even when you're not great at something, and I think it's helped me in science in a lot of ways, helped me think about things differently. and certainly, if you want to do research that kind of crosses borders, it doesn't have to be some international collaboration, but just it helps you to be more open to collaborating with somebody with

different ideas. the more people you spend time with who aren't exactly like you, the better anything will be, and I think learning a second language is just the fastest and easiest way to come to that realization. if you're in a room with like-minded people, you're going to be saying the same couple of ideas over and over again. but if you add more voices from different experiences, that's going to open up a lot more possibility. and I think those are all skills and things you learn really easily through doing a study abroad or learning another language.

Miranda envisages a career as a professor at a research university in the future because that occupation can provide many more opportunities to carry out research in different parts of the world.

Anna: Nursing and public health

Anna (age group 25–30) was raised near a university town in the Midwest in the predominantly Latvian community her family had joined after emigrating from Latvia. As a bilingual, she considers language learning relatively easy. Also, having frequently assisted her grandparents in navigating English-medium situations, she developed understanding and empathy for non-expert language users from a young age. Her international experiences in youth included family journeys to Latvia and outdoor trips to Central America such that study abroad in college, in and of itself, was not particularly novel to her. Another long-lasting influence was her background in theater arts:

> I think through theatre, there's always this desire, hunger to learn about the human condition, like why we are the way we are, and what motivates us, and what drives us. and I remember an acting teacher always saying there are those universal desires of love, understanding, and acceptance. so I think those are some of the things that drive me. [...] we are supposed to connect and create and liberate in the world. that's what I think humans are supposed to do in this very finite bizarre experience we have on a much longer trajectory in terms of the history and lifespan of the earth or the universe. that's what we can do amidst this very brief chaotic time.

Anna attended a large, Midwestern public university initially as a theater major but soon realized that she was drawn to 'more utilitarian' pursuits. She changed her major to international relations, although without 'any real sense of direction.' In a course on medical anthropology, the PBS documentary *Unnatural Causes* prompted dramatic realizations concerning links between health outcomes and inequalities in education and wealth. At the time, she decided that she would enroll for a master's degree in public health, to tackle those problems. However, her study abroad experience flipped that plan.

Given her experience of taking French courses since high school and her particular interest in racial disparities and the historical context of colonialism, Anna decided to study abroad in Senegal, with health as her program focus. When she arrived, she first stayed in the capital city of Dakar for about a month, living with a host family and taking courses on international relations, French and Wolof. Then she moved to a rural internship site in Sokone and worked at a hospital for two months, during which time hands-on experience in health care changed her direction: 'I want to be a nurse, because healthcare issues are interesting and I love this one-on-one experience. [...] I don't really want to study world problems. We have enough problems in the US. I want to go tackle healthcare in the US.' Returning from study abroad with renewed and changed ambitions, she spent the following year catching up on the prerequisites for nursing school.

> I tell people all the time that I credit Senegal to me becoming a nurse, me going into healthcare, and ultimately coming back and being able to reflect on our own inequities in the US. you don't need to look far to go solving problems. but sometimes it takes an experience to kind of step outside of that, to kind of come full circle.

After obtaining a second BA degree, in nursing, Anna worked for two years in emergency rooms and in surgical oncology where she grasped the rewarding nature of treating health issues but also realized that she could not be involved in preventing them. Encountering chronically ill patients, including those without health insurance, convinced her that she needed to 'go to work on the system.' When we met her, she was pursuing a PhD in nursing science at a university on the West Coast, studying 'nutrition with the lens of health equity and social determinants of health and chronic disease prevention.' She did not know whether she would later pursue a traditional academic pathway or a role in a public health department or in policy development. Regardless, she is dedicated to 'improving healthy food access and food policy, especially for marginalized populations, low-income populations.'

Hailey: Market strategy

Growing up in Hawaii, Hailey (age group 31–35) began Japanese studies in high school to accompany friends who were heritage learners. She did not suspect at that time that a language she had 'stumbled into' would have an important impact on her life. At the liberal arts college that she attended on the West Coast, she majored in English literature and intended to become a journalist. Meanwhile, minoring in Japanese, she continued to study that language throughout college, although she 'wasn't sure that it would fit into my career necessarily.' Nevertheless, her professional path was strongly influenced by a sojourn in Japan, during which seemingly banal circumstances nevertheless provoked developmentally significant reflection. In the fall semester of her junior year, she studied abroad at a university on the outskirts of Tokyo.

> if you've ever been in Japan, you'll know that advertising is <u>everywhere</u>. it's just a part of your entire existence there. so you'll be riding on a train, and then they'll have ads on literally the handle that you'll hold to stand up on that train. and so I guess I got really curious about advertising more broadly, as a result of that. so I came back in the spring, and I ended up getting into an internship at a magazine, mostly working with their advertising department, just because I was curious about it.

During her senior year, Hailey interned at a large American newspaper on the West Coast and applied for Fulbright US Student Program to Japan. It happened that the newspaper offered her a full-time role, while simultaneously she received the Fulbright. With the newspaper agreeing to hold the role for her, she went back to Japan for a year, enrolling in intensive language study at a university in Kyoto during the first half of her stay and carrying out research on how the internet was impacting the Japanese newspaper industry during the second half. When she returned from the Fulbright-sponsored sojourn, she worked at the newspaper for three years, seeking out new business opportunities and revenue streams. Knowing that eventually she would have to leave this job, given the fragility of the newspaper industry, and taking into account her desire to work for a company that is 'pure online,' she applied for three roles at a leading multinational technology company and was accepted for one based in Australia. She moved to Sydney and worked there for two-and-a-half years, helping travel brands to better understand how consumers were using the internet to make decisions across different markets. Then she transferred to the company's West coast office and did similar work for another two years. Wanting to 'pivot into strategy work' in her career, she decided to pursue a master's degree at a prestigious business school in New England. She took many courses on finance and entrepreneurship, which was 'super eye-opening' for her, as she had no prior formal education in business. She particularly enjoyed the international nature of that program, with a diverse student body and an opportunity to spend a month in Peru consulting for a local business.

After obtaining her MBA, Hailey returned to the multinational technology company. She works in their central strategy team and helps to solve a broad range of problems, such as how to 'make our ads products work better in places like India and Indonesia where consumer needs and business needs are fundamentally different than they are in the US and Europe.' Though she only uses Japanese intermittently in her daily work – for instance, in helping to translate surveys targeted at the Japanese market – she thinks that language study 'forces your brain to think differently, you have to stretch different muscles,' and that it 'broadens your perspective on the world in a way that is crucial for you to be successful in almost any role.'

> I work for a very large US company that tends to develop products specifically for the U.S., and that's great. but the reality is there's a whole lot of the rest of the world that uses our products on a day-to-day basis and loves our products on a day-to day basis. and I often find that I am the person in the room that will raise the hand and be like, cool, how do we think about this for other markets as well?

Hailey is 'a super huge advocate for the liberal arts.' While a liberal arts degree may not directly translate into a career path, she believes that 'the skills that you get in liberal arts give you more optionality' and that 'it actually affords a lot broader experience' in the 'longer term game.'

> when I started applying for full time roles out of undergrad, this is before I found out that I got the Fulbright, so I was <u>terrified</u> to not have a job? so I applied for tons of things, but mostly in the business realm. and I just remember sitting in a room with somebody at, a private equity firm, and it was for a marketing role, and she said to me, you're an English major, why are you here right now? and I said, you know, it's funny, I think that the parts of my brain that I have to use to write a compelling paper in a literature class are actually very similar to what an economics major might be doing. so I get a piece of poetry or a novel, and I have to break that story into its component parts. I have to kind of re-stack the information into something else. and then I have to convey a message against it. that's not too dissimilar to what a math major or an econ major would be doing. the data is just different. it's words and themes. it's not numbers. and she was like, <u>whoa,</u> I never really thought about it that way. I was like, yeah, it so requires you to be deeply analytical, it's just analytical about something that is not necessarily traditionally thought of in that way.

In terms of her future, when we interviewed her Hailey was 'trying to decide if I continue on the path of my given team or if I switch roles' in the company. She is leaning towards the latter, to 'push myself in a different direction' and work within the company's product groups. She also wants to live abroad again if the possibility arises. Despite these uncertainties, she does 'feel like I couldn't work anywhere that didn't have kind of a global view of products,' as 'there's always going to be a part of me that is driven by things that are different from just the U.S.'

Owen: International insurance

Owen (age group 25–30) grew up in a New England city suburb as part of an Irish American family that retained ties to their country of origin and encouraged the children to be 'open to seeing the world.' He attended a private university in his home region, studying business and majoring in finance with the hope of becoming an investment banker in Manhattan. When he applied to study abroad, he chose Budapest as his destination, because he was 'in kind of a rebellious mood' at the time and thought: 'I'm going to go with nobody. I'm going to be on my own. I'm going to go to somewhere completely different. [...] and I'm going to try to meet new people, and just step outside of my comfort zone.' Looking back, he said in the interview: 'that's a hundred percent what it ended up being,' calling the study abroad experience 'incredible' and highlighting its significant and long-lasting impact on his life. For Owen, it was primarily the social interactive nature of the experience that led to perceiving a contradiction between his previous, more insular lifestyle and the potential for dramatic enrichment through international contacts. He established friendships with other participants from around the world, leading to longer-term relationships and serendipitous coincidences that benefited him personally and professionally. He understood in a profound way that people coming from different cultures may think and act differently: a realization that has ultimately helped him to build international business partnerships. Also, he realized that moving to a place with a different culture, language and way of life was not only doable but also enjoyable:

> so I definitely came back a lot more confident about – why not do something outside of the U.S.? and not just why not? it's what I want. I love being outside of my comfort zone and being challenged in that regard, and finding a way to fight through whatever adversity might come due to languages or culture and ending up having an awesome time.

Following a spring semester in Hungary, Owen went directly into an internship at a bank in Manhattan. At the end of his stay, his Brazilian supervisor assured him that given his background and work ethic he could make a successful career in finance; however, if he wanted to work in international contexts, he would have to learn at least one language beyond English. Owen returned for his final year in college focused on finding a way to get into international finance and studying Portuguese due to Brazil's status as an emerging market at the time. After college, the 'fallout of the 2008 financial crisis' had a negative effect on Owen's job prospects. Somewhat reluctantly, he accepted a position in internal audit at a large insurance company. Still dreaming of an international career, however, he began to explore options available within the company, since it had a global reach. On the same floor where he was working, there was a team involved in internal audits for foreign operations with occasional travel abroad. He became determined not only to join that team but also to revive his high school Spanish and to develop his ability to the level required for business communication. These efforts were fruitful, and four years later he was sent to Ecuador to participate in an audit that took place entirely in Spanish.

After successfully transferring to the international internal audit team, Owen realized that although traveling outside the country was highly enjoyable, he was 'still checking other people's work,' which was not his preferred occupation. He discovered that there was an area of the company called surety, which was both attractive to him and more in line with his college studies. He began to contemplate and plan a transfer to the international surety team. To achieve this goal, he moved to another city on the East Coast to learn how to underwrite surety bonds in a domestic capacity, taking a career risk and temporarily leaving behind the international travel he had enjoyed on the audit team. About two-and-a-half years later, an opportunity came up for a post in surety in Mexico, and he secured this position.

When we met him, Owen was in his third year of assignment in Mexico City, working entirely in Spanish and trying to 'bring new business to the company through negotiations with brokers.' He said, 'I couldn't be happier about where I'm at in my career, and a significant portion of that is just due to the language learning.' In terms of the future, he plans to take a similar long-term assignment in Europe after his current post in Mexico ends, to further strengthen his resume. Then he will return to the US and focus more on the personal side of life, while still working in the international capacity of the company. He aspires to 'rise through the international side of the company and just keep pushing it for as far as I can get up the corporate ladder and see where I end up.'

Max: Psycholinguistics and systems engineering

Max (age group 36–40) grew up in the suburbs of a Midwestern town and attended Catholic schools for 13 years with 'mostly white, middle-class kids.' His general curiosity and desire to experience the world, and the encouragement of his high school Spanish teacher, together influenced his decision to attend a private university in a neighboring state with a strong reputation for its study abroad programs. As a double major in psychology and Spanish, after three semesters of advanced language study, a term in Salamanca was an integral part of his academic program. While he was there, he participated in a language program designed for international students from all around the world. He credits his host family there for indelible memories of holiday celebrations and for their strong support of his language development (see Chapter 6). Max considers study abroad to be a 'force multiplier' for language learning, not only because of greatly increased exposure, in comparison to classroom instruction, but also because it provides rich access to cultural nuances:

> I have no doubt in my mind that studying abroad was the biggest influence on my ability to not only make those advances in proficiency, but to be become more engaged as a student, to want to learn more. within the first month [...] when I was studying in Spain, I could tell that I was just more engaged and thinking about the language both analytically, but also experientially, trying to connect it to my own life in ways that I wasn't doing in my high school, or even college Spanish classes.

In addition to furthering his language ability, study abroad 'kick started' Max's career aspirations. In observing his own and his fellow students' progress toward competence in an additional language, he became intrigued by individual differences. In his case, a contradiction arose between the similarity of his own and a friend's learning context and differences in their language development:

> I remember noticing that a good buddy of mine, his vocabulary was going through the roof. but his fluency and his accent were still very stunted. [...] I was working really hard and focusing on losing the American accent, sounding [...] a little bit less like a foreigner, but my vocabulary was just small compared to his. so I was like, <u>wow</u>, that's really interesting. we're both in the same place. we're in the same classes. we're hanging out together all the time. but we're both getting something different from this experience. why is that?

As a psychology major, Max was attracted to the cognitive dimensions of these differences, and eventually chose to pursue graduate study in psycholinguistics at a major state university in the North Atlantic region. For his master's thesis, he carried out an investigation of individual differences in vocabulary learning during study abroad, collecting his data in Salamanca, which allowed him to visit his host family there. Later, for his PhD research, he implemented studies on the ways in which bilinguals retrieve words from memory and how they control which language they are accessing and manage conflict between languages. Subsequently, he secured a position as a scientist at an applied research center on the East coast, and for 10 years continued to focus on second language acquisition while also examining ways to enhance language instruction, including through various technologies such as virtual reality applications. In that post, he was working to support mission-driven and results-oriented federal agencies 'trying to [...] have an impact to benefit society [...] and I was finding that I really enjoyed supporting government agencies directly.' Recently, he has taken up an opportunity to use his technological and quantitative analytic skills in private enterprise. As a systems engineer, he continues to work primarily with government agencies to address advanced data analytic needs through his company's technology products. Having only just begun to pursue this new career avenue, he is not sure what the future will bring, but knows that he would like to keep abreast of language learning research and does not rule out the possibility of further participation in that field in years to come.

Antonia: Hospitality and catering

For Antonia (age group 51–60), it was not a vocation per se that was discovered in study abroad, since she was destined in the longer term to join a family business in the hospitality field. Rather, it was learning about the richness of Italian culinary traditions and farm-to-table practices that ultimately helped her to internationalize her company's offerings and expand their community reach. While she was growing up, Antonia's first-generation Italian American parents ran a small business selling produce in the capital city of a Midwestern state. The Italian language was not present in her home growing up, apart from some elements of the southern variety that her grandmother spoke. Like many immigrants in the 1920s, her grandparents had been eager for assimilation on behalf of their children: 'their goal was to learn how to speak English and have their children be American [...], they wanted to be integrated into the American culture as quickly as possible and be given a fair shake without being profiled.'

At the local state university, Antonia majored in Italian, in part to explore her heritage and in part because language study would give her 'a ticket to study abroad.' She studied in Italy three times during her undergraduate years: summer sojourns in Bologna and Rome, where family connections provided her a homestay, then a full senior academic year in Bologna. Early on during that year she met her future husband whose family embraced her and introduced her to their way of life. Her parents-in-law had a farmhouse outside the city, where they kept livestock such as goats, rabbits and chickens, tended chestnut, olive and fruit trees, and cultivated terraced hillside gardens and orchards with nut trees and pomegranate bushes. Her mother-in-law made fresh pasta, polenta, regional breads, jams and canned tomatoes. As a city-dweller, Antonia had seen both wholesale and retail aspects of produce marketing but she now saw 'what can be done with food from farm to table.' Her first taste of a zucchini flower is the dramatic moment that she has retained in memory to mark the discovery of Italian culinary culture:

> I learned how to eat a zucchini flower when I was 19, but I'd never seen anything like that [...] in 1986 that was not something that was common in the United States unless you were involved in some sort of high-end gourmet restaurant. [...] I think it had an impact, completely, because not only did I have the farm to table experience, I saw the production

side. [...] there were cherry trees. there were rosemary bushes. so it was a total sensory experience that was life-changing. to learn all of that and also to learn a different language – you're learning a language but you're also learning a culture and new ways to eat. so you have this sensory part of it as well.

At the conclusion of her study abroad program, Antonia remained in Bologna for four years, until she missed her family of origin too much to stay away any longer.

With the family's encouragement, her brother had started a restaurant when he was 19 and Antonia was 17. That business flourished, dividing into two restaurants, one a gourmet dining room and the other a casual eatery, and adding a catering business. Antonia joined this enterprise when she returned from Italy, and later saw it continue to grow until a decade later it was sold to a supermarket chain and operated with a cafeteria, a catering service, a coffee company and a prepared foods division. Largely due to mismanagement and financial woes, the supermarket chain was eventually sold to a hedge fund for its real estate assets but Antonia retained the catering business, which has since operated from three locations. She is the general and primary sales manager but she also works with the culinary team to create menus and develop ideas while overseeing the entire process of operating catered events: 'it's not only administrative but it's also very hands-on.'

Antonia continues to travel abroad and bring back new ideas for dishes and parties that can be re-created for her clients including, recently, an elaborate dessert created by a Parisian pastry chef and an event with an Italian ski lodge theme. On a community level, she has led her company toward willingness to engage seriously and creatively with the needs and desires of local international civic groups. Her catering company regularly researches and develops culture-specific menus for Asian, South American and African groups:

> our willingness to be able to do this research and to really, to learn the cuisine of another culture is exciting to us. and I think a lot of that stems from my original experience, being able to experience something for the first time and [...] bring that back and share that with others. it was amazing.

On an organizational level, she promotes continued education for her staff through culinary trips to cities such as New York, San Francisco and Paris, so the people who work for her can share a broader vision of their craft regardless of their background and previous ability to travel.

4.4 Conclusion

This chapter opened with findings from our survey demonstrating that study abroad has a consistently high impact: across age groups, and on employment choices and relevant skills, further developing interest in language learning and working in internationalized contexts. The qualitative data provide another, complementary view on this impact, delving into the life histories of individuals whose professional callings were discovered through study abroad. With this combination of data sources, we present a broad and particularized portrait of the ways in which the career-related impact of study abroad is historically constituted, offering some insights into why and how this practice changes lives. This chapter has focused mainly on career choices that emerged from study abroad experiences; in the next chapter we present survey findings related to motives for language learning and study abroad along with the stories of participants for whom those experiences were pursued as part of a more general quest for identity.

5 Quests for Identity

5.1 Introduction

Although the main theme of this volume is the careers of language study abroad alumni, by no means do we intend to convey the message that this experience is interpreted only, or merely, in utilitarian terms. Indeed, when asked how they believed they had changed because of study abroad, many if not most survey takers provided short-answer responses to do with transformation, often phrased as 'becoming': less myopic, more accepting of others, open minded, confident, mature, courageous, socially engaged, well-rounded, focused, adaptable, equipped to handle change, smarter, etc. 'Balance,' wrote one participant, 'you need to work hard, but you need to pause and enjoy a meal. Study abroad taught me how to balance my soul.' 'This question,' wrote another, 'is too hard to answer in a small box. I'd say I was more alive, open, sensitive, and excited and driven to learn more.' For other participants the first responses that apparently came to mind were directly to do with discovery of identity. One wrote: 'I developed a strong sense of who I am, the type of person I want to be, and what kind of people I want to surround myself with.' Another responded:

> Wow, I can almost write a book for this question… I feel I am a completely different person, especially after my first study abroad. Each study abroad helped me view the world differently and made me look at everything from much broader perspectives than I would have if I stayed in my country town for the whole life.

In this chapter we first pursue the question of why: Why did our survey participants elect to study languages, and why did they decide to study abroad in the first place? Survey responses clearly indicate that, in initial decision-making, utilitarian motives took a back seat to what Kramsch has described as 'desire':

> For many language learners, desire is the need for a language that is not only an instrumental means of communication but also a way of getting in touch with oneself, of finding personal significance through explicit attention to articulation and meaning. Adolescents and young adults are not satisfied with the convenient answers given by the slogans that surround them in their standard mother tongue, nor do the ready-made identities offered by the marketing industry and the global economy

offer them anything to dream about. Like rap and hip hop, a foreign language can reveal unexpected meanings, alternative truths that broaden the scope of the sayable and the imaginable. (Kramsch, 2006: 102)

Having reviewed related survey findings, we then turn to professional life history narratives illustrating quests for heritage or other identities.

5.2 Motives for Language Learning and Study Abroad

We begin by examining the selections made by our survey participants from a pre-established list of possible reasons for language study. Participants were asked 'What are the top three reasons you have chosen to study languages?' from this list including a range of motives (e.g. employability, personal fulfillment, interest). Table 5.1 ranks participants' reasons for choosing to study languages, based on cumulative counts for their top three selections. In addition, data about participants' primary reasons are provided.

Table 5.1 clearly demonstrates that our participants were primarily interested in access to another culture, ability to navigate in a global world, and enjoyment, an aspect of language learning that has traditionally been greatly underestimated in comparison with negative emotions such as anxiety (Dewaele & MacIntyre, 2014). Analysis of participants' first reasons only tends to reinforce this general conclusion, although fewer participants selected 'useful for my career or employment' as their primary reason for choosing to study languages (11%). These results suggest that while employability does play a part in shaping motives for language learning, its contribution is relatively minor in comparison to these other, less utilitarian rationales. Also, participants

Table 5.1 Reasons for language study

Reason	Total		First reason	
	n	%	n	%
To fully experience and understand another culture	3433	70.08	1256	25.64
An essential skill to have in a global world	3198	65.28	1126	22.98
I enjoy learning languages	2603	53.13	1012	20.66
Useful for my career or employment	1982	40.46	544	11.10
I am good at learning languages	965	19.70	177	3.61
To satisfy a language requirement for studies	839	17.13	257	5.25
Interested in learning a language that is part of my heritage	756	15.43	308	6.29
I have someone close to me who speaks this language/these languages	713	14.55	184	3.76

Note. In Table 5.1 the denominator used in percentage calculation was the total number of survey respondents, i.e. 4899.

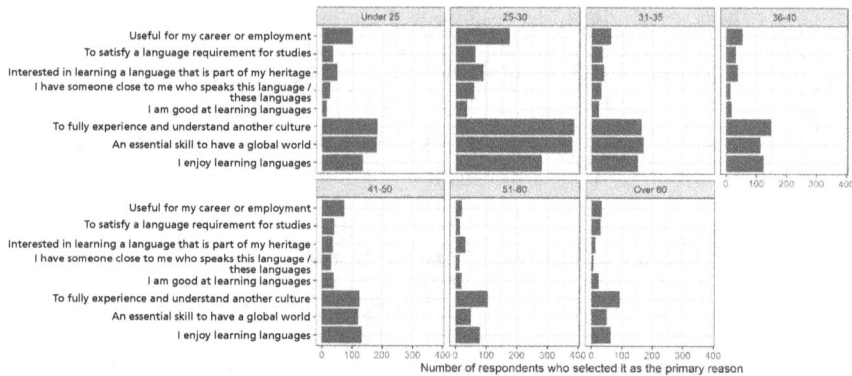

Figure 5.1 Reasons for language study as a function of age

who selected 'To satisfy a language requirement for studies' as their first reason are in a minority. To understand whether a time or age factor may be shaping these findings, we additionally examined respondents' first reasons for studying languages as a function of age, as show in Figure 5.1.

Figure 5.1 shows counts for each age group. In all cases, the most frequently selected primary reason for studying languages included 'to experience another culture', 'enjoyment of learning languages', and 'to develop essential skills in a global world', suggesting that many of the participants' reasons to study languages appeared not to be strongly influenced by age. That is, curiosity about the world, including a desire to learn about new cultures, appears to have remained the key reason for language learning across the different age groupings of our participants.

This said, since the interview data revealed a tendency for younger participants to be more career-focused in general than their older counterparts during their youth, we scrutinized, by age group, the responses to the question concerning career utility of language ability. These data show an important difference in the extent to which younger versus older participants included this option among their top three choices: nearly half the under 25 group (47.6%) as compared to 32.4% for the 51–60 age group and 34.1% for the over 60 age group. Although the older participants obviously have the benefit of hindsight and presumably, in many cases, of established professional identity positions from which to assess this issue, we suspect that these data do in fact provide some quantitative evidence to support our claim about generational changes in career focus.

Our survey also investigated motives for study abroad, once again with an item where participants selected their top three reasons from a list of fixed options. Figure 5.2 presents a visualization of the counts for each reason, showing that desire to live abroad and to learn a language were by far the most selected. These findings are consistent with those

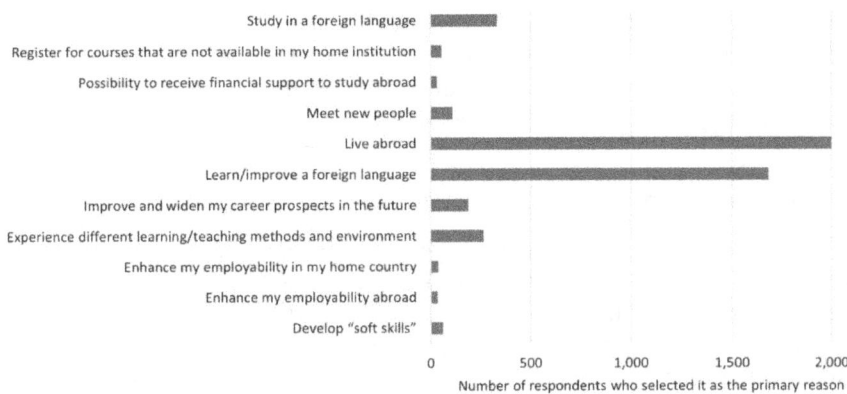

Figure 5.2 Motives for study abroad

tabulated for the question about language study, showing that the experience of life abroad itself was important for these alumni. Also, once again we see that enhanced career prospects and employability do not appear to have been major contributors to motives for study abroad even though, as illustrated in Chapter 4, in hindsight alumni do perceive strong links between international education and their actual careers.

These trends are also found among alumni of different ages, indicating that living abroad and developing language skills have long represented key reasons for study abroad in our sample.

5.3 Quests for Identity

When language learners go abroad in pursuit of understanding another culture, of broadening 'the scope of the sayable and the imaginable' (Kramsch, 2006: 102) or of understanding themselves and their heritage, what can they find? For some of our interview participants, dramatic developmental experiences in study abroad are best interpreted as prominently tied to heritage-related or other aspects of identity. Frances, for example, traces the awakening of her African diaspora consciousness to a short stay in the Dominican Republic, and later pursued this awareness during study abroad in Ghana. Courtney traveled to Asia twice as an undergraduate, in part because she follows the Bering Strait theory according to which her Navajo ancestors originated there. Appropriately, given her self-selected pseudonym, Afrika was drawn to South Africa as her study abroad destination. Hoping to expand her awareness of South American cultures, Carmen traveled to Chile as a Mexican American Spanish major and recounted one of the few stories of perplexity and disappointment in our interview data. For still others, study abroad prompted identity-related realizations unconnected to heritage. Moira found that the dramatic change in her social environment and her connections to a new peer group conveyed the freedom to claim a queer identity. Grace spoke of the discovery of an adventurous personality, and Thomas of the expansion of horizons he felt necessary to become a good doctor.

Frances: International education and creative writing

Frances (age group 36–40) grew up in New York City's sphere of influence, a descendant of working-class African Americans who migrated from the rural South to the urban North during the first half of the 20th century. Her parents 'didn't have a lot of money' but they were determined to broaden their children's outlook through reading, visits to museums, plays and other performances, and summer vacations involving travel, including a trip to Canada: the only time that Frances ventured outside the United States before college. Frances spent her early childhood in a predominantly black town. When she was in the sixth grade, the family moved to an Italian American town that had recently seen a 'huge influx of immigrants.' Here, she found herself gravitating toward like-minded, studious, multilingual classmates from all around the world. Spending time with the 'kids who were smart and interested in school' led to friendships with Chinese, Filipino, Vietnamese, Thai, Egyptian, Indian and Puerto Rican peers along with exposure to a wide variety of religious and culinary traditions. When visiting these friends' homes, she noticed a parallel with her own experiences of language use. At school, she and her friends were the 'quiet little nerdy ones,' but when using their home language, they were uninhibited and loud, just as she was when using African American vernacular English in the comfort of home.

At the prestigious small liberal arts college that Frances attended, as an anthropology major, she encountered some students from privileged backgrounds who had grown up with servants, posh boarding schools and frequent travel abroad. Peers continued to play an important role in developing her international perspectives. During the summer after her freshman year, she was invited to join a friend's family in the Bahamas. Two years later, she experienced cognitive-emotional drama that 'awakened (her) African diaspora consciousness' during a summer trip to the Dominican Republic with her best friend. Until that point, she had been unaware of the fact that this diaspora extends outside Anglophone countries in the Caribbean (and, as she would later discover, to Central and South America as well) in part because her best friend never mentioned her family's African origins, preferring to identify as Taino (indigenous), Spanish, or simply Dominican. Frances also saw first hand how personal identity can become complex abroad:

> when I got to DR it was my wake-up call, because I saw so many people who look like me and I was just, wait a second, these folks are black. oh

my God, they're <u>black</u>, you know? everywhere I looked I was awestruck. <u>she's</u> black and <u>he's</u> black, and look at <u>him</u>, <u>he's black</u>. and they're looking at me like, you're Dominican, right? why aren't you speaking Spanish? be proud of yourself. I'm like, I <u>am</u> proud of myself. well, stop speaking English, speak Spanish. we know you can speak. you are <u>lying</u> to us.

Later, Frances opted to undertake formal study abroad in Ghana, a destination that often attracts African American heritage seekers (Landau & Chioni-Moore, 2001; Whatley, 2017). She turned down an opportunity for university study in Ghana due to her preference for a semester-long program operated by a progressive study abroad organization that included homestays in both urban and rural areas, and a full month of independent fieldwork. Frances had also likewise turned down the opportunity to study abroad in Mali, where she would have continued her French studies in addition to learning a local language, because she preferred the Ghana program's academic focus on the history of the slave trade and the African diaspora. Students were encouraged to tailor fieldwork to their interests, and Frances pursued a project on indigenous medical practices and how these are incorporated into orthodox medicine. In addition to attending a plant medicine conference, she interviewed local healers such as midwives, herbalists and bone setters. 'I was learning in a way that I had never done before, because it was so hands-on. […] you're in the field and you're observing things that you've read about.' This was taken to an unexpected extreme when one of the bone setters, assuming she wished to apprentice with him, demanded that she put down her field journal and observe, and then that she treat one of his patients, fortunately, only for a sprain.

Frances' language education began in middle school, the earliest opportunity available in her public school system. She would have preferred to learn Spanish but the Spanish teacher had a reputation for presiding over 'party classes' where fun was prioritized over learning. So, Frances took up the study of French in the eighth grade and continued to study that language in high school and college. In comparison to the serious middle school French course, her high school classes were of lower quality, so Frances took matters into her own hands and began teaching herself by listening to a French-medium radio station, recording songs, transcribing the lyrics and singing along. Only later did she learn that speaking French would be of value to her in navigating travels in Africa.

In Ghana, she and her cohort received tutelage in Fante and Twi, two related Akan languages. The language instruction in the program came under sharp criticism by students for being surface-level and unsystematic, in part because Frances' cohort was the first with a majority of African American students who truly wished to learn these languages. Later, she came to understand some broader, related issues to do with the nature and documentation of these languages as well as social norms surrounding foreigner identities. Firstly, Fante and Twi are tonal languages, which makes them intrinsically more difficult for Anglophone learners than languages that do not mark phonemic differences in this way. Secondly, Fante and Twi are related but not identical, with, for example, many differences in everyday lexis. Finally, expectations for local language ability among foreigners in the community are low, and Ghanaians expressed awe at foreigners trying to speak local languages, sometimes acknowledging these languages' reduced standing compared to English, an official language and lingua franca inherited from the colonial era. Out of a strong interest in learning a language her ancestors might have spoken and an interest in showing politeness and respect, Frances began to master the very complex systems of greetings in the local community. Although use of the full greeting system is in decline in favor of English, particularly in urban areas, traditional salutations were a crucial form of politeness, with a refusal to greet interpreted as a violation of Akan sociocultural norms. Moreover, they varied according to many factors, such as level of formality, age, status, gender, clan or royal family membership, time of day, concurrent activity (e.g. eating, grave digging or childbirth) and the day of the week on which a person was born (marked by automatic day names) (Agyekum, 2008).

During her sojourn abroad, Frances began taking notes to support creative and essay writing related to her experience and aspirations to represent Africa in non-stereotypical ways based on first-hand observations. After college graduation, she received a Fulbright grant for another year-long sojourn in Ghana, this time to carry out research for a novel examining race relations and the slave trade in the 18th century. A few months before departure, she hired a tutor in Twi, and, for a few weeks in Ghana, she had a tutor in Fante. The only dictionary Frances was able to procure had been written by Christian missionaries and contained entries relevant to a third local linguistic variety. As a result, when Frances attempted to communicate, some people found her language 'all mixed up.' Despite this, she developed sufficient competence in the local language to overhear, understand and comment on gossip, much to the surprise and consternation of her hosts and associates. She also became so adept at appropriate greetings that she would sometimes be put on impromptu display ('hey, say something to her') as an extraordinary foreigner who 'knows the protocol.'

She then pursued a Master of Fine Arts (MFA) with an emphasis on creative writing. When graduating with her MFA, Frances knew that she wanted to remain involved in academia for the intellectual stimulation, but also that she did not want to teach. She found her way to achieve this by serving as an academic and study abroad advisor, promoting the benefits of international education, particularly for students wishing to visit Africa.

Meanwhile Frances has gone on to publish short stories, essays, and memoir excerpts, and to win a long list of prominent awards, fellowships and writing residencies. She has completed the above-mentioned novel, and an accompanying screenplay as well as a memoir. She is working on a short story collection inspired by her family's experiences during the Great Migration, the 20th-century relocation of some 6 million African–Americans from the rural south to the urban industrial north to escape poverty and entrenched practices of racial discrimination. In her memoir, among many other topics, she revisits and explores episodes of conflict in racial identification and the complexification of her American notions of blackness, such as an incident in Ghana where she was labeled as 'red.' She is also the host of an online radio show featuring Congolese and other African pop music, and has learned Lingala, a Congolese vehicular language, mainly through the same basic technique that she applied to learning French: listening to and studying song lyrics. In the future, Frances would like to continue learning languages, especially Spanish, French and Lingala, and to develop her musical abilities by playing the guitar in the Congolese style. She will continue to pursue publication of her written works. Eventually she would also like to organize an exchange program involving African American and Ghanaian students to overcome 'misinformation and ignorance on both sides' and to 'get kids together to be able to see each other and talk to each other and experience each other's cultures.'

Courtney: Secondary education

> Y á' át' é éh. Sh í' é í Courtney [...]. yinishy é. Kinyaa' áanii nishłí. Naneesht' ézh íT áchii'nii 'é í b á sh íshch í ín. T áb ą ąh í 'é í dashicheii. T ód ík' ǫzh í 'é í dashin ál í. Ni'deetiind ę́ę́' naash á.'Ak ót' éego 'é í asdz ą́n í nishłí.

> [Translation] *Hello. My name is Courtney [...]. I am from my mother's clan, the Towering House Clan. I am born for my father's clan, the Zuni-Red Running Into Water Clan. My maternal grandfather's clan is the Water's Edge clan. My paternal grandfather's clan is the Salt Water clan. I am from Teesto, Arizona. It is in this way that I introduce myself as a young woman.*

When we met Courtney (age group under 25) she was an honors senior at a state university in the Southwest, majoring in secondary education with minors in Navajo and Asian studies. Courtney had grown up entirely on the Navajo Nation reservation, in a 'very traditional Navajo home,' surrounded by a loving family who encouraged and modeled maintenance of tribal cultural and religious practices while also nurturing her aspirations to learn about the rest of the world. Her father and her aunt are both teachers and instilled in her a great respect for education.

The contradictions that Courtney faces between mainstream and Navajo worldviews are woven throughout her story. In her education classes, the notion that punishment and humiliation are not appropriate ways to guide children was presented to her as new information, but Courtney had already learned long ago, from her family, that talking that way allows 'negative spirits to enter your child.' Her interest in East Asian language and cultures stems in part from the Bering Strait theory, according to which human migration from Asia to the Americas took place more than 20,000 years ago, but her parents reject this notion as inconsistent with the Navajo creation story. Most importantly, for the Navajo the homeland is revered: 'so, the land is very sacred to us. we take it very seriously. she is our mother.' This means that one does not leave the land without a serious reason. At the same time, however:

> I can't sugarcoat the reality of how sad it is to be on the reservation where [...] we have the highest proportion of – how do I word it correctly – depression, alcoholism, suicide rates, murder, missing indigenous women. it's so very apparent on the reservation, so [...] there was always this thought that if I go beyond the reservation borders what is there for me to learn? what can I possibly do to avoid making my life nothing.

In addition to all this, there is a strong belief among her people that setting foot on land where wars have taken place and many people have died is dangerous: one of those spirits could attach itself to you, with evil consequences.

Given these beliefs, Courtney's parents were none too pleased with her proposal to go on a summer intensive language and culture program in Japan after her freshman year, with a visit to Hiroshima. Courtney appealed to the reasoning that her people need perspectives from outside the reservation and that education is a common good if travelers abroad intend to return to the reservation, which she did. At the last minute before the application deadline, her parents ceded: 'and finally they were okay, if you're going to go there we'll do some ceremonies and say some prayers, because we know you are going to come right back.' In the program, Courtney traveled around Japan and developed beginning level proficiency in Japanese, which she then enhanced in a language course back in her home university. She witnessed a situation in which a group of Japanese middle schoolers inquired about her identity, and no one, including the American and Japanese professors, was able to answer their question without the term 'Indian,' which caused 'a little pain in my heart.' By the following summer she had become more adept at seeking funding for study abroad and spent a month in Seoul becoming acquainted with Korean language and culture. Although no Korean instruction was available at her university, Courtney continued to refine her knowledge as vice-president of the Korean language and culture club.

Courtney is quite certain that her long-term future will be on the reservation, where she will take up teaching while also seeing to the needs of her aging parents and grandmothers. She sees this not only as a just return for the caring nurture she has received but also as part of an overall commitment to the well-being of her people. In the meantime, she hopes to spend a few years as an educator in Asia, with the length of her stay negotiated with her parents. Apart from learning about other ways of life and bringing this wisdom home, she sees herself as an informal ambassador for indigenous peoples. By way of illustration, she recounted an incident in which she and a Zuni friend had dressed in their traditional attire and were approached by a woman requesting a photo with her child and 'the pretty Pocahontases.' That was 'kind of hard to swallow.' She wants to integrate her identity and culture into her instruction and to show the world that indigenous people are still present and are poorly represented in Disney movies.

> I'm going to go get my education. I'm going to learn all I can. and then I'm going to come back, because that's just the way it is. we can't further ourselves as a tribe, as a people, if we don't care about our own. [...] okay, so in five years, I would have done as much as I could with teaching abroad. and in 10 years I will be back situated in the reservation as a schoolteacher living in my old home, taking care of my parents. and doing the best I can to expose my kids to the world that lies beyond the reservation, while also telling them, know your culture be familiar with your language because that's what we have. that's what we've <u>always</u> had. and that's how you can present yourself on the international stage where you don't have to just say it as kind of a token, I suppose. you don't have to say it because it's just something that you look like. you can say it with pride. I am Native American. I am an indigenous individual. recognize me and recognize that we are still here.

Prior to the Covid-19 crisis, Courtney had been accepted into the JET program (Japan Exchange Teaching) beginning in 2020. With that dream deferred, she is enrolled in graduate school and is pursuing a master's degree.

Afrika: Online language instruction

A life-long city dweller, Afrika (age group under 25) is a recent graduate of a large, Midwestern state university where she majored in music and in African and African American studies. She is a classically trained violinist who enjoys experimenting with jazz and other genres. Her parents encouraged her to develop her talents by providing lessons from age 5 onward and sending her to music-focused summer camps. For Afrika, music and language are closely intertwined. She observes that both can enhance communication across borders. Her initial fascination with K-Pop music led to her passion for Korean. The story of her attraction to languages begins with an anecdote about music: When Afrika was participating in a middle school choir, the teacher requested suggestions of songs, and one student proposed 'Adiemus,' a new-age composition by Karl Jenkins that uses an artificial language. Afrika loved it so much that she 'was listening to the entire album and singing along to it, not just humming the notes in it but pronouncing the syllables too, so my brain was already picking up how other languages felt.'

Afrika has been studying Korean since her first year in high school. She had to wait until she reached university to take a formal course in that language for one semester but, in the meantime, she researched and used a wide variety of online resources for independent study (see Chapter 6). At the same time, she is investing in learning Biblical Hebrew to enrich her understanding of the Christian scripture in context and has begun to apply her knowledge of one Asian language to another: Japanese.

Afrika took up the study of isiZulu in a formal classroom context to prepare for her summer study abroad in South Africa, where her experience of belonging to a racial majority for the first time provoked cognitive–emotional drama akin to that of the participants in Anya's (2017) study of African American sojourners in Brazil:

> when I went, I was very, very excited. my parents were excited for me. and when I was on the plane, it shows as you're flying where you are, and we were flying down the middle part of Africa, crossing Ethiopia and Kenya, and I was just <u>bawling</u>. I'm sure people thought I was insane. but I was just thinking about how my ancestors were brought over in <u>chains</u> across the <u>sea</u>, and I'm flying back with my full will intact. I'm flying back by <u>choice</u>. and this will be the first time that my feet are touching the soil that my blood comes from. [...] when I went it was such a different experience, feeling normal, I guess. with no one looking at me or glancing at me, maybe looking but not looking like, you know, I am different from anyone. I felt at home. I don't think I've ever, ever had that experience anywhere I've been.

Sponsored by the department of African and African American Studies, this faculty-led program included coursework at local universities in Pretoria, a rural sojourn, and an independent research project. Since Afrika's research involved the study of traditional Zulu music, she set about meeting local musicians and using her own violin to connect with them through improvisation. Particularly while in the rural area that her group visited, she was grateful to have studied the isiZulu language to enhance her interactions with the people she met. She made many local connections and she retains her South African personal network through social media.

After graduation, Afrika immediately began an internship with a local museum, assisting research on Ghanaian art. Subsequently she took a job as a music teacher in a public school, where she found herself overwhelmed and alone with classes of 30–40 unruly children. Now, during the Covid-19 era, she is making ends meet by teaching English and elementary Korean online. Her dream for the future would be an extended stay in Korea to further improve her language ability while steeped in Korean culture and traditions. She knows that she would like to become an advocate for language study and perhaps also a teacher.

Carmen: International education administration

Carmen's (age group 36–40) family emigrated to the US from Mexico when she was 3 years old, and she was raised in a Midwestern metropolis. Her family returned to Mexico every two years, so she had experiences of mobility from an early age as well as awareness that she 'had more family somewhere else.' To further pique her interest, she also had elder brothers who enjoyed traveling internationally and recounted many stories when they came home. Although her parents did not attend college, 'education has always been ingrained [...] and super valued in my family.'

Carmen attended a local public university, majoring in photography and minoring in Spanish. While she had always been interested in international experience, she was a first-generation college student and the very notion of study abroad was therefore unfamiliar to her:

> I never made the connection. I didn't know that was part of college experience until I met a couple of students and they told me that, oh, this is where I'm going to go. and I'm like, wait, <u>wait</u>, you mean you're going here and studying, <u>what</u>? so that blew my mind. and I navigated college all by myself, so it wasn't a problem for me to be like, okay, I need to go to this office, I have to figure this out on my own, and I did. I went more than a couple of times. I went to talk to advisors and see if this was even like an option for me. and I figured out how financially I would pay most of my expenses. [...] and that's really how it went down. it was through the help of my advisor, through my perseverance, and just my motivation.

Carmen spent a spring semester in Rome, taking Italian language classes and several courses in cinema and photography at Rome University of Fine Arts. Observing her program cohort, she quickly realized that 'not many underrepresented students were studying abroad.' She said: 'It was a cohort of thirty something students. [...] I would say ninety percent were white, and ninety percent were female. Myself and another Latina student were the only two Latina students in that program.' In Rome, many locals asked her if she was Peruvian or Ecuadorian since there were many immigrants from these two countries in Italy at that time. With her still developing Italian language proficiency, she found it challenging and confusing to explain her identity. If she said she was American, people would be confused and say, 'But you don't look American.' On the other hand, if she said she was Mexican, people would reply, 'Then why don't you live in Mexico?' Nevertheless, she so enjoyed her experience overall that she decided to study abroad again. As a Spanish minor taking many literature courses, she had always wanted to go to South America, and she selected a semester abroad program in Chile. Her description of the racism she encountered during this experience echoes that of 'Lidia,' a Chicana participant in Mexico who was received with suspicion by her host family as a less-than-ideal representative of the US and was disfavored in comparison to another guest of low Spanish language proficiency and European heritage (Riegelhaupt & Carrasco, 2000):

> when I talk about my experience in Chile, it's a little bit more different than my experience in Italy. you would think that because I'm already a Spanish native speaker I can come by as a Chilean or any Central or South American person, but I actually had a more difficult time acclimating. people were not as open as I thought they would be. as soon as I would open my mouth, people would already say like, oh, you're a Mexican. and I'm like, yeah, I am. and then they would mimic Spanish Mexican slang. and I'm like, you know, that's a very specific Mexican slang in a very specific place in Mexico City, so yes, I'm Mexican, but I'm not from there. so that was a little bit frustrating. people were more intrigued with the other students than me. they would just look at me and be like, oh, and who are you again, oh, why are you here, we usually get white students to study abroad to our country, not students like you. and I'm like, okay. so I was always perplexed that they had no interest in my background. [...] they would never be like, oh, okay, tell us more, or we're intrigued. it was just like, oh, okay.

Carmen was shocked to see 'how people would just with no shame talk about their dislike of certain groups of people,' because she grew up in a very diverse neighborhood and was accustomed to meeting people of varied backgrounds. With her outgoing personality and conscious efforts not to allow these hostilities to ruin her whole experience, she 'would just hang out with people that really wanted to hang out with me or get to know me.'

After graduation, Carmen pursued wedding photography for several years while also serving as an assistant schoolteacher to make ends meet. Realizing that she enjoyed working in education, though unsure about the specific capacity, she decided to pursue a master's degree in linguistics. She then planned to work in curriculum development but spent six months seeking a relevant job. At that point she expanded her options and found employment in the department of financial aid at a small public university, where she used Spanish in presenting information to parents and students. During her time there, she sought her second master's in higher education leadership, and it became clear to her that her place was in education abroad.

When we met, Carmen had just taken up a position as a study abroad advisor at a private university. Drawing on her own experiences, she expressed a strong desire to help students from under-represented groups to understand and take advantage of international education opportunities. Her own study abroad experiences help her when counseling students:

> it depends obviously on the student and who I'm talking to. I'm not going to put my experience as an example because everyone is different and everyone has different perspectives. but if they do ask what opportunity is there, I tell them study abroad is something that you have to experience. I don't glorify it, nor do I sugarcoat it. I do tell them that they might experience various things, such as hostilities [...] or situations where your identity might be questioned or where you might not fit in or where it might get really uncomfortable. so you have to learn how to, how to deal with uncomfortable situations.

Carmen is actively engaged in efforts to diversify participation in study abroad. One of the projects she has been contemplating is to 'start some sort of pipeline' to introduce the notion of international experiences early in education, especially in poorly resourced schools where there are few role models, and the very idea comes to seem 'far-fetched.'

Moira: Mechanical engineering

> I think of studying abroad and learning Spanish [...] as a crucible moment for me, a transformative moment because there were a lot of very real challenges and struggles that I had, and also it was [...] the start of so many of my passions and interests and kind of pushed me to develop into who I am now. so it was an amazing experience, in part because it was so hard.

Moira (age group 25–30) was raised in a Midwestern college town and spent the summer after her junior year of high school in rural Nicaragua doing volunteer youth development work with a non-profit organization. In addition to improving her Spanish language skills, that experience placed her in an environment 'drastically' different from anything she had experienced before. Amid poverty and other disadvantage, she witnessed and came to appreciate the village's open-door practice of sustaining community ties. Although she came from a dairying region, the first time she milked a cow was in Nicaragua. She headed off to her state university bound and determined to study abroad, although it would be no simple matter to integrate this experience with her curriculum in mechanical engineering.

Moira took up a minor in Spanish and lived in Buenos Aires for six months of her sophomore year, during which she encountered a variety of challenges but overcame most of these. She quickly perceived that the variety of the language spoken in urban Argentina did not correspond to what she had previously learned; at first, she became deeply frustrated by her near total inability to understand. This problem was particularly dire in one of her integrated courses on the social history of Latin America, requiring extensive reading and delivered in Argentine Spanish by a professor who, according to a classmate, talked 'like he had potatoes in his mouth.' Having never before struggled to prevail as a student, the course was a 'rude awakening.' Though she had little background in history or social science, Moira survived by becoming engaged in the local students' practice of dividing up the readings and preparing simple summaries to share with each other. In the meantime, her command of everyday local Spanish increased quickly to the point where she became impatient with the slow pace and exaggerated enunciation of another of her professors, who oversaw a course for foreigners. Near the end of her sojourn, she traveled to Peru where, she proudly declared, the people she met thought she was from Argentina.

Although Moira certainly did not fit in with her host family (see Chapter 6), the social affiliations she developed in Buenos Aires had a strong and lasting effect. In the early days of her sojourn, she was lonely, but determined to form ties with local people and to speak Spanish as much as possible. One of the strategies that succeeded for her was volunteering to teach English to a small group of young professionals who then invited her to join them for a holiday picnic, and to play a role in a short film. Another was to take advantage of the program's language-buddy exchange and trade English for Spanish conversation with a young woman whom she still considers a friend. Perhaps most consequential of all was her decision to join classmates from her social science course at a demonstration protesting violence against women, the first in what has subsequently become an international movement. After the march concluded, she was unsure about how to navigate the public transit system to return home; her classmates suggested that she accompany a woman and her girlfriend who lived in Moira's neighborhood. On the bus they exchanged phone numbers, and soon Moira was invited to a house party. Moira had 'had things turning in the back of [her] mind about maybe I liked girls before then' but had chosen not to acknowledge these feelings. However, that party was the scene for a dramatic cognitive–emotional realization:

> once I was in Argentina I had all this incredible space to explore who I was. and I was surrounded by all these people who I'd just met. and so I could be anything to them. and so, that gave me the kind of space and freedom. it was a perfect opportunity to start thinking oh, I actually <u>do</u>

like girls. [...] so the first time I came out to anyone was in a room full of a dozen people I'd never met before.

The woman she had met on the bus became Moira's 'fairy gaymother' and extended her a warm welcome into a wide community of local queer friends who met regularly to socialize in bars and in each other's homes. By the end of her sojourn Moira was proud of the relationships she had built in Buenos Aires and of her ability to 'participate in life in Spanish.'

On return to her home campus, Moira once again felt a bit isolated, particularly since she knew very few gay people. She solved this problem by helping to found an LGBTQ engineering group, an activity she then reproduced at her first place of employment, a manufacturing company where she worked in research and development as well as product design and quality assurance. Two years later, she applied and was accepted for a stint in the Peace Corps, to work on a water engineering project in Peru. Without the pandemic, she would have departed for this post in April of 2020. Instead, when we spoke, she had deferred her Peace Corps service and was planning to spend the summer working for a family fishing business in a remote part of Alaska. In the longer term, Moira hopes to combine her interests and passions to build something she can be proud of. She would like to return to Latin America, live in Spanish again, and become involved in water infrastructure work. She is beginning to shift her focus from mechanical to environmental engineering and would love 'to do something that integrates the engineering side but then also has a social side, like doing good for people, the community, the earth or the environment.'

Grace: Chemical engineering

Grace (age group 41–50) was raised in the suburbs of a Midwestern city with parents who were determined to send her to college and enable an escape from working-class origins. Travel was limited to local destinations or visits to family in the US. In fact, when she set out for Europe on a backpacking trip in her third year of college, this angered her father, who cited the sacrifices of his immigrant grandparents as a reason not to venture beyond US borders.

Near the end of her college years, Grace had completed all the requirements for a degree in chemical engineering but wasn't quite ready to face the job market. Looking for a way to avoid graduating, she began to investigate study abroad. She had studied German, so her advisors suggested Germany, but Grace had already been there on her European tour and found it 'to be just like Minnesota,' her home state. She had also studied Russian, so an engineering fellowship in Russia was proposed, but Grace was not confident in her ability to navigate a 'dangerous' chemical facility in that language. 'A lot of the world speaks Spanish,' she reasoned. Before long she had signed up for a program in rural Venezuela that required no previous knowledge of the language, even though the program did not offer language courses for beginners.

At the time, Grace knew very little about South America and nothing about Venezuela. Her language ability was so limited that she didn't know the Spanish word for 'welcome' and could not recognize the sign being held up at the airport by the program employee who had been sent to greet her. At the same time, in the small town where she was located, there were very few speakers of English. With no appropriate Spanish courses available, Grace took matters into her own hands; with the help of a dictionary, many local interlocutors, and the 8-year-old daughter of her host family, within three months she became capable of navigating everyday life tasks such as using public transportation or shopping:

> my whole experience was going into shops and just talking to the shop owners, stopping people who were working, talking to people on the street, talking to people sitting on a park bench, talking to other people. I just tried to talk to anybody.

At that point, her program should have ended; but Grace was not ready to leave and conclude her language learning experience. After years of considering herself to be introverted, she was discovering that she could be gregarious as necessary, much like the participants in the LANGSNAP program who claimed greater confidence and independence after a year abroad (Tracy-Ventura *et al.*, 2016). Much enamored of South America and her new personality, she developed an extensive network of local social connections; she wanted to 'get to that next level' and extended her program to a full year.

Upon returning to the US, Grace completed her undergraduate degree in chemical engineering and foreign studies, with a concentration in Spanish. She then set about looking for employment that would allow her to return to South America and encountered many negative reactions to that aspiration. After four or five months, she interviewed for a job in a laboratory that had rejected many previous candidates, and began her career in research and development, which is extremely rare. She worked under a 'great mentor' who appreciated the intrepid spirit that had led her to immerse herself in an unknown language and culture and who pushed her to continue expanding her professional horizons. This mentor encouraged her to take a job in a factory and learn how to operate a pilot plant.

While she was there, Grace was contacted by a leading oilfield services provider with an offer of a job in South America. After three months of arduous training and testing, she was told that she would be posted in Brazil, only to find out at the airport that her destination had been switched to Bogotá, Columbia: 'They're trying to find someone who they can just keep dropping into new locations […] so that obviously landed me the job.' For four-and-a-half years, Grace enjoyed living in Columbia and learning cutting-edge technologies with this firm. She had no intention of returning to the US at that point but, when oil prices fell dramatically in the early 2000s, she was laid off and lost her visa. She attempted employment with a domestic semiconductor company in a clean room for a year, but found that she could not 'work in this little box by myself.' She returned to Colombia and accepted employment as an English teacher while waiting for the oil market to improve. Once again, however, she was recruited, this time by a multinational corporation headquartered in the US. She has since worked for this company, first in a variety of research projects that have earned her fourteen patents, then, after taking a master's degree in international management, on the 'business side' of the enterprise. She then realized that she strongly prefers to exercise her creativity and talent for 'weaving the thread of connections' to 'make something totally new' and has returned to work in laboratory settings as the company's front-end innovation officer, currently working on medical applications – yet another field that is new to her. For the future, she cannot envisage settling into one technology pathway but will continue to change and learn while also stepping up her efforts to provide mentorship to younger colleagues, particularly women.

> the end of the story, I would say… the biggest thing I got out of this study abroad experience is just different ways to look at a problem, and knowing that you'll […] enjoy the experience and you'll make it through to the end, right? you don't know what that path is going to look like. you can't predict it. just go for the ride, right? just have fun with it. and it happens over and over again.

Thomas: Anesthesiology and pain medicine

For our Zoom interview after the Covid-19 crisis began, Thomas (age group over 60) appeared in his office at the Californian Veteran's Administration hospital where he currently works, seated in front of a 'Clyde,' a full-sized skeleton festooned with masks, gowns and other personal protective equipment. Covering the skull was a mask made of a paper bag with two eyeholes punched in the front, such that the entire array of gear looked very much like a scarecrow. The bag was labeled 'PAPeR.' Thomas explained that the acronym PAPR stands for 'portable air pressurized respirator,' in other words, 'the things that we are supposed to be wearing, that look like the astronaut suit,' but this, he said, 'is paper.' During a mock code in the intensive care unit, there was a shortage of PAPRs, and Thomas had apparently worn this paper bag on his head in protest: 'Tell them this is what we are using.'

Thomas was raised in town of about 2000 inhabitants, in north central Kansas, 'the heart of Uncle Sam.' He was the fourth of five children in a Catholic family he qualified as 'lower middle class.' His father owned a series of retail operations: first a creamery, then a Gamble store, then a hardware outlet and, finally, a heating and air conditioning appliance concern. There were some family influences on his desire for travel. Having grown up during the Great Depression, then weathered the Second World War as adults, his parents were 'world-weary.' However, once the appliance store was operating, they were able to take advantage of group travel to Europe and the Caribbean courtesy of the Whirlpool manufacturer of ranges and refrigerators, which offered these trips to reward sales. Some of his older siblings were engaged in the social movements of the 1960s, including a sister who hitchhiked to India from Europe with her boyfriend.

Among our participants' stories, Thomas's is the most dramatically emblematic of the youthful insouciance toward careers that is characteristic of his generation. He had decided that he wanted to go into medicine by his mid-teens and attended the local public state university to major in microbiology with this goal in mind. He is careful to specify that he also wanted a liberal arts education that could include language study, and this prompted him to choose a Bachelor of Arts curriculum with French honors. At his own expense, he went abroad to France for the first time after his freshman year, on a summer program that included group travel, courses at the Sorbonne in Paris, and independent travel. He fell in love with Paris, and this 'was the beginning of the end.' Two years later, when the standard practice would have had him spend the summer studying for the MCAT (Medical College Admission Test), instead he bought a Eurail pass and spent two months traveling in Europe with a friend who was a literature major and inspired him to read for pleasure.

> and the more I read, the more I wanted to read. and the more I realized that [...] I needed to know more about the world. that's what it came down to, and if I was going to be a good doctor, I needed to know more than just growing up in small town Kansas.

Thomas pursued this knowledge about the world with genuine passion. After the second summer in Europe, he dropped out of college, retaining temporary part-time work as a teaching assistant and bench scientist in a microbiology lab. When the semester ended, he hitchhiked to California and became 'a ski and rock-climbing bum.' In the following fall, after moving to the New Mexico Rockies to continue rock climbing and skiing, he and his sister participated in a month-long benefit for epilepsy awareness involving bicycling throughout Colorado. As his sister had never been to Europe, she and Thomas planned a bicycle tour there for the following summer. Returning to Paris at the conclusion of that trip, his sister's social circle introduced him to a divorced, Trotskyist professor of sociology who needed an au pair. In exchange for room and board, Thomas agreed to become a 'manny' for the professor's highly articulate child: for the next year, he learned a great deal of French from a three-and-a-half year old. In the meantime, to earn money, he worked 'illegally' at night for the Hertz rental company, driving cars around the city to wherever they were needed. In this way, during his sojourn in Paris Thomas became affiliated with a group of 'pretty radical' veterans of the 'May 68 uprising' and enjoyed a social life that included a trip to the Alps for communal living in a ski chalet, thanks to the largesse of wealthier group members. By this time, he had been away from school for three years, had read extensively and had toyed with the idea of becoming a writer. He had also met the woman who would eventually become his wife, a French citizen of Valencian origin.

Thomas' first attempt to complete his undergraduate degree did not work out as planned. He returned to Kansas, accompanied by his girlfriend, after a 'Green Card marriage.' However, at that point she was less than pleased with life in a small American university town, and soon returned to Paris. Undaunted, Thomas convinced his professors to allow independent study, and promptly joined her there; still early in their relationship, they had their second Green Card marriage in Paris. At that point Thomas found a job as an English teacher in a school that offered language instruction by contract as continuing education for adults. Eventually he became the union delegate for the school and led a successful sit-in strike, negotiating in French on behalf of his colleagues for the establishment of salaries rather than hourly pay, a universal raise and supplemental health insurance. To prepare for this event, he had read all the relevant laws and union regulations. Thomas then segued into a full-time job at a Tex-Mex restaurant in the Marais, an artsy quarter of central Paris, where he started as a waiter and was eventually promoted to manager. During this time, his wife became pregnant with their first child. When the restaurant closed, he stayed at home with the child for a year, eventually concluding that it was 'time to get serious.'

The family moved back to Kansas again, and Thomas completed undergraduate degrees in microbiology and French literature. He turned down a full scholarship for a combined MD/PhD because of uncertainty about the amount of time that would be needed to complete the research requirement. With a scholarship from the Air Force, he then attended medical school; as an active-duty Air Force officer, he completed a residency in anesthesiology and a fellowship in pain management. Altogether he stayed for 20 years at the same Air Force hospital in San Antonio while his three children were growing up. When the children had left home, he decided to take a 'break': this turned out to involve a 6-week stint with Médecins Sans Frontières (MSF)/ Doctors Without

Borders in the war-torn Democratic Republic of the Congo, where his ability to speak French was highly useful.

> now that was probably one of the most extraordinary experiences of my life. there's no question about it. it was awesome in the best and the worst ways, just seeing people die left and right. [...] I was outside on the walkway and I heard what I thought were fireworks and I'm looking around and nobody's moving. what kids have <u>fireworks</u>? because honestly, these are poor people there. most of the people in the courtyard were family members that were cooking or cleaning because they had to cook the meals for the patients. they had to empty the bedpans for the patients. nobody was moving. and then I saw my MSF driver duck, <u>duck</u> underneath and run inside a building and I realized, <u>those are AK47s,</u> that's not <u>fireworks</u>!

Following this adventure, Thomas took an actual break in Paris with his wife, then worked for a few years in temporary positions back in the US, including one in which he visited the homes of Medicare patients to ensure that their healthcare provider organizations were properly seeing to their needs. In that position he was a first-hand witness to the extremes of economic disparity in his own nation, entering the homes of the wealthy but also those of 'hoarders,' 'cat people,' 'dog people' and people with holes in their floor or in the roof of their house. Eventually he settled on a post in the Veterans' Administration in California, where he currently works, in part because this frees him from the constraints of negotiating with insurance companies and allows him to practice medicine as he sees fit.

As we concluded our conversation Thomas returned to his story's initial theme: the need he felt for diverse life experience in his youth in order to become a good doctor:

> your imagination is fueled by your experiences, right? your ability to think critically might be steeped in a scientific basis, but your ability to imagine new ideas and think outside the box a little bit? it's going to depend on your imagination and your imagination depends on your experiences.

Furthermore, 'for a doctor, for example, empathy is one of the most important things you can have,' and one of the ways to gain an empathic stance is through the exhilarating but also humbling experience of learning to express yourself in another language.

5.4 Conclusion

In this chapter, we first scrutinized survey findings related to our participants' motives for language learning and study abroad. Although pervious chapters have demonstrated the clear links that many alumni perceive between practical employment-related opportunities and on-the-job skills, here we show that their initial reasons for engaging in language study abroad tended not to be utilitarian. Rather, the majority of participants studied languages to explore other cultures or because they believed that language ability is crucial for life in a globalized world. They chose to study abroad for the experience of living outside their home cultures and as a means of enhancing their language ability.

We characterize the life history narratives in this chapter as quests for identity because their main themes are to do with discovery or development of the self through the cognitive–emotional drama of study abroad experiences. In the interviews, we happened upon four examples from the 756 participants who claimed a heritage identity as a reason for language study: Frances, whose African–American diaspora consciousness was awaked by sojourns in the Dominican Republic and Ghana; Courtney, whose belief in the Bering Strait theory of Native American origins inspired travel to Asia; Afrika, who combined her interest in language and traditional Zulu music in South Africa; and Carmen, who used her sojourn in Chile to refine her academic language abilities. For Moira, it was travel to Argentina and the formation of new social ties that gave her freedom to claim a queer identity. Grace gave herself a formidable challenge at the end of her college career by sojourning in Venezuela with no prior language training, an experience that she believes changed her personality and prepared her well for the flexibility and adaptation she would later require at work. Sensing in his youth that mundane experiences in Kansas were not enough to develop the wisdom and empathy necessary for the medical practice he desired, Thomas embarked on a multi-year, multi-job adventure in Paris. All these stories, each in their own way, illustrate how desire for otherness in language and in life, satisfied through study abroad, can contribute to the formation of desirable selves.

6 Exploring Features of Study Abroad Programs

6.1 Introduction

In this chapter we combine survey and interview data to examine the long-term impact of certain study abroad program features. We begin with some background information about contexts for language learning from the survey, showing that university classrooms and study abroad have retained their relevance even as many younger learners turn to online resources. Interview data also show that the spread of communications technology has influenced the qualities of the language learning experience in general. We then consider duration, a topic that is of contemporary concern among language educators since there is a marked trend toward shorter sojourns. Our survey data show that many US-based language learners study abroad more than once, while our interview data demonstrate how even short-term programs can be impactful, depending on the sociocultural and economic life horizons of participants. We then consider residence options from the survey, complementing these findings with interviewee narratives of their most memorable program experiences, usually homestays. Finally, we compare survey and interview findings about the experience of returning home after a sojourn abroad.

6.2 Background: Contexts for Language Learning

In this section we provide information from the survey about the contexts in which our participants claimed to have learned languages. We also include snapshots from our qualitative data to illustrate striking changes in the role of technology across the generations represented in the project.

6.2.1 Survey findings on contexts for language learning

To understand the specific role of study abroad, participants were asked to select all learning contexts for each of the languages that they claimed. The results, shown in Figure 6.1, show that the most common context is the university classroom, followed by study abroad and high school courses.

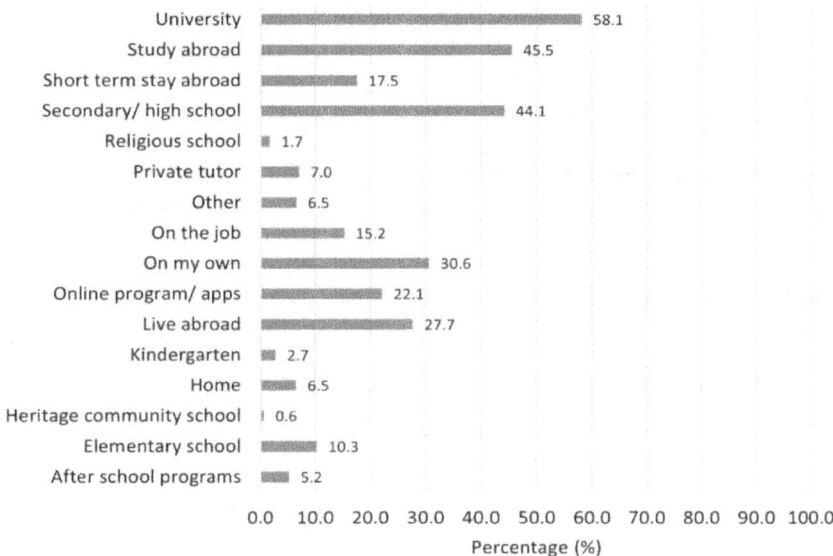

Figure 6.1 Contexts for language learning

Many participants claimed to have learned their languages independently ('on my own'), on the job, or using online apps. Even though online language learning opportunities are popular, overall, they do not appear to be outstripping more traditional contexts for language study, such as face-to-face classrooms.

However, the qualitative data suggested that there may be generational changes in approaches to language learning, given the salience and availability of online resources; among the interviewees in the groups aged 30 or less, several reported having set out to learn on their own (see below). Therefore, we examined three contexts ('university,' 'on my own,' and 'language learning apps') by age group to produce Figure 6.2. This figure shows that while university-based learning has indeed remained constant, as might be expected, in comparison to older learners, more younger participants claim to have learned languages on their own or using apps. Based in part on the accounts of younger interviewees, we assume that learning on one's own includes significant use of online resources.

6.2.2 Snapshots of generational changes in technology for language learning

The evolution of technology has always exerted a formative influence on the nature of study abroad as a context for language learning, particularly in recent decades during which the rise of online social networking

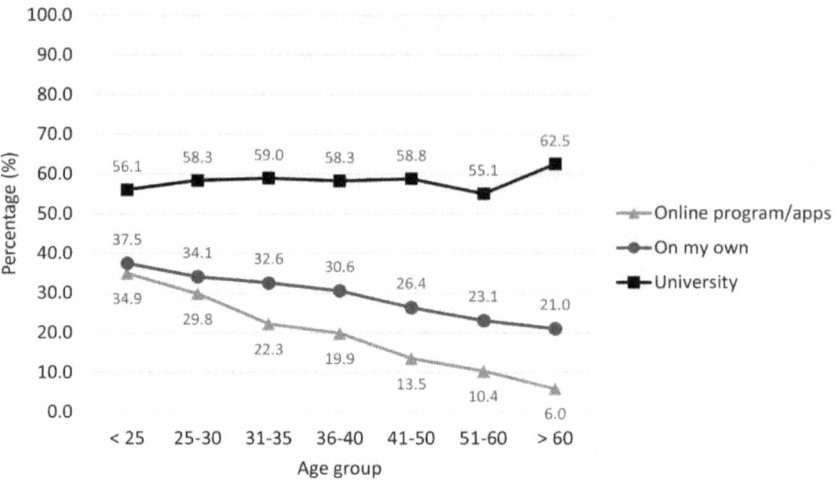

Figure 6.2 Generational changes in contexts for language learning

and easily portable, personal communicative environments have changed the fundamental meaning of physical places or locations. Many of our participants who studied abroad before the advent of the internet were careful to note this aspect of their experience, particularly as it relates to the relative inaccessibility of communication with home during times of stress or crisis. However, in this section, we will briefly examine what our participants' stories reveal about the role of technology specifically for intentional, focused language learning. When they deliberately set out to learn a language, what resources were available and how did they orient to them?

For this purpose, it is instructive to compare some comments from one of our more senior participants, Mark (age group over 60), with those of the youngest interviewees. Mark is a retired Foreign Service Officer who learned Chinese and Japanese, and whose accomplishments include having become the first adult-onset learner of Korean to qualify as an interpreter in delicate diplomatic encounters. During high school Mark was placed in the college-bound track and was required to study either French, Spanish, German or Latin. In an early manifestation of his identity as a 'language jock' (see Chapter 3), he challenged a friend in a race to learn the antiquated Fractur script that appeared on the cover of their first German textbook. During their second year of German study, however, a new teacher arrived equipped with a new method:

> Mr. R. came along with his Wollensak recorder and offered the oral, aural methods and, speaking sentences and learning dialogues and saying the language from the word go. it was a revolution. nothing like that had ever occurred in any language. of course, that I'd ever heard up to that time.

The Wollensak was a sturdy, stereophonic, high-fidelity reel-to-reel tape player advertised in 1966 as featuring an 'exciting Sound with Sound famous quality and durability.' The approach was clearly the audio-lingual method, also known as the Army Method or New Key, based on a structuralist analysis of language paired with a behaviorist understanding of learning. It is common knowledge among applied linguistics that this approach, along with its theoretical underpinnings, has long been discredited and has in some circles become something of an object of derision. For this reason, it is refreshing to imagine the enthusiasm with which it was received by a teenage language buff in a semi-rural 1960s high school classroom.

As for the younger participants, several of the interviewees who were 30 years of age or younger reported having learned their primary languages partly or mainly on their own, in informal settings or using online apps and social media platforms. Afrika and Hugh are among the 39 respondents in the under 25 age group who wished to learn Korean. However, courses in that language were either inconvenient or unavailable on their campuses. Afrika has never taken a formal course in Korean but she is an astute user of language exchange websites, familiar with the ones that are 'good for finding motivated people.' As a beginner, she used a messaging app that includes a translation feature to facilitate interactions. Now that her proficiency is more advanced, she schedules continued conversation with her exchange partners on Zoom or Skype. Afrika's language ability is such that she now teaches beginning Korean online and produces publishable subtitles for pop music videos. Since Korean was not offered on his home campus, Hugh also took it upon himself to start moving toward proficiency in that language using online resources before studying for a semester in Seoul. While in Korea he took advantage of an 'English learning zone' at a university café to meet local students who would then participate with him in an informal, friendship-based language exchange.

Owen did not discover his strong motives to learn Spanish and enjoy an internationalized career until the end of his studies and the beginning of his working life. After his request for paid tutelage in that language was turned down at the insurance company where he works, he became solidly determined to learn it on his own, based on the elements he had acquired in high school. He first convinced friends on his work team to organize a weekly lunch where conversation took place in Spanish. Then he decided to surround himself with Spanish in his personal time:

> so pretty much for the past six years I only listen to music in Spanish [...] I usually come in, grab a coffee, read a couple news articles, just force myself to do it in Spanish, make a notebook of the words that I don't know, and find my coworkers who speak Spanish and just engage with them and practice, and basically I did that. I had a couple, for

transparency, I did have maybe one or two girlfriends along the way that also spoke Spanish. so kind of practice with them or their families, but it really was like 2012 to 2018 anything I could do Spanish-wise, I did it.

After receiving a tip from a colleague, before he interviewed for his current post in Mexico, Owen spent $30 on a popular self-teaching commercial textbook program primarily so that he could claim to have had some formal instruction in Spanish. All this effort paid off and he got the job.

On one level, these short vignettes illustrate the dramatic changes in accessibility to language resources via technology made possible over the period of history with which we are concerned. Whereas Mark was astonished to be exposed to 'authentic' German language utterances, thanks to the widespread distribution of home and classroom tape recording, Owen simply took for granted that he would encounter no difficulties in finding ample materials for Spanish reading and listening online. Afrika and Hugh's *ad hoc* personal Korean learning programs rely on the navigation and critical appraisal skills characterizing digital literacy for their generation. On another level, these findings suggest that the declines in language enrollment announced by the Modern Language Association (Looney & Lusin, 2019) may not entirely reflect the extent to which young Americans are studying languages. There may well be many like Afrika, Hugh and Owen who are pursuing their language-related goals, but without recourse to the knowledge and guidance of language educators. If true language learning expertise is to be applied in these situations, this suggests a role for teachers and programs in helping students to evaluate, select and use appropriate materials from among the many online resources at their disposition. It also suggests a role for explicit metalinguistic awareness in language teaching: for instance, to help learners appreciate the various dimensions of communicative ability (e.g. grammatical/formal but also pragmatic, sociolinguistic, strategic capacities) rather than relying entirely on 'folklinguistic theories' (Miller & Ginsberg, 1995; Zhuang & Kinginger, 2022).

6.3 Program Duration

As indicated in our survey findings, and in demographic data made available in annual IIE Open Doors reports, one of the most visible trends in US study abroad is toward sojourns of decreasing length. Short-term programs, defined as lasting eight weeks or less, accounted for 64.8% of American study abroad in the academic year 2018–2019, prior to the pandemic, up from 52.1% in 2005–2006 (IIE, 2021a). According to Dietrich (2018: 552), these programs are attractive to students because they allow for time abroad without interfering with 'real life,' that is, on-campus activities, graduation requirements, relationships or work. For non-traditional or low-income students with family or work commitments, short-term sojourns make study abroad a feasible option.

While short-term programs contribute to the democratization and diversification of international education, this trend has given rise to concern about the extent to which these programs make substantive contributions to the learning that is normally attributed to study abroad. Thus, the applied linguistics literature reveals a recent preoccupation with demonstrating the benefits of the short-term sojourns that have now become the norm. These studies have shown that students can make meaningful progress toward language proficiency and intercultural competence in short-term programs (e.g. Cubillos *et al.*, 2008; Duperron & Overstreet, 2009; Issa *et al.*, 2020). In comparison to longer programs where students are left to their own devices to structure the use of time and seek integration within local communities, they may in fact present certain advantages if they are appropriately designed (Dietrich, 2018). Cubillos and Ilvento (2013: 505) note that short-term study abroad fosters determination to learn languages and can serve as a 'recruitment and retention tool' for language departments. Evidence exists to show that participants in these programs perceive their personal and intellectual impact and that they become more inclined to study or travel abroad again (Dietrich, 2018).

In our survey, participants were asked about the length of their program(s) and could indicate the length for up to four programs if they had studied abroad multiple times. The total number of responses received for this question was 6562. Overall, most respondents completed programs that were relatively short in length: one semester (2–5 months; $n = 2582$, 39%) or shorter (2–8 weeks; $n = 2173$, 33%). A small proportion of participants completed programs for one academic year (6–11 months; $n = 1284$, 20%) or longer (12+ months; $n = 523$, 8%). Thus, most respondents completed programs that lasted less than one academic semester.

Figure 6.3 shows the ways in which the proportions of the different program lengths have changed over time in our survey data. These data indicate that programs of all durations occurred over the different time periods, albeit with small differences. Perhaps most clearly, while stays lasting 2–8 weeks have remained relatively constant over time, semester-long stays appear to have increased over time. The data also indicate that stays of one year or greater have reduced over time. Of all programs reported to take place before 2000, the proportion of semester-long programs is 26%. In comparison, this proportion increases to 46% for study abroad programs that took place after 2010. In addition, the proportion of stays lasting one academic year has more than halved over time: 31% of programs in our sample lasted one academic year before 2000, but this proportion is 13% for respondents

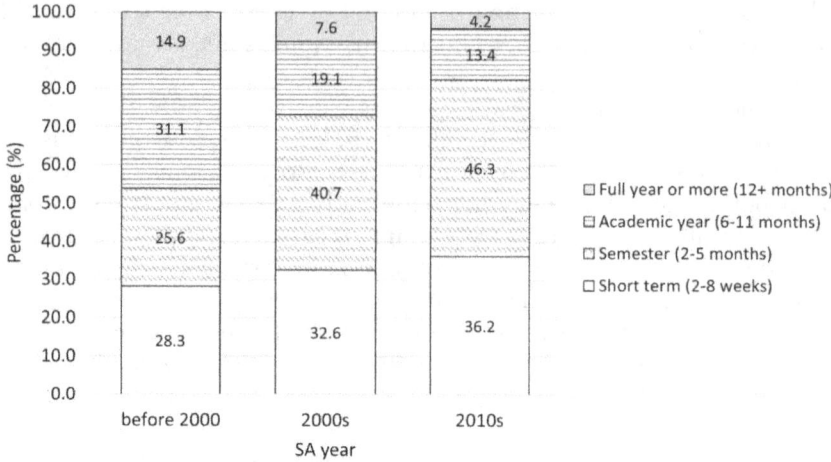

Figure 6.3 Duration of study abroad programs by time period

who studied abroad since 2010. These data indicate that study abroad experiences today are typically shorter, with semester-long sojourns being the most frequent.

In addition, and in response to questions arising from the qualitative phase of the project, we used the survey data to explore to what extent alumni had undertaken multiple sojourns abroad and what the durations of those sojourns were. This analysis is based on the total number of respondents who reported at least one duration for their program(s) ($n = 3696$). Overall, just over half of respondents participated in one program only (52.4%) and approximately one-quarter of respondents participated in two programs (26.4%). In comparison, fewer survey respondents completed three or more programs: 469 respondents (or 12.7%) had completed three programs and 318 respondents (or 8.6%) had completed four programs. Although these frequencies are comparatively low, they do indicate a substantial number of participants with large amounts of experience abroad. Taken together, therefore, just under half our sample had participated in at least two programs.

Examining the question of program length through the survey and the lens of 54 individual life stories permits several observations. Firstly, in both the survey and the interviews it is quite common for these participants to claim multiple experiences of study abroad, sometimes with one or more short-term programs in secondary school or college followed by a longer sojourn. Also, to prolong their time abroad, a number of these participants also pursued organized or sponsored experiences following graduation that do not appear in Table 2.7. These include Fulbright scholarships (Maryse, Hailey), government- or university-sponsored teaching fellowships (Jo, Freida, Emma, Anton), on-site employment with their previous study abroad program (Maryse, Amelia, James) or the Peace Corps (Mark). This finding very much aligns with claims about the ways in which study abroad leads to more investment in matters international or to desires for transnational identities (Tullock, 2018). It also suggests that the practice of assessing linguistic gains or other desirable outcomes (e.g. self-efficacy, intercultural competence, motivation, etc.) in pre- and post-designs involving only one study abroad timeframe at a time, or confining matters to the college years, does not adequately capture the learning trajectories or achievements of many multilingual Americans.

Secondly, regardless of program length it is quite rare in our interview data for participants to claim little or no interest in an international dimension to their professional lives. For the younger participants under the age of 30, it is often too early to determine where these aspirations will lead: whether Hugh will be able to join the Foreign Service, Blair will become an attorney involved in pro bono work for immigrant populations, Courtney will teach in Japan, Lily will find satisfying work in international education, or Afrika will be able to sojourn in Korea. Others began their careers with an international focus but then followed inclination or necessity into new endeavors: Beverly (age group 31–35), for instance, struggled to secure stable employment in study abroad administration and is now an accountant, while Andrea's (age group 51–60) career led from an international role in government service, to marketing consulting and then, in a dramatic mid-life shift, to mental health counseling. Only two participants, Slug Cactus (age group under 25) and Pamela (age group 51–60), provide counter examples, a lukewarm disposition on the part of Slug Cactus, and a complete disavowal of interest in international work for Pamela. Notably, both interviewees described only one study abroad experience in a program with instruction delivered in English and little attempt to encourage local social integration.

Thirdly, in these data, especially among the younger participants (under 35), there are in fact cases where only short-term sojourns are reported. These include Courtney's two summers in Japan and Korea, Leonora's study trip to Morocco, Mary's homestay in Spain, Miranda's stay in Ecuador, Afrika's time in South Africa and Felicity's two forays to the UK and Spain, further described below. All these participants but one have actively maintained or enhanced additional language skills or have directly invested in international endeavors. Courtney hopes to teach in Japan, Mary has learned elements of Somali to interact with immigrant parents in the urban schools where she works, Miranda found employment with a non-governmental environmental group in Paraguay, Afrika teaches and learns Korean online and Felicity moved to Spain. For Leonora, study abroad awakened a desire to foster intercultural understanding at home, through peace education. Among our older participants (over 50) as well, however, there are also such reports. Mark, a retired Foreign Service officer who eventually mastered Korean and Chinese, did not officially study abroad in college at all, but traces his passion for international affairs to a summer stint as a volunteer in Nigeria. For Thomas, who was reared in rural Kansas, a summer trip to France launched nearly a decade of adventure in that country and elsewhere before he settled into medical studies, and later volunteered in the Democratic Republic of Congo for Doctors Without Borders. Catherine, who established a distinguished career in government service and learned several languages that are considered difficult, was inspired to pursue international work by a short-term stay in the UK. In sum, whether the participants are young or not, whether the study abroad is short term or longer term, the meaning of these experiences is best understood in terms of dramatic cognitive–emotional experience (perezhivanie) in the context of whole lives (Coleman, 2013).

Finally, to elaborate on this latter point, understanding the impact of study abroad is much enhanced by awareness of its place in any individual's sociocultural history and class-related life horizons. For individuals coming from families of privilege or from relatively cosmopolitan backgrounds, including expectations of travel, mobility in general, and ease in diverse settings (e.g. Khan, 2012), a typical college sojourn of any length may not be attractive or necessarily lead to dramatic revelations. This aspect of student circumstances may help to explain why, in our interview data, non-traditional destinations are mostly the province of students with relatively privileged or international backgrounds (see also Doerr, 2012; Trentman & Diao, 2017). For instance, Anna, already bilingual in English and Latvian, chose Senegal; Victoria, having lived in a community of expatriate medical personnel with her Irish and South African parents, went to Niger; Emma, who attended an elite college preparatory high school, studied abroad in China and then immediately after graduation moved to Russia for work as a teacher. For students of lesser means, however, any amount of time abroad can provoke development through drama. To illustrate this claim, here we present the narrative of Felicity, whose international journey began with a very short-term (3-week) stay in the UK.

Felicity (age group 31–35) was raised in a southern Tennessee town of approximately 10,000 inhabitants, near the borders with Mississippi and Alabama. She believes that she may have inherited some of her bravery from her father, who traveled to work on offshore oil rigs beginning when she was 12 years old. During her college years, she cast about in search of an appropriate concentration for her studies, first choosing dance education, then child and family studies, then English, and finally global studies. She transferred from one school to another twice, starting at a branch campus of the local public university. Her studies there were interrupted after two years, then taken up once more at a community college located near home and allowing her to commute from her parents' residence. It was at this college that she received a 'random email' about study abroad opportunities that sparked her imagination:

> when I read the email, something lit up inside me, and I asked my parents, I said, could I do something like this? and they said, well, how much does it cost us? well, they have summer programs and those are the cheapest ones, because they're short, and I know they have a scholarship.

Felicity duly composed an essay and received funding for a 3-week stay in London. Afterwards, she had an 'unstoppable and insatiable desire to go for more.' She moved to a larger university, this time another state school where she met her global studies advisor at a campus event promoting study abroad. During the two summer months she spent in Spain, she met the Spanish man who would become her husband.

Felicity returned to Spain after graduation on a student visa, enrolling in a course on teaching English as a second language and then teaching for the Ministry of Education. The couple then moved back to the US for several years during which she worked as a wedding planner. Ultimately though, they realized that 'they weren't really happy in the U.S.,' gave up the 'expensive Green Card' they had procured for her husband and returned to Spain. Felicity now lives in Madrid and works as an admissions officer for a university there offering a business curriculum in English. She expresses pride in her ability to navigate everyday circumstances in Spanish, although she does not routinely use that language at work. She feels at a disadvantage for language learning, having begun in earnest as an adult, and compares her struggle to 'building with a very broken foundation.' When she returns home to Tennessee every other year, her relatives are often at a loss for topics of conversation, knowing very little about her life. She feels most at home among other Anglophone expatriates, regardless of their national origins. In concluding her remarks, she explicitly mentioned some limitations on her imagination in her younger years:

> I never imagined I would live any further than Nashville. [...] an hour and a half from home was the furthest I ever thought about. [...] when I did the study abroad programs in the summer, at first I thought that was all I can do. I didn't think I was strong enough to live in another country. I would never have thought about an entire semester abroad. that would have been <u>terrifying</u>, because I didn't think I was strong enough, and the joke was on me. I'm certainly strong enough to live on my own and live in another country where things are completely foreign and make that my home.

In our view, Felicity's story offers useful insight into the cognitive–emotional drama that can be provoked by study abroad, even if it is short-term, for students of limited means. Like Alice, the working-class subject of Kinginger's longitudinal study (2004), Felicity interpreted international education as a pathway toward cosmopolitanism unavailable in her community of origin and a way to develop personal strength.

6.4 Residence Options

In applied linguistics and language education, contemporary debate about the relative value of different housing arrangements during study abroad has largely centered around questions of effectiveness for language and other learning. Quantitative studies have compared pre- and post-proficiency outcomes of housing types (homestay vs. residence hall or shared rentals), and to date have yet to provide solid evidence of the superiority of one over the other (e.g. DiSilvio *et al.*, 2014; Magnan & Back, 2007; Vande Berg *et al.*, 2009). Qualitative studies have documented the highly variable nature of experiences both in homestays and in university housing, pointing to the significance of the ways in which students and/or hosts interpret their roles and their general dispositions toward their circumstances (e.g. Diao, 2014; Iino, 2006; Kinginger, 2008; Kinginger & Carnine, 2019; Kinginger & Wu, 2018; Kinginger *et al.*, 2016; Pryde, 2014; Shiri, 2015; Wilkinson, 1998). Findings of the LANGSNAP project have suggested that it may not be housing arrangements per se that ultimately matter: rather, Anglophone students of French or Spanish who made the most progress toward advanced language proficiency in that study had displayed 'a clear vision of the ideal multilingual self, flexibility and resilience [and] emotional engagement.' These characteristics nurtured 'intensive relationships which challenge L2 proficiency and drive forward development' (Mitchell *et al.*, 2017: 247–248) in whatever work-, study- or leisure-related settings were available to them.

Our survey respondents were asked to indicate the nature of the housing arrangements in their programs, whether they had lived in a homestay or a dormitory, and if they shared these accommodations with local people or with other Americans.

Table 6.1 shows that overall, living with a host family (65%) was reported to be more common than living in a dormitory (38%). More respondents indicated living with American students (44%) than living with host country peers (23%). Indeed, these tendencies appear to hold across our different age groupings (see Table 6.2). For example, living with a host family is consistently a more common feature of respondents' experiences than living in a dormitory. Among respondents under 25, for instance, 29% had lived in a dormitory, whereas 64% had lived in a host family. Similarly, among respondents aged 60 or older, living in a host family (73%) was nearly twice as frequent than living

Table 6.1 Residence options during study abroad

Residence options	n	%
Living with a host family	3167	64.7
Living in a dormitory	1862	38.0
Living with American students	2151	43.9
Living with host country peers	1129	23.0

Note. In Table 6.1 the denominator used in percentage calculation was the total number of survey respondents, i.e. 4899. Each respondent could select more than one option.

in a dormitory (39%). In terms of living with American students versus host country peers, our results indicate some small changes over time. For example, while living with American students was more frequent than living with host country peers among the under 25s (50% vs. 18%), respondents aged 51–60 and over 60 indicated greater balance between these options (35% vs. 26% and 37% vs. 23%, respectively).

With the qualitative data from the current study, it is possible to address questions about residence options from a different angle and possibly also to contextualize perennial scholarly interest in proving the relative impact of homestay experiences. In comparison to apartment or dorm stays, homestays, and the relationships that characterize them, however ephemeral, appear to be memorable. While the participants in our study did recall the general structure of their residence hall housing arrangements, when prompted they typically did not offer details, although one interviewee recalled a positive experience in an urban international student housing complex, another praised the eco-conscious nature of his residence hall, and two brought up retrospective concerns about safety. Homestays, however, place students in circumstances that can immediately challenge expectations and generate the kinds of cognitive–emotional drama that drive development. Thus, in many instances they provoke long-term reflection, often with particular lived experiences (perezhivaniya) retained as contributions to the overall coherence of life stories. This can be the case

Table 6.2 Residence options during study abroad by respondents' age

Age group	Living with host family	Living in dormitory	Living with American students	Living with host country peers
	% (n)	% (n)	% (n)	% (n)
<25	64.3 (464)	29.1 (210)	49.9 (360)	17.5 (126)
25–30	56.7 (842)	42.2 (627)	48.5 (720)	24.5 (364)
31–35	70.3 (481)	34.5 (236)	41.1 (281)	21.5 (147)
36–40	71.3 (390)	36.9 (202)	39.1 (214)	23.8 (130)
41–50	69.0 (412)	40.5 (242)	40.4 (241)	27.8 (166)
51–60	67.4 (229)	45.0 (153)	35.3 (120)	25.6 (87)
>60	72.7 (226)	38.6 (120)	36.7 (114)	22.8 (71)

whether or not the memories associated with homestay living are entirely or even mainly positive, and whether or not the episodes in question were particularly consequential on the surface, at the time.

6.4.1 Homestays

Of the 54 participants in our interviews, 30 claimed to have lived in homestays at some point during their experiences abroad, thus mirroring the proportions in the survey. Their stories about this aspect of study abroad are just as variable as those to be found in the broader literature on this topic. In these materials several study abroad alumni recounted dramatic moments in homestays as integral to their professional life stories, either in entirely glowing terms or as challenges that ultimately contributed to their adult pursuits. Others recalled pleasures of homestay life, such as culture-specific holiday celebrations or receiving language-related assistance from children. Still others retain memories of obviously conflictual situations in the home. Finally, a few of our participants encountered primarily transactional approaches to the homestay either on the part of their hosts or on their own.

Two of our participants described relationships with study abroad host families that have endured and continue to enrich their lives. In response to our request for photographs of meaningful moments related to international experiences, Jo Kapusta (age group 36–40) forwarded a picture of her 'Japanese grandpa.' When she arrived in Tokyo as a participant in a year-long high school youth exchange program, with very little proficiency in Japanese, this man was waiting for her at the airport. He gave her a tour of the city, introducing her to his associates as his 'American daughter' and he then accompanied her to his home in southern Japan. Since then, Jo graduated from college and spent five years in the JET (Japan Exchange Teaching) program, then pursued an advanced degree in international education, ultimately accepting her current post with a Japanese organization promoting educational exchanges between Japan and the US. According to Jo, throughout her career her Japanese grandpa has been instrumental in helping her to secure the social and institutional connections necessary for success. On the last day of her most recent month-long business trip to Japan, he invited her home where she learned that he was in the early stages of dementia, requiring in-home care. Nevertheless, she recounted a joyous reunion during which she was included with other members of the extended family in a session involving photographs of her former host as a child and stories about his life before the war. Ultimately, Jo attributes her embrace of Japanese culture to his efforts:

> I really owe a lot to him, he was always very encouraging, especially when I was still very new to Japan, and my Japanese was not good at all.

but he introduced me to a lot of important people in my life and taught me values that are important in Japan. so I think that's the reason that I've really embraced the culture and why I also feel so embraced by the culture and why I do consider myself a third culture kid.

For Rose (age group 41–50), a high school French teacher whose case is presented in Chapter 3, a year-long college-level sojourn in eastern France nurtured the development of a close relationship with a host family. Rose's parents had insisted that she try living in France on a shorter-term basis before making a commitment to stay the year, and she participated in a 6-week summer program after her first year of college. That experience was 'not the greatest,' in large part because her host family was 'in it for the money.' When it came time to choose a housing arrangement for her longer sojourn, she set aside her reservations and opted once again for a host family. Her hosts, a school librarian, a teacher and their three adult sons, became her lifelong 'French family.' This relationship began when she 'chose to become part of the family,' rather than spending her spare time with other students, and they 'really brought [her] into the fold.' She was invited to join the family for leisure outings, longer vacations, and trips to the family farm to procure fresh produce and meat. On her 21st birthday, her American boyfriend joined her and the family on a day-long excursion through local vineyards. The family also agreed to host a small group of Rose's German friends, former study abroad participants at her home university, although they also used this occasion to teach Rose about the history of their region, Alsace-Lorraine, which has long endured the brunt of Franco–German rivalry and war mongering. They also told her about the wartime suffering of their relatives, including a grandparent who had never recovered from an encounter with mustard gas during the First World War. Her host parents checked her homework, provided home-cooked meals with conversations resembling a 'ping-pong match,' and asked her into the kitchen to learn their recipes. When a conflict arose with one of her professors, after an illness prompted a missed class, Rose had to work hard to convince her hosts not to intervene on her behalf. Her host father shared his crossword puzzles well before Rose was able to contribute to completing them. Rose and her host mother together took part in an aerobic exercise class, which was 'hysterical,' when they compared their own performance to that of the professional ballet dancers also enrolled.

> and oh my gosh, the talks, the conversations, the laughter, the news was always on in the background so that, and they did that for me, because they like it quiet but they did that so that I could hear the news and ask them questions. which, as an adult I understand how cool that was. they didn't have to do that. I just assumed, and they didn't tell me that until the end of the year, but we laughed, we talked.

Rose remains in continuous touch with her host family through social media, and visits regularly when she accompanies students on summer trips to France.

For the academic year he spent in Paris, Steven (age group 51–60), now a professor of European history, chose a homestay over a bed-and-breakfast arrangement because he 'wanted the complete immersion program.' To his delight, he was placed in the home of an elderly couple who were former settlers in North Africa (known at the time as 'pieds noirs') and survivors of the Holocaust. His host mother had learned a smattering of English while 'hiding out with the resistance' and helping to conceal the location of Canadian soldiers behind German lines. While they were discussing the 1940 British naval attack on the French ships at the port of Mers-el-Kabir, to prevent them from falling into German hands after the Allied defeat in the Battle of France, Steven's host father casually mentioned that he had been present at that event. Six days out of each week, his hosts provided an elaborate home-cooked dinner and, although he had no prior experience in the kitchen, Steven was invited to learn his host mother's culinary secrets, an ideal language learning situation because of the immediate physical presence of objects and processes. In this way, he greatly expanded his vocabulary to include terms for foods, utensils, spices and techniques. His host father had recently suffered a stroke that had affected his short-term memory, such that in addition to engaging Steven in nightly telling-your-day routine at dinner, he also tended to repeat the same questions from day to day, a practice that Steven also deemed very helpful for language learning:

> so every day at dinnertime. I was grilled by him and he wanted to know […] who did you meet, he was very very French. […] what beautiful women have you met, did you get their telephone numbers, why not, you should take up smoking. all French women smoke. you have to offer them cigarettes. it's a come on.

Steven's host father was no longer officially permitted to smoke but, after dinner, he would invite his guest to join as he strolled and enjoyed his daily clandestine cigar. Having graduated from an illustrious Grande École and served in an upper-level administrative post, he had many highly placed friends ('generals and ministers') and would permit Steven to 'tag along' to gatherings, thus offering a glimpse into the social lives of the elite.

Steven recounted an anecdote from the beginning of his stay in which he displayed the profound naïveté of a rural American's initial observation of Paris. While exploring his new neighborhood in the 18th arrondissement, next to Place Pigalle and Place de Clichy, he had noticed women out alone at night, and commented to his hosts that the area must be very safe:

I said to Madame [...] I was like, gosh, this place is so safe for me because like there are women out at like all hours of the night. she nearly <u>died</u>. she's like, well don't talk to those women, whatever you do. Monsieur was just like, oh, he was just roaring with laughter, was like you should ask 'em for a cigarette. and then they told me what that was [...] talk about going from a small village in upstate New York to Paris, you know, huge change.

Two of our participants directly attribute career aspiration to conflictual situations and the accompanying cognitive–emotional drama they encountered in homestay settings. Bonnie (age group 51–60) was raised in a blue-collar, working-class household and eventually joined the Foreign Service before turning her attention to international education administration. Through the auspices of a sister city arrangement, she went to France on a high school summer exchange program and had her first glimpse of the mundane level at which surprising cultural differences can operate. On the first morning in her semi-rural homestay, she woke up and prepared to take a shower as usual. However, when she located the bathroom, the shower stall was in use for storage of boxes. Perplexed, still in her bathrobe, and operating with a very low level of proficiency in French, she presented her issue to the family using mime, and received in reply one of the few words she could understand: 'Samedi. Samedi.' When it dawned on her that the members of this family only took showers once a week, as was typical in more remote settings at the time (Ross, 1995), she was amazed. She still recalls that first Saturday in the home and the fact that she was offered the first shower that day. Bonnie presented this anecdote along with her personal theory about reactions to cultural differences, which is remarkably similar to the observations of Alred and Byram (2002):

> I think everybody's got a switch that, when they travel outside the country for the first time, either they are amazed and enthralled and that switch is flipped and they think, oh my God, there's a whole world out here I knew nothing about! I want to see more, right? or they say, oh my God, I want to run home and stay in my bed. this is too much.

Upon her return home, Bonnie announced to her parents that she wanted a job that would pay her to travel.

For James (age group 36–40) 'being in France for a year was kind of an awakening on a lot of levels, now in retrospect I would say it's where [...] my sociological imagination was awakened because you deal with so much culture shock.' Now a professor of sociology at a university in France, having grown up in Baltimore, James traces much of this awakening to life with a host family that was '<u>really, rea::lly</u> different' from his family of origin in terms of culture and social class. At the time, the program he attended normally recruited host families from the upper echelons of society. James was placed in the home of a wealthy, highly conservative, practicing Catholic family with three children, all significantly younger than James. Because he is gay and had been raised in a middle-class home with progressive values and little attention to religion, at first he was alienated and considered a request for a different family. However, he soon realized that this family's central location (a 'gigantic apartment in the middle of the city') would be advantageous for his social life outside the home; in fact, as the year progressed, he developed a strong and active local social network through Gay Pride events and activism within an HIV prevention organization.

In contrast to the findings of other studies examining rich patterns of language socialization at homestay dinner tables (e.g. Kinginger & Carnine, 2019; Lee *et al.*, 2017), James found himself in a 'semi-adult child position' and was fed pedestrian fare, such as chopped hot dogs and rice, in the kitchen with the other children. There were dinner parties, during which the host parents used their formal dining room and served more refined dishes, but James was never invited to those events. Neither did he join the family for holidays or vacation trips to their secondary residence in Spain. The family warned him against inviting his own friends into the home, lest they become jealous of his spacious and well-appointed quarters. The main social tie he formed in the homestay was to the family's housekeeper, an immigrant from Madagascar who was a constant presence 'cleaning the house, doing laundry, folding, cooking.' To some extent, the housekeeper took James under her wing, inviting him for Christmas, a wedding anniversary party and other family events such that he felt much closer to her family than to his official hosts. All of this was 'so foreign to [him] on a class level as well as a cultural level' that, in retrospect, he believes that the homestay, though 'complicated,' made a major contribution to his desire for a career as a sociologist.

For some of our other participants, homestays remain memorable but contribute less to the overall account of realizations taking place in study abroad. Erik (age group 41–50, see Chapter 3) spent a year in a major Japanese city, and later became an entrepreneur. His most important learning occurred at university, where he mixed with a group of other students determined to improve their language proficiency in a rigorous program that required presence on campus every weekday from 8 until 5. For the first six months of his sojourn, he lived with a couple who had three small children and another on the way. Their home was located in a distant suburb of the city and required a 2-hour commute, most of which consisted of walking up or down a tortuous mountain road while dodging oncoming traffic (see Durbidge, 2020 for more cases illustrating the significance of homestay geographic location). Moreover, when he returned home after each school day, Erik was expected to contribute to the upkeep of the home and to child minding. In winter, it became abundantly clear that there was no central heating in the home. Erik also remembers some occasions during which the couple entertained business associates and he was included, that the first time he woke up having dreamed in Japanese took place there, and that he had never been in better physical condition in his life before. However, in the end his circumstances simply became too arduous, and in the spring semester he moved to another homestay, closer to the university.

From her semester in the suburbs of Tokyo that eventually launched a career in market strategy (see Chapter 4), Hailey (age group 31–35) recalls a home that 'defied every stereotype people have of Japanese families.' Both members of the couple worked outside the home and, despite his commute into and out of the city, the father was present at dinner every evening. This couple had met while they were both abroad in New Zealand to learn English and retained a desire to expose their children to other places and people, including student guests and the six or seven others who had preceded Hailey. After a typical evening, during which Hailey received assistance in learning to write from the couple's 7-year-old daughter and the whole family watched television, Hailey and her host mother sometimes stayed up late discussing 'cultural' or controversial topics in English that were beyond her current level of Japanese proficiency. In this regard, she considers herself 'very fortunate' in her homestay placement.

Anna (age group 25–30) is a nurse now preparing a PhD in that field. Her sojourn in Senegal included a month in the capital city, Dakar, followed by a 2-month internship in a small-town hospital near the Gambian border, both with homestays. Anna had not planned to pursue nursing prior to this time but the internship had a profound influence on her ambitions (see Chapter 4). She did not form a close relationship with her hosts in Dakar, perhaps because she was newly arrived and somewhat disoriented. However, during the internship she enjoyed an experience more akin to a whole-village stay than to a simple in-family residential experience. She was overwhelmed by the hospitality of the people she encountered, particularly the casual way in which strangers, including herself, were invited into homes for meals taken from communal dishes:

> the culturally normative thing is there's never not enough food. you- just everyone cuts, you know, you get a slice of the pie and the room cuts out a portion of that and everyone eats a little less to accommodate the other person. I just remember that really hitting me because in the U.S. it's like, God forbid you invite another person to dinner. we need to rearrange everything and plan and blah, blah, blah. it's like the people are really present there. and so communal, and I knew that the U.S. was a more individualistic country [...] but it kind of really brought it to the front of my mind.

Outside Dakar, where French is commonly used, Anna discovered a real need to develop some proficiency in Wolof, the main indigenous language of Senegal; most of the patients she treated did not speak French. She developed strong admiration for the elaborate, ritual expression of respect expressed in Wolof greetings. As documented in Irvine (1974: 168) these greetings are obligatory in every encounter, 'whenever two persons are visible to each other.' They are traditionally performed in rounds consisting of a salutation, at least one question about the welfare of the interlocutor, questions about the whereabouts and health of the interlocutor's family and praising God. They are also expressions of social status based on various criteria (age, gender, caste and achieved prestige), with the person of lower status performing the greeting, a fact that Anna did not mention and may not have perceived. Instead, she interpreted this ritual as indicating that 'people really want to ask how we're doing.' In any case, she was particularly impressed by the normal response to a 'How are you?' question, which she considers 'one of the most beautiful things I've ever heard.' According to Irvine (1974) a typical greeting sequence would open as follows:

A: Na ngga def? [How do you do?]

B: Maanggi fi reh. [I am here only.]

(Irvine, 1974: 171)

Anna's language learning process was facilitated by the 'extremely close' relationship she nurtured with her hosts, one of the wives in a polygamous marriage, her daughter, and the housekeeper. At one point when the house was being remodeled and the daughter had just married and moved to her husband's home, Anna shared a bed with the two other women in the household: 'It was like we were three girlfriends having a slumber party and I just remember thinking this is so wild and wonderful, and it felt like me and my mom at home.' Her host mother also helped her to comprehend local norms for behavior: for example, instructing her to slow down when she was walking to avoid making others worry. On this topic she concluded: 'there were parts of Wolof that were really enlightening,' stating that on her return from Senegal her parents noticed that she was unusually 'calm and in the moment.'

Frances (age group 36–40) studied in Ghana for a semester and eventually became an award-winning creative writer (see Chapter 4). Most impactful for her was a research project examining indigenous medical practices. Her program 'really focused on getting you involved with the local community' and included two homestays, one urban and one rural. In the city, she was astonished by the relative luxury of her accommodations. Whereas some other students in the program were doing without modern plumbing or were sharing rooms with host family children or grandparents, she had a 'huge' room to herself, with her own bathroom and electric water heater. She was also surprised, in the rural area, to find that her hosts were not living in 'huts with no electricity,' although she did have to accustom herself to sharing one water tap with a grandmother, her daughter, two small children, some cousins and some renters. Two decades later, Frances is still in contact with some members of this family.

For other participants, the memorable aspects of homestays have mainly to do with culinary practices or holidays. Beverly (age group 31–35) lived for a year in southern France with a family that included two adult children who had left home, a teenage son, a father and a 'mother hen' who was 'used to taking care of people' and was 'such an amazing cook.' This host mother would shop daily for fresh ingredients and invest considerable time in preparing the convivial family dinners that have traditionally characterized French culinary culture (Fischler & Masson, 2008). Beverly particularly recalls the challenges posed to her at the dinner table. She was required to partake of a dish of frogs' legs and to overcome her apprehensions about eating beans to taste a regional specialty, cassoulet (made of beans, duck and pork in a recipe that calls for 34 steps on the *Bon Appétit* website). Just after high school, Lily (age group 25–30) spent a gap year in France, including a homestay in Paris with a 'playful' family who would make fun of her for some things, including her American aversion to certain dishes. She remembers one night when her host mother had prepared a rabbit tagine: 'she just plops this tagine in front of me with all these beautiful vegetables around essentially a whole rabbit. I just looked at it and it was my favorite animal as a kid. and I was like, really?' Fortunately, Lily was excused from eating the rabbit and offered an alternative dinner. On another occasion, her host father courteously removed the heads from the shrimps on her plate, helping her to feel 'loved and welcomed' despite her issues around certain aspects of French culinary practice. During her academic year in Beijing, Emma (age group 31–35) lived in a small apartment with a mother and her 12-year-old daughter, and recalls being included in birthday celebrations, including her own, during which longevity noodles, 'a noodle that doesn't end,' were served. As a college junior, Max (age group 36–40) arrived at his study abroad destination in Spain, Salamanca, just after the New Year's celebration that spring. A few days later on 6 January, his host family observed the Día de los Reyes, or Three Kings Day, commemorating the arrival of the three wise men in Bethlehem following the birth of Jesus. The whole family was present along with guests, and 'it was just a really loud chaos to me because I couldn't understand a word.' Tradition calls for a cake that has a small model of a king or queen baked into it, and for the person who happens to receive this gift to be treated as monarch of the day. Max turned out to be that randomly chosen person: 'They made a big deal of it, and I was just, oh this is cute. I have no idea what's going on. I'll have to look at it later.' He still has that little gift and keeps it on the desk in the office where he works as a system analyst.

In addition to Hailey and Steven (whose host father's loss of short-term memory and tendency toward repetition had made of him a useful conversation partner for a learner), several other participants noted that they had received language-related tutelage from host family members, particularly children. During the year he spent working in Paris as an au pair for a divorced professor, Thomas (age group over 60) received daily instruction from his highly articulate 3-year-old charge. During her semester in Chile, Freida (age group 41–50) encountered some difficulties with her first host family, an unwillingly childless couple who treated her like a baby. After two weeks in that situation, she moved to the household of a professor with three children, one of whom had 'some sort of delayed development' and became her 'best Spanish teacher ever.' Grace (age group 41–50), who arrived in Venezuela with no knowledge of Spanish whatsoever, attributes her rapid attainment of basic conversational ability to the 8-year-old daughter of her host parents, who craved attention and 'wanted to talk to [her] all the time.' Once the daughter realized that Grace was incapable of responding, she took it upon herself to teach, pointing to objects and naming them:

> I would ask her to come with me into town and we would just go to the shops and I'd say how do you do this? how do you do that? what's that called? […] and I would say within three months I could go anywhere I wanted, ask for anything I wanted and get my point across. now, grammatically correct, no, but I could communicate sufficiently to live there and get around, catch the bus, go shopping, get what I wanted.

Two participants described homestay experiences in largely negative terms. Moira (age group 25–30) made a homestay arrangement independently from her semester-long program in Buenos Aires. Her own family in the Midwest had hosted a student guest from Argentina who then proposed to return the favor, offering Moira the opportunity to share a rented apartment with her and her sister, also university students. Through this experience, Moira learned that in Argentina the departure from home for college tends not to represent the same rite of passage toward adult independence that it often does in the US. Although the parents did not live in the city, they nonetheless insisted on maintaining strict supervision of their children and anyone else in the apartment. The sisters repeatedly and unsuccessfully attempted to impose their parents' rules on Moira, forbidding her from going out alone in the evening or from frequenting certain areas of the city reputed to be unsafe. Moira's alienation from the host family was cemented when she was directly told never to allow black people in the apartment.

Carmen (age group 36–40), who is Mexican American, studied in Chile and encountered favoritism toward people of European descent in many contexts, including in the home she shared with a middle-aged woman, her mother, sister and husband, and another study abroad participant from the Basque country. Guests in the home would be confused as to why a Mexican student was present but they would not pursue the question with Carmen. At dinner, served every night at 8:30 or 9:00, most of the attention went to the other student, leading Carmen to conclude that she was 'not that interesting.' Over the dinner table, the hosts would recount stories about the white, female students they had received in the past, including a shocking one in which their brother, at the peak of his youthful allure, had seduced one of their guests even though he was married at the time. Although she was alarmed at the 'harsh' classism and racism she observed, this did not dampen Carmen's enthusiasm for learning to use Spanish for academic purposes, nor for the Chilean variety of that language, and she has gone on to work in the study abroad profession hoping to contribute to its racial and socioeconomic diversity.

Several alumni noted the largely transactional nature of their homestay arrangements, whether this preference was exhibited by their hosts or on their own part. Anton (age group 51–60), who works in international development, spent an academic year in Paris living with a 'nice, fairly well-to-do family right on one of the big boulevards,' and an American friend. He was quite content with this arrangement since some other students in his cohort lived with elderly women on small pensions who relied on the income from hosting and would not arrange convivial meals, preferring to set out small portions of food 'suitable for an old widow.' In Anton's homestay, dinner followed a ritual beginning with the evening news and lively discussion with the host father, who had served in the Pompidou administration, and proceeding with a traditional, multi-course meal. While they were officially there, Anton and his friend were treated as members of the family; however, at the end of the contract they were no longer welcome: 'When it was done, it was done, and I had a day to get out.' On the assumption that the family would be interested, Anton brought his brother to meet them, and was rebuffed.

Both Miranda and Blair brought a transactional understanding of the homestay of their own to the arrangement. At the time of her 2-month summer stay in Ecuador, Miranda (age group 25–30), a marine biologist, was not yet aware that Spanish would play an important role later in her life. She lived with a woman who worked full-time and her son, who was frequently absent, such that she 'mostly talked to the housekeeper and the dog.' In any case, Miranda was in Ecuador to pursue her interest in varieties of nature, and most weekends were devoted to field trips and exploration of local eco-systems. For Blair (age group under 25), the entire study abroad experience functioned as a metaphorical pressure release valve. By his own admission, Blair was rambunctious in his early youth, socializing with the 'wrong crowd' and skipping school to enjoy other activities. He had no interest in following his paternal family line into a local military academy until he was denied admission and required to take an alternate route to the academy via community college. The lives of academy cadets are strictly regimented and subject to rigorous, constant physical and mental discipline. Thus, for Blair, study abroad for a semester in Valencia was a 'way to break up the monotony,' and make his college years more bearable. He remembers living with a widow who ran a boarding house and spoke the local language rather than standard Spanish. However, his memories of that experience and of his academic pursuits in general while in Spain are somewhat vague because he was 'hell bent on doing other stuff,' such as numerous weekend trips to other European countries or Spanish cities, in the Grand Tour tradition. Following graduation, Spanish still played a role in Blair's life, helping him to communicate with co-workers in the construction industry while he saves money to attend law school.

6.4.2 Other housing options

Fourteen participants claimed to have lived in various kinds of residence halls during their time abroad but, as noted above, their comments about these accommodations were relatively limited in comparison with those about homestays. Participants who lived in short-term housing or hostels during summer programs did not mention learning affordances in those settings, apart from Mark (age group over 60), who lived in the school he was helping to rebuild in Nigeria. As a retired Foreign Service Officer, Mark traces his fascination for international affairs to this first sojourn abroad. He remembers a Peace Corps volunteer in the village who had his underwear ironed to prevent screw flies from boring into his flesh, and also remembers listening to the BBC on a shortwave radio:

> it was so completely exotic and foreign. we sat there by the light of the kerosene, I think it was a mantle lamp, and I watched the geckos hunting on the walls for the insects. and we listed to the British news with a British accent, and the world news. and it was just, it was a complete ((laughter)) opening up to international affairs and all.

As for shared rentals, the only extensive comments were from Tim (age group 25–30) an ocean engineer who attributes much of his language development to the French roommates with whom he shared an apartment during his first semester in France. Subsequently, during his internship he lived in a group house with ten French-speaking fellow newcomers to the city:

> that was an extremely happy time for me 'cause it was just […] we're all like kind of, everyone was new to the city. and so we're all kind of

discovering it all for the first time together. um, so we'd all go out together and hang out all the time. so, and of course it was all in French. so it was good to at that point be able to speak to them in a normal way.

Two participants shared happy memories of life in residence halls. During her year abroad in France, Amelia (age group 25–30), who is now an arts journalist and playwright, lived in the American House of the Cité Internationale Universitaire de Paris, a private foundation and park established after the First World War to promote exchange between students of varied national origin. For Amelia this situation was 'incredible,' offering her a first experience of independent life, with her own room but also access to people from all over the world. Peter (age group 31–35), who now works in renewable energy, lived in Freiburg, the 'solar capital of Germany' and recalls his astonishment at discovering the car-free eco-district of the city where he lived in former French barracks that had been retrofitted with solar and green roof components. His dormitory was also near the Heliotrope, the first building in the world to capture more energy than it consumes by physically rotating to expose its solar panels to maximum sunlight. So, he said, 'a lot of interesting technology that [he] was exposed to as a young 19-year-old at the time […] that wasn't something that [he] was seeing in Minnesota.'

Clementine (age group 41–50), now a practitioner of acupuncture, was the only member of her cohort who elected to live in the 'foreigners' dorm' in downtown St Petersburg, as it turned out, with Russian roommates who wanted to live close to their school. The others were pursuing a 'real college experience' and opted for university residence halls in the distant suburbs where, ironically, the real 'foreigners' were located; at the time most Russian students lived at home and did not require dorms. In addition to being inconvenient, these dorms were dangerous. Clementine's program was closed the following year after a student who refused to pay protection money to the local gang died after being thrown out of a window. Looking back at this experience Clementine feels that, overall, it was highly beneficial, especially after growing up in a small town. On the other hand, now that she is adult she is surprised at how little supervision or attention to safety were provided by the program, especially 'given how wild things were there.'

Pamela (age group 51–60), now an attorney in probate practice, attended a trimester-long program in a major city in southern France. Designed for business majors, the program offered two weeks of intensive tutelage in 'survival' French followed by courses delivered in English. The students were housed in a bare-bones residence hall in a remote part of the city with 'no security, no person on site to keep us secure.' Pamela recalls that she and her roommate were robbed in the middle of the night and that in public she was 'careful not to stand out like Americans, make ourselves sort of targets.' She stated explicitly on the survey that study abroad had convinced her not to pursue an international career.

6.5 Returning Home

As noted in Chapter 1, the immediate aftermath of study abroad is a rarely studied phenomenon, although some research has indicated difficulties in campus or classroom reintegration for some returnees. Our project included questions about returning home from a sojourn abroad, both in the survey and in the interviews. The survey question focused on institutional provisions mainly, whereas in the interviews participants made clear that their challenges were primarily emotional. In the survey, participants were asked after returning to your home university, how difficult was it to (i) find appropriate language courses to continue studying the target language; (ii) find courses of interest; (iii) integrate experiences abroad into the program of study; (iv) meet students with interests in international affairs; and (v) connect with members of the international community on campus. Participants responded to these statements using a sliding scale of 0 to 10, with 10 representing 'very difficult.' Overall, participants indicated few considerable difficulties integrating back into university life following study abroad (see Table 6.3).

As part of the interview, participants were asked to reflect on the experience of re-entry to their home campus and to comment on whether they remembered any provisions in place to offer support for returning students. For some, these questions were not particularly relevant, either because they had not in fact returned home after study abroad, or because the sojourn took place in the relatively distant past and such details had faded from memory. In answer to the first question, participants chose to comment on various phenomena such as intense desire to share newfound enthusiasm about host cultures with unreceptive audiences, boredom and isolation, changes in desired life direction, and 'communicative lingerings' (Sicola, 2005), especially a temporary inability to adapt to interactional norms at home. As for

Table 6.3 Descriptives for survey questions about returning home after study abroad

Statement	Mean	Median	SD
Find appropriate language courses to continue studying the target language	3.31	2	3.58
Find courses of interest	2.79	2	2.96
Integrate study abroad experiences into program of study	3.18	2	3.18
Meet students with interests in international affairs	3.23	2	3.00
Connect with members of the international community on campus	3.74	3	3.03

the second question, from the perspective of the participants at least, it would appear that program efforts to accommodate returning students have been a largely *ad hoc* affair, and that re-entry to on-campus life is best facilitated at smaller colleges with cohesive communities, particularly those colleges with significant participation in international education.

Some participants portrayed their younger selves, on return from study abroad, in a quite unflattering light. For Gloria (age group over 60), homecoming to a large Midwestern public university after a year in Madrid was 'tough.' In interactions with her parents and classmates she was 'horrendous,' angry about the weight gain she associated with American food, constantly forcing everyone to listen to the Spanish records she had brought home and unable 'to understand why the whole world didn't want to go to Spain.' Despite her relatively cosmopolitan upbringing (see Chapter 3), on arrival at her private university after a sojourn in Niger, Victoria (age group 36–40) experienced 'the world's worst reverse culture shock.' She had become 'this insufferable don't-you-know-people-are-dying-in-Africa sort of person' and struggled to re-adapt. Amelia (age group 25–30) gave up a job she had secured in Paris after a year there and 'cried the whole way home.' She roamed the streets of small-town Connecticut with a camera, documenting everything that was wrong, including the pastries at Dunkin' Donuts. In line with the perennial image of France in the US (Kinginger, 2016; Levenstein, 2004), Andrea (age group 51–60), who had also spent a year in Paris, returned to her small liberal arts college as a 'French sophisticate,' with a new wardrobe, wine glasses and a smoking habit. Heather (age group 41–50) returned to her public university's campus in Texas from a year in Russia attempting to convince all her friends to eat borscht and salads made from beets, but 'they weren't as excited as [she] was.'

Other participants focused less on their attempts to share new perspectives and more on the isolation and general ennui they experienced as returnees. Anton (age group 51–60) returned to the leafy rural campus of his small liberal arts college after a year in Paris to a year of lackluster 'senioritis' and a perception of the campus as 'homogenous.' After a semester in Korea, Hugh (age group under 25) found the environment of his private, Catholic university and the absence of any language-related challenges to be profoundly boring. Jessica (age group 36–40), who had no previous international experience prior to her semester in Mexico, commented on alienation from her former friends, including a long-term boyfriend, with whom it had become 'hard to relate.' Erik (age group 41–50) had been obliged to choose between study abroad and the business-related internship that most of his classmates had enjoyed, and initially perceived himself as out of step in the race to an entry-level job.

Still others, whose life stories are described in Chapters 3, 4 and 5, had discovered new vocations or aspects of their identities during study abroad and remember the aftermath as a time of transition or turmoil. Following a semester in Senegal, during which she discovered her vocation as a nurse, Anna (age group 25–30) traversed a period of 'existential chaos,' seeking a new identity and professional pathway, and spending most of her time alone, frantically attempting to adjust to a science-based curriculum. Moira (age group 25–30), who had found the courage to claim a queer identity while studying in Argentina, was also isolated at home for a time, since her original social network did not align well with her new perceived self. Freida's (age group 41–50) passion for social justice had been awakened while she was in Chile, and she became disenchanted with the work required to complete a major in English literature upon her return. After a sojourn in Hungary and an internship at a Manhattan bank, Owen (age group 25–30) was squarely 'focused' on achieving a career in some form of international business.

Another theme present in some participants' narratives is a phenomenon termed 'communicative lingerings' by Sicola (2005) in a study of the linguistic aspects of reverse culture shock among long-term expatriate returnees. Such 'lingerings' include the unintentional display of 'foreign' communicative behaviors and the perceptions of home culture communicative style as strange (see also Dewaele, 2008, on multilinguals' divergence from local sociolinguistic norms). Sicola's participants were shown to recruit elements of other languages to complete expression in English, and to experience difficulty in re-adjusting to interactional norms for physical and social distance. For Sicola, communicative lingerings are an index of the depth of acculturation while abroad as well as of participants' appreciation for host cultures' communicative practices and the underlying principles they represent.

While no specific question about this topic was posed to our participants, several of them recalled memories related to perceptions of interaction or politeness influenced by their socialization while abroad. For instance, after a year in Russia Heather (age group 41–50) found several aspects of communicative style at home to be 'jarring.' These include the overall volume of conversation in public spaces and her own tendency to stand or sit a bit closer to her interlocutor than was locally appropriate. Heather also expressed a strong affinity for the Russian practice of not smiling when encountering a stranger, having been forced to do so in childhood: 'I always hated being told to smile. [...] I remember just always feeling bad about myself. Then I got to Russia and I thought, oh my gosh. People do that. It's okay.' (This is a mirror image of the accounts given in Konstantinovskii and Voznesenskaia (2009: 18), where Russian students returning from Western countries wearing a smile are quickly rebuffed, cursed at and considered 'not normal.') During a sojourn in southwestern France, Beverly (age group 31–35) had grown accustomed to informal conversations with strangers in public settings such as supermarkets or other shops and attempted to continue with this practice at home in the suburbs of New York City, to no avail. Erik (age group 41–50) returned home from a year in Japan with a strong tendency to translate certain features of Japanese politeness into English, such that his father instructed him to 'stop saying thank you all the time. [...] people are going to think you're crazy.'

As for institutionalized provisions offered to study abroad returnees, our participants offered few recollections, often stating outright and with conviction that there were no such arrangements on their campus. Carmen (age group 36–40), who had recently taken up a post in international education when we spoke, did explain that the attempt to convince students at her urban, public university campus to study abroad at all was quite effortful, and that perhaps there were no additional resources available for add-ons to programs. In any case, overall, the picture that emerges from the interviews is one in which re-entry has been informally facilitated on small campuses with tight-knit communities, particularly those where a high percentage of students go abroad. In these situations, the students are personally known to the faculty, who can then calibrate expectations for academic performance or find teaching roles for them. Upon return to his small liberal arts college in the South, Steven (age group 51–60) was recruited to co-teach French language courses, received individual instruction to enhance his advanced literacy skills, and lived in a 'French bubble,' regularly invited to dine with Francophone professors in various disciplines. James (age group 36–40) attended a small liberal arts college with an international focus and emphasized the benefits of returning to campus with a cohort of fellow study abroad participants and a sense of 'tradition in the program' that 'smoothed over' any potential alienation. Like Steven, James and his cohort benefited from flexible expectations of the faculty, demanding courses appropriate for their needs, and the presence of Francophone people in informal settings, in this case including exchange students from France working as teaching assistants. As returning students in similar institutions, Jessica (age group 36–40) and Laura (age group 51–60) also served as language tutors, and Laura also opted to live on the 'international' floor of a residence hall. Astrid (age group 36–40) and Victoria (age group 36–40), who attended the same prestigious private college on the East Coast, both noted that study abroad was very common among their classmates, and that this shared history facilitated their re-entry process. Hailey (age group 31–35) was able to rejoin a group of four students who had lived in Japan in an advanced language course. Max (age group 36–40), also enrolled in a small college with an emphasis on international education, is the only participant to mention having been involved with the orientation process for the next class of study abroad participants. Among all the participants who attended larger, public universities only one recalled efforts to integrate the knowledge and abilities accrued during study abroad into local courses or extra-curricular offerings: through a connection to a faculty advisor and based on her year-long sojourn in Spain, Gloria (age group over 60) received an invitation to co-teach an advanced-level course on cultural geography that was 'totally an absolute fun experience.'

6.6 Conclusion

In this chapter we have reviewed some characteristics of study abroad programs in the light of our quantitative and qualitative data. We have shown, for example, that homestays are a preferred housing option and that, in our data at least, these are more likely than other arrangements to generate the kinds of cognitive–emotional dissonance that drives development and remains in memory as a contribution to long-term catharsis. Concerning the return to campus after study abroad, in the survey we queried mainly curricular issues and found these were perceived as unproblematic. The interview data, however, unveiled multiple and complex emotional dimensions of this transition.

Another highlight of this chapter is the discussion of program length that we can provide in a mixed-methods study. Research in applied linguistics and language education typically focuses on gains in proficiency or other attributes from one program or sojourn at a time. It is true that many of our survey participants reported only one study abroad experience. However, because so many interviewees described multiple sojourns, we re-examined the quantitative data for evidence on this question. Findings show that just under half the survey respondents had studied abroad more than once. Among those individuals who participated in two programs, there is a tendency (46%) for the second sojourn to be longer than the first (26% for the second sojourn to be shorter; 28% for the two sojourns to be equivalent in length). Thus, our materials suggest that understanding how language study abroad contributes to transnational disposition requires a long timeframe. For example, if we had only examined the first of Rose's homestays in France, we would have missed the life-changing personal and career-related development sparked by the second. Further, with our interview data we can contextualize and interpret the longer-term meaning of brief study abroad for students like Felicity. We can also discuss the overall ontological significance of study abroad in the context of 'whole lives' (Coleman, 2013).

7 Multilingual Dispositions and Lessons for Life

7.1 Introduction

In this final chapter we consider two related themes: the development of multilingual dispositions (Canagarajah, 2007), including the ability to communicate politely and effectively in international groups that include speakers of English as a lingua franca (ELF), and the ancillary or unexpected benefits that our participants claimed to have derived from language study. We first discuss the long-term multilingual nature of study abroad as a learning context, as described by interviewees of various ages. We then briefly consider survey findings showing that participants value highly the intercultural communication skills that they believe helped them to secure employment. As noted in Chapter 2, an interview question about the use of ELF was added to our protocol after that topic emerged spontaneously in the first sessions. Here we employ our interviewees' responses to that question as a way of unpacking the notion of intercultural communication and relating it to the more contemporary, language-oriented construct of multilingual disposition. Notably, many of our participants agree that experience with otherness, and with struggles for self-expression in a new language, have made them better speakers of English in international settings. Finally, participants mentioned several benefits of language learning beyond the ability to use languages per se for communicative purposes at work. As an attorney, Jessica does not use her Spanish proficiency at work but finds it quite valuable for her volunteer activities. Peter described an analogy between the process of learning German and problem-solving in general. Emma, who has learned Spanish, Chinese and Russian, applies her awareness of language to her work in technology development. Max believes that his ability to be flexible and adapt to divergent professional jargon is attributable to his language learning.

7.2 Snapshots of Language Immersion Over Time During Study Abroad for Anglophone Students

Among students, educators, program directors and the public, study abroad has traditionally enjoyed a reputation for immersion such that students are surrounded by a constant stream of 'high-quality contextualized exposure' to language (Isabelli, 2007: 333) and can enjoy an effortless process of 'easy learning' (DeKeyser, 2010: 89). However, research has clearly demonstrated that the nature of study abroad as a language learning environment is highly variable and depends upon the dispositions of all parties (e.g. Kinginger, 2008). In recent years, Anglophone learners have been shown to encounter particular challenges related to the ubiquity of English as a lingua franca and need to deliberately foreground their goals. The LANGSNAP project, for example, aimed to capture the everyday linguistic practices of contemporary study abroad in relation to language learning. The study followed 56 British students majoring in French or Spanish using Language Engagement and Social Networks questionnaires and various measures of language development. Among the major findings of this research is that study abroad today is 'a multilingual and intercultural experience, involving virtual as well as face-to-face relationships, and the maintenance of long-term social relations alongside those created during the sojourn itself' (McManus et al., 2014: 112). New research emphasizing the 'multilingual turn' in study abroad (Diao & Trentman, 2021) may at last orient the field toward a permanent recognition of the fact that study abroad settings are diverse linguistic ecologies that were not designed for the extraction of language competence by visiting students.

Our interview data suggest that, with or without the contributions of internet-based communications technology, US-based learners abroad have typically encountered multilingual realities throughout the historical period in question. The only description of an intensive immersion in an apparently monolingual society we received was from Mark, who lived in a remote area of Korea in the early 1970s but was there to teach English for the Peace Corps. During his first year as a volunteer in a rural Egyptian village, Anton was somewhat similarly immersed in Arabic but was able to rely on translated interactions during meetings to improve his comprehension. Among the other participants in the 51–60 or over 60 age groups who commented on this topic, Steven mentioned that his host mother helped him on his arrival by using her command of English, and Maryse related the following anecdote about her efforts to foreground her needs as a learner of French in a service encounter during her first trip to France:

> when I got to France that first summer I remember I asked for something in a store in probably bad French and the person answered in English. and I asked- replied in French, and he said something in English and I replied in French, and he said in French, you win Mademoiselle. and I thought that was just lovely.

Freida (age group 41–50) lived in a homestay in Chile for a semester during which her hosts feigned lack of English proficiency until the last day of her stay to further her language development. Emma's (age group 31–35) host family in China had hoped that she would be available to tutor their daughter in English, but that possibility was shut down, presumably by the local program administration. Patrick (age group 31–35) was counseled by his home university study abroad office to choose Granada over Barcelona if he truly wished to learn Spanish, because he would be less likely to meet speakers of English; however, the principle frustration in language learning that he described was about situations elsewhere in Spain, where 'people would generally just talk to us in English, when they saw a pale person dressed strangely.' In short, in our data, there is abundant evidence to show that study abroad is, and for a long time has been, a multilingual context.

7.3 Becoming a Better Speaker of English as a Lingua Franca

It is easy to see that the worldwide spread of English (see Chapter 1) has deleterious effects on the so-called immersion environment that study abroad represents in the popular imagination. But is it also possible that Anglophone language learners can benefit not only from their own attempts at self-expression in a language other than English, but also from many opportunities to observe and use English as a lingua franca? Certainly, our survey respondents value the intercultural communication skills queried there: asked to rate on a scale from 0 to 10 how important these skills were in securing employment we received a median response of 8 ($SD = 3$). Our initial interview protocol did not include a question about the influence of language learning on our participants' use of English. However, over time, as we queried general satisfaction and benefits derived from this process, we noticed that our interviewees often mentioned that their personal struggles with language had influenced their approach to interaction with other multilinguals, particularly with speakers of English as a lingua franca (ELF). Having discovered this organic theme in our earliest collected data, we began including a specific question on that topic.

ELF is defined as the use of English among speakers of diverse first languages (Jenkins, 2011) with native speakers included if at least one speaker is a second-language user of English (Mauranen, 2018). ELF studies have been in existence for decades and have now produced a significant body of research that we will not attempt to review here. However, we do note a consensus among scholars concerning the general absence of severe miscommunication among ELF speakers (Cogo & House, 2018) and around the abilities required to achieve this. Canagarajah (2007: 926), for example, notes that ELF does not exist as a system 'out there' but is constantly in the process of becoming and evolving in specific interactional contexts. Speakers of ELF derive their competence for 'cross-language contact and hybrid codes' from their multilingual lives. They 'are able to monitor each other's language proficiency to determine mutually the appropriate grammar, phonology, lexical range and pragmatic conventions that would ensure intelligibility.' They employ pragmatic strategies to pre-empt and resolve misunderstanding, enhance efficiency and build rapport (Liu & Kinginger, 2021). Successful use of ELF also implies certain dispositions, including openness to negotiation and the unexpected, and positive attitudes toward variation in speech. Further, because multilingual communication requires constant situational adaptability, becoming a user of ELF normally requires considerable extra-curricular learning in 'actual contexts of language use and practice' (Canagarajah, 2007: 933).

In addition to documenting the remarkable capabilities of ELF users, this literature also examines some challenges confronting monolinguals engaged in multicultural work settings. Cogo (2016: 369) terms this 'a native speaker problem,' citing other studies showing that native speakers working in a multinational corporation are less comprehensible than non-native speakers (Charles & Marschan-Piekkari, 2002), and that in general they are relatively less efficient in their accommodation of communication (Sweeney & Hua, 2010). This problem is in fact widely documented in studies showing that when interacting with ELF speakers, native speakers tend to use culture-specific idioms and obscure vocabulary while imposing their own communication norms (e.g. Crystal, 2003; Seidlhofer, 2000). Cogo's own work within a multinational banking corporation shows that socialization in this community of practice normally leads to the type of multilingual disposition described by Canagarajah (2007) for all employees, with some exceptions who display arrogance 'when they speak to English L2 interlocutors as if they were speaking to L1s, without any accommodation in terms of speed or idiomatic expressions' (Cogo, 2016: 375). However, Cogo is careful to point out that this form of insensitivity can emerge with speakers of any language background.

Does language study abroad in 'actual contexts of use and practice' enhance the ELF-related abilities of Anglophone, US-based learners? That is, do they develop the disposition and capabilities for negotiation and accommodation that are necessary to avoid turbulence in multicultural interaction? To answer this question would obviously require a research design documenting what learners actually do in the settings where they learn and work. In the meantime, once we began querying this issue in our interviews, it became clear that most of our participants believe that they have become better users of ELF. Some of them, particularly those with recent and intensive work experiences involving multilingual colleagues, were able to provide articulate folk explanations of this phenomenon or examples of specific illustrative events. In this section, we provide some selected examples of this phenomenon.

Miranda (age group 25–30) recounted having been on the receiving end of monolingual insensitivity in Spanish during the time she spent working for an environmental group in Paraguay. Many of her local interlocutors spoke very quickly and without attending to the lexical range of their talk to enhance intelligibility. These and other, similar experiences have 'completely shaped' Miranda's approach to interacting with ELF speakers. She makes conscious efforts to speak as clearly as possible, and explicitly mentioned some of the monitoring and accommodation strategies characterizing expertise in ELF:

> of course, when they're stumbling or are struggling, I think it's definitely shaped my reaction to that and kind of trying to sort out, do they need me to just sit here and be patient, or do they need me to kind of fill in some words for them. as you meet somebody you gauge maybe their level of embarrassment over things like that. I always try to relate to myself to whoever I'm talking to, to understand I guess what they need from me as an English speaker to get through the conversation. I think it's been a very active thing on my mind anytime I'm speaking to somebody with English as their second language.

Owen (age group 25–30), who currently works in Mexico City for a multinational insurance company, has also noticed the 'native speaker problem' among some of his colleagues who have no study abroad or language learning history, and speak '100 miles an hour using slang and local colloquialisms' that pose challenges to ELF users. As a result, in such interactions he goes out of his way to avoid vernacular expressions and to use Spanish–English cognates whenever possible. Helen (age group 31–35), a pediatric occupational therapist, mentioned a similar strategy to choose words 'that would maybe be more optimal' with interlocutors for whom English may be 'a second, or third or fourth language.' Because she regularly works with Spanish-speaking patients and their families, she has 'adopted' frequently used Spanish cognates into her professional English language repertoire. Eleanor (age group 31–35), a professional linguist, recounted an incident in which she was observed by her companions as she conversed with a recently arrived friend from Italy whose English 'wasn't very good.' Prior to this occasion, Eleanor was not aware that she was particularly skilled at ELF interaction but, when she received a compliment on the ease with which she communicated in this setting, she realized that, like Owen and Helen, it was 'second nature' for her to invoke her background in Romance languages to improve intelligibility.

Having learned Japanese both in study abroad and in a subsequent Fulbright year in Japan, Hailey (age group 31–35) now works in market strategy for a large multinational tech company and certainly requires skills in multilingual communication. Hailey emphasized the lessons in humility she had learned, initially by measuring her stellar academic record in language courses against the realization, upon arrival in Japan, that her functional ability was low. Subsequently she came to understand 'how horrifically difficult English is, particularly when I think about idioms or spelling.' Hailey is able, at this point, to catch herself when she uses a culturally specific metaphor in a work meeting involving EFL speakers, to assign blame for the problem to herself, and then to quickly repair the miscommunication she has caused:

> last week [...] I was in a meeting with people on my team, one is Lebanese, and one person is Malaysian. both of them speak great English, like fine. and I was in that meeting. and I said the phrase, I'm not willing to die on that hill, and they both looked at me like, what? and I was oh alright this is an American idiom that I think is probably derived from war time. it just means that this is not something that I will [...] it's not something that I think is so crucial that I will do everything to get. and they're like, oh, okay.

Astrid (age group 36–40) is a former learner of Chinese who has worked in affordable housing finance with immigrant groups. Her comments on this topic relate less to language per se than to the empathy she can summon from her own experience in China when she encounters individuals of diverse backgrounds who are at a loss for words. For Astrid, study abroad is 'a shortcut to empathy':

> if you grow up as like an athlete or middle class white kid, you've never really been uncomfortable. I mean, I'm sure you've been uncomfortable, but you've never been in a setting where you were not – and I'm not trying to sort of be all Social Worker about it – but you've never <u>not</u> been the center. and so when you go to a foreign country, it may be your first experience even if you get re-centered because you're white, and people look at you and treat you like you're a movie star. but you still have some amount of the experience of not knowing what's going on and feeling like people might be laughing at you, even if they're not. eating something that wasn't what you thought it was [...] all those experiences of, like, I am not in control. I think it's easier then to look at the person who's an immigrant and sort of say, like, golly, they must be pretty disoriented right now [...] like, hey, I remember what that feels like.

Similarly, Mary (age group 31–35) contextualized her remarks on language learning and empathy with reference to her career as a teacher and aspiring urban high school principal. For Mary, having learned Spanish and some Somali brought insights into the complexities faced by immigrant school pupils coping with classroom talk in English. Rather than classifying these students as 'slow processors,' teachers should try to understand that errors are due to 'the patterns they have in their home language,' and that comprehension requires an arduous process of translating everything twice: 'I think when you yourself have been that student in the class, who's like, okay, I know I want to say this, how do I say this? it kind of gives you that understanding a little more.' Mary also believes that to 'connect and relate' to ESL students, it is paramount for teachers to pronounce their names as accurately as possible. In her administrative roles, she has observed that monolingual teachers tend to abandon that effort much more quickly than do teachers with histories of language learning.

Victoria (age group 36–40), who now works in global public health, has learned commonly taught languages (French and Spanish) and has also attempted to master Hausa, Zarma, Tamil and Setswana. Her admiration for the accomplishments of multilinguals has grown deeper through life and work in Africa, where she routinely encounters individuals for whom English is a fifth or sixth language:

> having struggled in any one of those languages, Hausa in particular, I have such an admiration for people who speak those languages. so, yeah, if they're struggling in their sixth language when they're talking to me, I'm not going to count that one against them. I just think of the times that I have struggled and the amount of patience people have shown with me.

In fact, according to Victoria, the value in language study abroad resides not just in the realm of the immediately practical but also in 'learning how to struggle.'

7.4 Unpredicted Benefits of Language Learning

In addition to the value of world language or ELF proficiency for professional roles per se, one of our participants elaborated on the use of language outside formal working contexts and three others described certain capabilities that they attributed to the experience of language learning. When we met Jessica (age group 36–40), she was working as legal counsel for an international non-profit organization that provides products and services for graduate business programs. Inspired by a high school Spanish teacher, she had chosen to enroll in a small liberal arts college known for its emphasis on study abroad. She had participated in two back-to-back study abroad programs in Mexico: first a summer program with a homestay, then a semester during which she lived with a Mexican roommate and took business courses in Spanish. While she was attending law school in the Washington, DC area, she focused on international business and legal components, worked for an international law journal, carried out a project about corporate governance in Mexico, and volunteered at an immigration clinic. After graduation, she worked for a large international law firm for several years, and then became an in-house attorney at the education-based organization. In addition to her day job, where Spanish is rarely used,

Jessica devotes significant time and effort to non-profit work. She is one of the founding members of a small but impactful organization that raises funds for people around the world suffering crisis and heartbreak, recently including families who had been separated at the southern border of the US. In this pursuit, especially in dealing with the immigration crisis, Jessica finds her Spanish ability 'incredibly helpful, though it's rusty.' She recalls the day when they reunited families separated at the border:

> It was amazing to be able to connect with those families, to talk to them about their experience, what they've seen, how long they've been separated from their children that were in the US and still in custody, and even more than that [...] to be able to connect with those kids who are going through what should have been the worst day of their lives [...] so being able to connect with them in Spanish was honestly the highlight for me of that experience. [...] It was rea:lly impactful to me to be able to make those connections.

Peter (age group 31–35) is employed by a renewable energy concern where he is regularly confronted with the challenge of working out how to move from 'an empty farm field to solar panels in the field.' This process requires technical know-how along with significant skills in negotiation with landowners and local regulatory offices. To achieve this, according to him, he applies the meta-awareness of problem solving he acquired as a learner of German. Peter's early language instructors, both at school and in the domestic summer immersion program where he later worked, clearly offered ample opportunities for playful activity in their classrooms, including games, songs and dramatic improvisation. They calmed his fear of errors and encouraged him to experiment with his own capacity for self-expression, otherwise known as strategic competence (e.g. Savignon, 1997), in situations where his command of the language was not completely adequate to the task: for instance, by designing activities requiring circumlocution. Now, Peter views various aspects of language, from irregular verb conjugation to telling jokes, as a 'puzzle' to be solved using whatever resources are available.

This process maps onto his current preoccupations at work, where he must 'be creative on the fly on how to solve something that [he] might not have perfect information about.' As an example, he cited a dramatic event at work when all parties agreed to the installation of solar panels on a rural property, and a bald eagle's nest (a 'potential killer' for the project) was discovered there. Due to habitat destruction and contamination of food sources, at the time these birds were safeguarded under the Endangered Species Protection Act. Even if this were not the case, Peter's commitment to environmental activism would orient him against the destruction of such a nest in the interest of a construction project. Rather than abandoning the effort, however, Peter carried out research on eagle nesting habits and consulted with the local government, eventually discovering that the nest in question was for hunting rather than birthing, and therefore could be located to another tree, thus saving the project. The puzzle analogy extends into a lesson on persistence:

> without this training through language where I had to puzzle through sentence structures and what I wanted to say, I'm not sure I would have been as comfortable pushing back on this roadblock and trying to find a way around it.

Emma's (age group 31–35) narrative illustrates the specific value of metalinguistic awareness for career achievement in various fields. Emma sojourned in Mexico for a semester while still in high school, having studied Spanish since the age of nine. In college she spent a month in Venezuela and a full academic year in China. After graduating with a major in business and Chinese, she 'spun a globe' and decided to go to Russia for a year as an English teacher affiliated with the program in Moscow that hosted students from her school. Having attained significant proficiency in three languages other than English, she then worked for two years as a paralegal clerk for an immigration law firm with no specific education for that position. She did, however, present the ability to learn new sets of terminology and to interact with people of divergent backgrounds 'very quickly.' Subsequently, she pursued screenwriting for several years before taking a temporary job transcribing for a large technology company that eventually became a full-time position. After several promotions, and with 'no science training,' she is now a project manager focusing on the semantics and pragmatics of natural language comprehension in the development of applications. 'That excitement about language,' she said, 'is why I was able to progress in my career.'

Max (age group 36–40) offered a short narrative illustrating how the experience of language learning can enhance collaboration in teams of diverse expertise. He recalls a time during his work in a psycholinguistics laboratory when communication in a newly united interdisciplinary team became difficult due to divergent understandings of constructs and terminology. 'Drastically different' knowledge bases and skill sets were represented on the team, which included cognitive psychologists, linguists, computer scientists and engineers. Furthermore, each discipline had its own vocabulary. For several months, misunderstandings about basic topics of conversation were rampant. However, he and his colleagues were eventually able to acknowledge that they were coping with a language barrier, and 'once we got that fluency in understanding how to communicate with each other, then our productivity and our collaboration really shot through the roof. [...] it definitely felt to me like going through the process of learning how to communicate in a foreign language.'

7.5 Conclusion

Since we included many details about the process and meaning of language learning in previous chapters, here we chose to examine what our participants explained to us concerning ancillary benefits such as approaches to problem-solving, metalinguistic awareness, and intercultural communication skills. Perhaps the most compelling and promising of our findings here have to do with these latter abilities, specifically multilingual dispositions and strategic approaches to enhance inherently cooperative communication in international contexts. While admittedly somewhat haphazard and prompted by an originally unplanned interview question, these comments suggest that the multilingual dispositions of language study abroad alumni might be a worthy topic of focused research examining actual practices in professional contexts. That is, the preoccupations of ELF research, much of which has been carried out among multilingual professionals at work, might also apply to helping Anglophone speakers avoid becoming part of 'a native speaker problem.' If it is true that language-focused sojourns abroad are not only a shortcut to empathy but also a source of specific strategies that speakers adopt to facilitate intercultural communication and the success of international working teams or groups, this would be a powerful argument in their favor.

8 Conclusion

8.1 Introduction

The aim of our project was to investigate the long-term impact of language study abroad in the careers and lives of Anglophone, US-based alumni. We were particularly interested in how language ability is valued and cultivated over the life span; the contributions of this ability to personal and professional opportunity and satisfaction; institutional or other support for language learning and use after study abroad; and the advantages and challenges that these learners experience. To achieve our goal, we designed a mixed-method study including an initial survey, then a life-history typology derived from the survey data to inform a principled selection of interviewees. In this chapter we will review some general highlights from the findings of the study, then consider what our study might offer to researchers, educators, policymakers and the public. Finally, we will review some limitations on the study and offer reflection on avenues for future research.

8.2 Highlights

As noted in Chapter 1, there is a strong ideological current running through interpretation of international education in the US wherein study abroad is a marginally useful decorative frill on the education of the privileged (Gore, 2005). Study abroad can also be interpreted in the light of neoliberal thinking on the role of education in shaping the self-governing marketable self or in the light of neocolonialist discourses of adventure. Although there are always exceptions in a study such as this, we have found that, in retrospect, most of our survey and interview participants clearly see a relationship between study abroad and their careers but most do not frame their motives in neoliberal terms. To recall: in the survey the most commonly chosen reason for language learning was 'to understand another culture,' and this finding was consistent across age groups. In the qualitative data, we see many stories of dramatic revelations through escape from humdrum existence at home quite like those described by Coffey and Street (2008). These include, for instance, the awakening of African diaspora consciousness for Frances in the Dominican Republic, Peter's discovery of eco-friendly practices in Germany, or Erik's realization, while in Japan, that language learning can be a serious and rewarding endeavor. In many of these stories, utilitarian motives take a backseat to what Kramsch has described as 'desire' for 'alternative truths that broaden the scope of the sayable and the imaginable' (Kramsch, 2006: 102).

In this book, we have shown that while a majority of language study abroad alumni work in education, that field is anything but monolithic and includes a variety of teaching, administrative and materials development roles. Beyond education, however, these alumni have roles in a wide variety of professions including business, healthcare, government service, engineering, sports, hospitality, law and the arts. Given our qualitative data, we have considered in detail *how* participants in various careers view study abroad as an academically strong source of professional development via the liberal arts curriculum. For example, as a market strategist for a major technology company, Hailey is an outspoken proponent of the liberal arts curriculum as a pathway toward imminently useful analytic skills. Thomas emphasized the importance of language study and international experience in the development of empathy, one key quality of good physician. Maryse found her language, writing and 'anthropological' observation abilities to be crucial to a career in banking and management consulting.

Another important finding of our study is that 65% of our survey participants claim to have used a language other than English at work, a somewhat surprising figure that bolsters assertions about the direct utility of this pursuit. In the qualitative data, we illustrated this finding with stories from a variety of professions, such as James' career as a professor of sociology, Anton's work in international development, or Tim's employment in ocean engineering for a French company. Our survey data also revealed remarkably high levels of multilingualism in our sample, with approximately 70% of participants claiming knowledge of two or more languages. In our qualitative materials we saw that, in the case of Valerie, learning one commonly taught language (French), can lead to the learning of another more difficult language (Russian) later in life. We also examined the experiences of polyglots like Steven, a history professor who has mastered six European languages in support of research, or the 'language jock' Mark who studied French and German in school, then moved on to master three Asian languages during his career with the Foreign Service.

8.3 Insights for Research

The major methodological highlight of the current study is the development of a life history typology to guide the selection of interviewees from the 2741 individuals who volunteered in the survey. The fact that more than half the survey participants wanted to talk about their study abroad is in itself a strong testament to the power of these experiences and the pent-up emotions surrounding them. However, it also presented the need for a systematic selection process of some kind. The typology established a structural link between the quantitative and the qualitative phases of the study, so that the life paths of the interviewees would mostly reflect the study as a whole, with a range of ages, careers, institutional affiliations, and socioeconomic backgrounds. As discussed in Chapter 2, this principled approach allowed us to avoid most cherry picking, though we did select some participants based on other criteria toward the end of the process. We believe that this way of organizing sampling in a larger-scale project represents an important step toward achieving the principled integration of approaches that is the hallmark of contemporary mixed-methods research.

Much of the applied linguistics research on study abroad is focused on the short-term impact of one program at a time, often with the assumption that the environment itself is deterministic and that the main duty of the researcher is to measure impact on various aspects of language ability or other desirable characteristics. In this project we have departed from our field's usual research practices in several ways. At the simplest level, by examining how study abroad is represented in the life stories of participants of various ages, we have taken a 'whole lives' approach (Coleman, 2013) to understanding the ontological significance of these 'reference points' (Alred & Byram, 2002). We can see, for example, that from a life history perspective one study abroad or language learning experience is often only part of a sequence that includes other significant formal or informal investment in similar pursuits.

On another level, we have advanced the claim that environments themselves are not deterministic: their role in development can only be understood as part of a dialectic that includes the psychology of the learner (Vygotsky, 1987). Individuals, with their idiosyncratic prior histories, partially constitute learning environments, which is why the 'same' environment will be different for different individuals. Further, it is in encounters with dramatic contradictions between past and present conditions that development occurs, and the resolution of these contradictions can become a long-term project (Lantolf & Swain, 2020). Therefore, study abroad, as a planned disruption in everyday living, can be (but is not always) a momentous occasion. Many stories in this volume illustrate this process: James, for example, is still working through the turmoil he experienced as a gay progressive in a conservative Catholic home; Antonia's first taste of a zucchini flower has come to symbolize the vast array of farm-to-table pleasures discovered in Italian and other international cuisines; Max eventually made a career of his puzzlement over individual differences in language learning processes.

This way of understanding the impact of study abroad also helps to contextualize current discussions about program length in response to a decrease in academic or full-year programs and an increase in short-term or semester-length programs. On one level, we can consider that just under half our survey participants had enrolled in two or more programs. On another, if the aim is to encourage development through cognitive–emotional drama, then the length of the program matters less than its learning potential for the individual student. To recall, Felicity's first study abroad experience was a 3-week excursion to the UK, not necessarily the kind of sojourn that would challenge a worldlier, middle-class student. However, since Felicity had never imagined traveling beyond the borders of Tennessee, the experience was so dramatic that it launched a long-term commitment to living abroad.

In this work we have responded to Tullock's (2018: 271) call for more research examining the lifelong dynamics of identity development and whether sojourns abroad that appear to have minor impact can serve as 'launching points for longer term transnational identities.' In fact, two of our interview participants, Valerie and Pamela, did attend the same university and participate in the same program in France at roughly the same time. Pamela's memories of the program are centered on perception of danger, and the main effect was to dissuade her from international pursuits. Valerie recounts an experience very similar to that of Ailis, a participant in Kinginger's (2008) study who spent every long weekend traveling to different European capital cities in the company of fellow Anglophones, investing very little in language learning. By her own admission, for Valerie study abroad was about freedom, mobility and enjoyment, and she was not at the time developmentally ready to assume control of her own use of time for investment in activities to promote language learning. However, in the longer term, Valerie's time abroad did in fact function as a launching point, with her record of language learning and international interests qualifying her to learn Russian and work for the Department of Commerce in Moscow.

8.4 Insights for Education

We believe that this study demonstrates robustly the significance of language study abroad in the lives of US-based adults whether or not they are among the 65% who have used their language ability at work for practical purposes. Many of our interviewees claim to have discovered a vocation or life goals while abroad, or to have developed capabilities beyond language crucial to their subsequent success. Beyond this, our study offers several additional insights for educators. Firstly, in the survey, we attempted to address the immediate post-study abroad phase with questions about courses and other institutional provisions, but these did not elicit a robust response. It was as if the return to campus was not problematic for our participants. In the interviews, however, a question about coming home elicited a broad range of strong emotions, from Amelia's pathos-driven photos of Dunkin' Donuts displays to

Freida's disenchantment with her studies. These findings suggest that if institutions wish to implement debriefing or other follow-up practices for study abroad returnees, attention to the affective dimensions of this experience is warranted.

Secondly, interviewees generally retained only vague memories of courses or other academic pursuits in comparison with recollections of homestays. In fact, Owen claimed that the most popular course among his cohort in Budapest was taught by an instructor who encouraged students not to come to class but instead to go out about town and enjoy life. In short, the academic dimensions of study abroad may well be important but they do not appear to be particularly memorable, at least in our materials. This phenomenon may well be related to ways in which local educational provisions are downplayed in US promotion of study abroad (Doerr, 2012). Furthermore, like the British LANGSNAP participants (Mitchell et al., 2020), few of our interviewees expressed need or desire for advanced academic literacy in their additional languages. Only those who in fact have built academic careers, like James, Steven or Laura, or who work in language-intensive government service, like Mark and Victoria, mentioned continuous effort to improve their literacy. Others conveyed skepticism about the value added from advanced language ability or their own capacity to achieve it. Erik, for example, is aware that he has not fully mastered the honorific register in Japanese but is not convinced that he requires it to function in business contexts, and Anton claimed that attaining high-level literacy in Arabic would require a full lifetime of devotion. Taken together, these findings suggest a tension between the need to re-value and integrate course work with life experiences abroad. They also suggest a need to promote the kinds of literacy development that might lead to more international career options and thereby to a larger population of Americans possessing the language proficiency or intercultural understanding necessary for participation in complex business or political negotiations (Trentman & Diao, 2017).

Thirdly, our study suggests a need for widespread recognition of study abroad as a multilingual setting where, unless they travel to remote, isolated destinations, Anglophone learners will inevitably and increasingly encounter versions of their own language in both formal and informal settings. On the one hand, this means that these learners require a strategic approach to foregrounding their identities as language learners, just as Menard-Warwick's (2019) participant Shana did. On the other, it also means that Anglophone learners abroad have many opportunities to develop their understanding and use of English as a lingua franca, enhancing their ability to function in international or otherwise diverse groups and likewise their competitiveness on the job market. In this study, interview questions about ELF practices were added to the agenda after the topic emerged in an impromptu manner, and many participants claimed enhanced intercultural communication abilities. Whether or not and how Anglophone students develop capabilities in this domain is an important empirical question that could be fruitfully addressed in future, systematic research endeavors.

Finally, although our findings about the perennial appeal of the classroom are reassuring, the growth of language learning 'on my own' among younger participants in our study is also an issue deserving the attention of language educators. We ignore at our own peril the fact that learners are constructing their own environments from among the vast array of resources now available, including various forms of computer-mediated communication, mobile-assisted learning, digital gaming, and social media platforms. Many such learners take up language development as a leisure activity (Toffoli, 2020). Among applied linguistics researchers, the phenomena surrounding language learning and teaching beyond the classroom now constitute a recognizable field, as witnessed by the appearance of a landmark edited volume (Benson & Reinders, 2011) and a Routledge handbook on this topic (Reinders *et al.*, 2022). Although much of this work centers on the learning of English, the experiences recounted here by Afrika, Hugh and Owen demonstrate the relevance of these changes for Anglophone learners of additional languages and suggest that educators seek an active role in helping their students develop metalinguistic awareness to guide their choice and use of informal learning affordances.

8.5 Insights for Policy

As noted in Chapter 1, one of the inspirations for this project came from a report of the American Academy of Arts and Sciences, *America's Languages* (2017), calling for renewed investment in languages to meet 21st-century needs in business, research and international relations. In this volume, we have documented the role of study abroad and language learning in launching the careers of Americans employed in a variety of fields and sectors. In our survey findings, we have shown that language learning is a perennial goal for the population we sampled, and that the majority of our participants from among the general educated public claim to have used their additional languages for purposes related to employment. Our interview participants explained several ancillary professional benefits they associate with their history of engagement with language learning, such as problem-solving skills, increased intercultural communication capabilities, and mastery of specific aspects of ELF to avoid becoming part of a 'native speaker problem' (Cogo, 2016: 369) during interaction in diverse groups. They have also helped us contribute to arguments in favor of homestays and other means of promoting local social integration for long-term impact. In Chapter 3 we illustrated the practical value of language other than English for education, business and entrepreneurship, healthcare, government service, engineering, sports management and the arts. In Chapter 4 we offered profiles of individuals for whom language study abroad involved the discovery of ambitious career aspirations in diverse fields such as nursing, marine biology, hospitality, renewable energy and market strategy.

In sum, our data thoroughly and repeatedly demonstrate the value of language study abroad for the career development of generative American adults, many of whom make important contributions to the well-being of their communities and display the features of global engagement outlined in the SAGE Project (Paige *et al.*, 2009): civic engagement, knowledge production, philanthropy, social entrepreneurship and/or voluntary simplicity (e.g. reducing consumption out of concern for the environment). At the same time our materials, including statistics on the history of program costs and the qualities of narratives gathered from younger versus more senior interviewees, also show an increased financial toll on families over the period under consideration, and a tendency for non-traditional destinations to be the province of relatively privileged students. That is, our findings add to the already well-established rationale for programs offering need-based financial support to students from under-represented groups and for the study of less-commonly taught languages (e.g. the Boren Awards). We have also seen that the meaning of study abroad depends to a great extent on the sociocultural and economic life histories and horizons of individual students, that is, the cognitive–emotional lived experience (*perezhivanie*) through which learning conditions are refracted. A sojourn abroad of any length or apparent intensity can generate significant developmental drama for students of modest means.

8.6 Insights for the Public

Another source of inspiration for this project was our long experience of conversations with students whose parents are anxious about their children's preparedness for employment, prosperity and satisfaction in life. Over the years, many students have explained to us that their desire for languages may be intense, but that they have been strongly enjoined to set aside language study in favor of pursuits, often business or management-related, deemed useful. Quite often, their parents simply cannot imagine any future involving languages that they have not themselves witnessed, and they associate language study with poorly remunerated teaching jobs only. Parents' concerns are fully understandable. Higher education represents a substantial investment for the average middle-class family and, to recall from Chapter 1, the cost of tuition at public universities has increased at double the rate of inflation since 1965. Study abroad often translates as added expense in lost wages and other expenses. In this book we have shown that language study abroad is a major contributor to readiness for employment in a wide variety of occupations. It is true that the majority of our survey participants are involved in education, but the types of positions they hold vary widely and include teaching, research, administration and materials design. In these and others among our life stories of individuals who have relied upon language skills for success in business, healthcare, government service and other pursuits we that hope students and parents will find reassurance about the meaning of language learning for personal and professional success.

8.7 Limitations of the Study

One visible limitation of this study is the fact that survey recruitment, and therefore the whole project, was biased toward people with a likely favorable predisposition toward language study abroad and a tendency to care about its future. To qualify for the survey, participants needed to claim proficiency in at least one language other than English and to have experience of study abroad. It is reasonable to suppose that those who showed the stamina necessary to complete the survey were particularly eager to contribute useful perspectives in support of the study's advocacy goals. Another related limitation is that in this publication we have not been able to include information from all the interviewees. More attention is required, in a future endeavor, to the stories of the few participants whose careers were in limbo at the time of the interview and the stories of the small minority of those for whom study abroad had a minor or negative impact. Finally, in this volume we have been unable to report on every aspect of the survey and have set aside certain of its themes for future analysis (e.g. specific features of language use, participation in volunteer work).

Unlike the longitudinal LANGSNAP project (Mitchell *et al.*, 2020), we did not collect linguistic data to examine proficiency maintenance or attrition. Such an effort would have been extremely complex given the range of languages in question and the limitations on our resources. Nevertheless, it means that we must rely on the subjective judgments of the participants themselves in evaluating their achievements. Given our own histories as language acquisition researchers, it is a bit discomfiting to claim in an academic publication that Person X knows Language Y with neither corresponding qualifications nor empirical evidence.

Our qualitative research design called for limited contact with participants in the form of one-on-one retrospective professional life history interviews. On the one hand, in many cases we were therefore unable to move beyond the perspectives of US-based alumni who may or may not have considered their own impact on local ecologies in their destinations and who may have been influenced by neocolonialist discourses of adventure and extraction of benefits for candidate members of the global elite (Doerr, 2012; Trentman & Diao, 2017; Zemach-Bersin, 2007). In this manner, our study ignores previous critiques of ethnocentrism in the study abroad literature, where only student voices are heard, previously issued by one of the authors (Kinginger, 2019b). On the other hand, a collection of more extensive data would have been impractical, and our procedure for member checking and partial co-authoring of our narratives demanded respect for individual narrative choices, both in terms of their idiosyncrasies and in terms of their recruitment of broader discourses.

Another limitation is to be found in some minor disparities between the planned design and the process by which the study was carried out. In announcing our mixed-methods approach, we claimed a sequential design in which the results of the first, survey phase would exert major influence on the second, qualitative phase. In practice, we did of course use the survey results in generating our life history typology for interview sampling. However, after this phase the study operated in some ways as if it had a concurrent design. That is, the survey results were derived, and the interview data collected independently, each process with its own aims. *Post-hoc* efforts to integrate methods at the interpretation stage have been attempted throughout this volume and also occurred when trends in the qualitative materials suggested the need for further inquiry involving the survey data, for example in considering the possibility that younger participants were more likely than their elders to have learned languages 'on their own,' or in seeking quantitative evidence to accompany the observation that many interviewees seemed to have undertaken multiple sojourns abroad (Chapter 6). Many advanced techniques for principled integration in mixed-methods studies rely on coding of the qualitative data, and thus are not appropriate for this study. Given the broad scope of this volume and its ambition to report the study as a whole, we are satisfied with our efforts to date. However, more integration might be possible in the future, while investigating particular, smaller-scale research questions for which both data types are pertinent.

8.8 Conclusion

At the time of writing, study abroad is little more than a dream for many young people whose lives and educations have been drastically altered by a global pandemic. The study abroad industry has suffered disproportionately, even to other forms of education, because it assumes that travel, social interaction, and encounters with others are normal, harmless and integral to modern life. The pandemic arrived while we were only halfway through the qualitative data collection process for this project. It required us, and everyone else, to drop everything and re-learn how to do our jobs. Writing this book during the pandemic has been a major exercise in persistence. Throughout the book we have acknowledged that alongside our research goals we have also wished to advocate for language study and international education. We persist in believing that these activities are in fact life changing, we have put forth our best effort to demonstrate this, and we hope for a brighter future in which young people with multilingual aspirations will once again routinely pursue their goals through travel and learning.

Appendices

Appendix A: Full Version of the Survey

#	Survey questions	Answer options
1	To agree to participate in this survey, please answer yes below.	Yes | No
2	Have you ever participated in a study abroad program?	Yes | No
3	Do you speak/ use a language other than English?	Yes | No
4–11	To what extent do you think your participation in the study abroad programs directly influenced each of the following: • Your selection of type of employer • Your selection of a field of employment • Your ability to use a language other than English at school or work • Your interest in studying a foreign language • Your interest in getting a job overseas • Your interest in working for a multinational organization in the U.S. • Your acquisition of skills that helped you get a job • Your acquisition of skills that informed your career choice	Rating on 0–10 scale (10 means 'great extent', 0 means 'not at all')
12	How do you think you have changed after completing your study abroad program(s)?	Open ended
13	Other than English, list up to five languages that you have learned or are learning?	A list of languages in alphabetical order
14	Which language(s) do you consider to be your native language or mother tongue?	A list of languages in alphabetical order
15	Where did you learn these languages?	Home | Kindergarten | Elementary school | Secondary/high school | After school programs | Heritage community school | Religious school | University | Study abroad | Live abroad | Short term stay abroad | Private tutor | Online program/apps | On my own | On the job | Other: please specify

(Continued)

#	Survey questions	Answer options
16	What year did you start learning these languages?	Open ended
17	In the past year, did you regularly use these languages to engage in the following activities? Mark all that apply.	Engaging in informal conversation/ small talk/ courtesy needs	Service encounters	Long and short phone conversations	Listening to radio/ podcasts/ audiobooks, TV/movies or other media	Reading news, blogs, social media	Surfing the Internet	Using social media, online chatting	Sending text/ SMS messages and emails	Writing a diary or blog	Engaging in community activities	Reading fiction, literature, scholarly writing	Volunteering to help people whose first language is not English	Other: please specify
18	In the past year, did you occasionally use these languages to engage in the following activities? Mark all that apply.	Same as above
19	In the past year, did you regularly use these languages with the people listed below? Mark all that apply.	Parents	Siblings	Grandparents or older relatives	Life partners or spouses	Close friends	Acquaintances	Fellow students	Teachers/ professors	Members of the wider community	Visitors who speak a language that I use/ am learning	Other: please specify
20	In the past year, did you occasionally use these languages with the people listed below? Mark all that apply.	Same as above
21	What are the TOP THREE reasons you have chosen to study language(s)	It will be/ is useful for my career or employment.	I need(ed) it for my studies to satisfy a language requirement.	I see it as an essential skill to have in a global world.	I am good at learning languages.	I am interested in learning a language that is part of my heritage.	Learning languages allows me to fully experience and understand another culture in which I have an interest.	I enjoy learning languages.	I have someone close to me who speaks this language/ these languages.
22	What were the TOP THREE reasons that made you decide to study abroad?	Live abroad	Meet new people	Learn/ improve a foreign language	Develop 'soft skills'	Register for courses that are not available in my home institution	Experience different learning/ teaching methods and environment	Study in a foreign language	Possibility to receive financial support to study abroad	Enhance my employability in my home country	Enhance my employability abroad	Improve and widen my career prospects in the future
23	Please indicate all study abroad programs for language or academic training you have participated in. Select each program from the list below. Please indicate the name of the program, the year the program started, what country you visited, and the duration of the program.	

(Continued)

#	Survey questions	Answer options
	• Program	Academic high school program	Academic Programs International	AIFS	American Councils Study Abroad, Research Abroad	American Overseas Research Center Fellowship	American Youth Leadership Program	Benjamin A. Gilman International Scholarship	CEA Study Abroad	CIEE	Congress-Bundestag Youth Exchange (CBYX)	Critical Language Scholarship Program (CLS)	David L. Boren Scholarship or Fellowship	Foreign Language and Area Studies (FLAS)	Fulbright English Teaching Assistant	Fulbright U.S. Scholar	Fulbright U.S. Student	Fulbright–Hays Scholarship	IES Abroad	IFSA–Butler	ISA	ISEP	National Security Language Initiative for Youth (NSLI-Y)	Semester abroad	SIT Study Abroad	STARTALK	Summer high school program	The Overseas Language Flagship	University sponsored study abroad	Youth Exchange and Study Abroad (YES Abroad)	Other: please specify
	• Year	2018	2017	2016	2015	2014	2013	2012	2011	2010	2009	2008	2007	2006	2005	2004	2003	2002	2001	2000	Before 2000
	• Duration	Short term (2–8 weeks)	Semester (2–5 months)	Academic year (6–11 months)	Full year or more (12+ months)
	• Country	A list of countries in alphabetical order
24	During your study abroad sojourn(s), did you participate in any of the following? Mark all that apply.	Living with a host family	Living with host country peers	Living in a dormitory	Living with American students	Participating in an internship	Taking host university courses	Taking host high school classes	Performing volunteer work	Being involved in close personal relationship(s)	Other: please specify
25	How did you pay for your study abroad programs? Mark all that apply.	Self-paid	Loans	School/ university scholarship	Government scholarship	Covered in tuition	Other: please specify
26–30	When you returned to your home university after your study abroad, how difficult were the following: • Find appropriate language courses to continue studying your target language • Find courses of interest • Integrate your study abroad experience in your program of study • Meet students sharing common interest in international affairs • Connect with other members of the international community on campus	Rating on 0–10 scale (10 means 'very difficult', 0 means 'not at all difficult')
31	Are you currently … ?	In school	Employed	Both	None of the above
32	In what ways do you think studying abroad changed your interests/ desires for future work?	Open ended

(Continued)

#	Survey questions	Answer options
33	After completing the highest degree, in what year did you start working?	2018 | 2017 | 2016 | 2015 | 2014 | 2013 | 2012 | 2011 | 2010 | 2009 | 2008 | 2007 | 2006 | 2005 | 2004 | 2003 | 2002 | 2001 | 2000 | Before 2000
34	What is your level of employment?	Part-time (less than 35 hours/week) | Full-time (35 hours/week or greater)
35	Is your job based in the U.S.A. or overseas?	Based in the U.S.A. | Based overseas
36	Which country are you based in?	Open ended
37	Do you speak the language of that country?	Yes | No
38	Where are you currently employed?	U.S. Federal Government | U.S. State or Local Government | Other Government | International organization (e.g. United Nations, World Bank) | Non-Governmental Organization (e.g. Amnesty, Red Cross, MSF, Oxfam) | Non-Profit Educational Institution | Other Non-Profit Organization | For-Profit Company | Multi-national company | Other: please specify
39	What is the position in which you are currently employed?	Staff | Middle Management | Senior Management | Technical | Chief executive | Other: please specify
40	What sector are you currently working in?	Agriculture | Business | Construction | Education | Energy | Finance | Health | International Affairs/ Development | Manufacturing | Media | Real Estate | Technology | Telecommunications | Transportation | Tourism (including Leisure & Hospitality) | Professional and Business Services | Other: please specify
41	Have any of your jobs required the use of languages other than English?	No | Yes: which language(s) have you used/do you use at work?
42	Have you used these languages for any of the following? Mark all that apply.	Negotiations | Client outreach | Researching/ work with original/ local sources/ searches | Supervising of and outreach to non-English speaking employees | Analytics | Marketing (internal and external) | Government relations | Work meetings | Writing work reports | Presenting at work related conferences/ seminars | Other: please specify
43	Tell us how you use your foreign language at work.	Open ended
44	Does your current job require you to travel overseas?	No | Yes: tell us about your work related travel (place, duration, frequency, purpose, etc.)
45–48	To what extent do you think each of the following made you a more competitive candidate for your current position? • Language skills • Intercultural communication skills • Major/ field of specialization • Knowledge of regional/ world affairs	Rating on 0–10 scale (10 means 'great extent', 0 means 'not at all')
49	What is the name of the college/ university which you attended as an undergraduate?	Open ended

(Continued)

#	Survey questions	Answer options
50	What is the highest degree you attained.	Associate's Degree (A.A./A.S.)	Bachelor's Degree (B.A./B.S)	Master's Degree (M.A./M.S., MBA, MPA, etc.)	Doctor of Philosophy (Ph.D.)	Juris Doctor (J.D.)	Medical Doctor (M.D.)	Other: please specify
51	What is the name of the college/ university which awarded this highest degree?	Open ended
52	In what year was this degree award?	2018	2017	2016	2015	2014	2013	2012	2011	2010	2009	2008	2007	2006	2005	2004	2003	2002	2001	2000	Before 2000
53	What was your major or field of specialization? Mark all that apply.	Area Studies	Business/ Business Administration and Management	Communications	Computer Science	Education	Engineering	Foreign Languages/ Linguistics	Health Sciences or Medicine	History	Humanities	International Relations/ Affairs	Law/ Legal Studies/ Law Enforcement	Mathematics	Physical Sciences	Political Science	Social Sciences	Other: please specify
54	When you were a student, did you engage in any of the following using your foreign language(s)? Mark all that apply.	Writing reports/ assignments	Making class presentations	Participating in language clubs	Presenting at professional or academic conferences	Reading journals, articles or other assigned readings
55	In what ways do you think studying abroad influenced your choice of major or field of specialization?	Open ended
56	What is the name of the college/ university you are currently enrolled in?	Open ended
57	What is the degree program you are currently enrolled in?	Associate's Degree (A.A./A.S.)	Bachelor's Degree (B.A./B.S)	Master's Degree (M.A./M.S., MBA, MPA, etc.)	Doctor of Philosophy (Ph.D.)	Juris Doctor (J.D.)	Medical Doctor (M.D.)	Other: Please specify
58	What is your major or field of specialization? Mark all that apply.	Area Studies	Business/ Business Administration and Management	Communications	Computer Science	Education	Engineering	Foreign Languages/ Linguistics	Health Sciences or Medicine	History	Humanities	International Relations/ Affairs	Law/ Legal Studies/ Law Enforcement	Mathematics	Physical Sciences	Political Science	Other: please specify
59	Do you currently engage in any of the following using your foreign language(s)? Mark all that apply.	Writing reports/ assignments	Making class presentations	Participating in language clubs	Presenting at professional or academic conferences	Reading journals, articles or other assigned readings
60	Are you currently … ? Mark all that apply.	Doing an internship	Searching for a job	Engaged in volunteer activities	On a fellowship: please name the fellowship	Other: please specify
61	Gender	Female	Male	Other	Prefer not to answer
62	Age	under 25 years old	25–30	31–35	36–40	41–50	51–60	over 60 years old
63	We would like to showcase alumni of study abroad programs. May we contact you for further information?	No	Yes: Please provide your name and email address

Appendix B: List of Project Partners

Universities

Arizona State University
Bentley University
Dickinson College
The George Washington University
Indiana University
James Madison University
Michigan State University
Northern Arizona University
Northwestern University
Tulane University
University of Kansas
University of Michigan
University of Minnesota
University of New Orleans
University of Oregon CASLS
University of Rochester
University of West Georgia
Yale University

International Education Organizations

Amideast
API Academic Programs International
CAPA Global Education Network
CEA Study Abroad
CET Academic Programs
IFA Institute for Field Education
IFSA Future Focused Study Abroad
ISA International Studies Abroad
ISEP International Student Exchange Programs
Spanish Studies Abroad
WYSE Travel Confederation

Appendix C: Topical Interview Guide

Please tell us the story of how you came to occupy your professional role/ your studies so far.

(Discussion of any photographs supplied).

Describe your college study abroad experiences.

Can you recall any experiences in your youth that inspired you to pursue international education and proficiency in languages other than English?

Did study abroad or language ability specifically play a role in your professional choices? How?

Do you continue to use the language (s) you studied while abroad, if so how?

What activities do you pursue to maintain or develop your proficiency?

For language learning, what was the specific role of study abroad as opposed to other aspects of your college education?

Can you describe some of the pleasures involved in language learning? What about frustrations?

What was it like for you to return to campus after study abroad? Were there ways for you to use your knowledge to contribute or continue to learn language?

Have you learned other languages for professional or personal reasons?

How do you envisage the future of your career?

Question added:
Are you better at speaking ELF?

Questions discontinued:
Do you believe that study abroad and language ability are valued on the job market?

In your view, what forces either help or hinder language development?

References

Agyekum, K. (2008) The pragmatics of Akan greetings. *Discourse Studies* 10, 493–516.
Allen, H. (2013) Self-regulatory strategies of foreign language learners: From the classroom to study abroad and beyond. In C. Kinginger (ed.) *Social and Cultural Aspects of Language Learning in Study Abroad* (pp. 47–73). Amsterdam: John Benjamins.
Alred, G. and Byram, M. (2002) Becoming an intercultural mediator: A longitudinal study of residence abroad. *Journal of Multilingual and Multicultural Development* 23, 339–352.
American Academy of Arts and Sciences (2017) *America's Languages: Investing in Language Education for the 21st Century*. Cambridge, MA: American Academy of Arts and Sciences.
Anya, U. (2017) *Racialized Identities in Second Language Learning: Speaking Blackness in Brazil*. New York: Routledge.
Bakalis, S. and Joiner, T. (2004) Participation in tertiary study abroad programs: The role of personality. *The International Journal of Education Management* 18, 286–291.
Barkhuizen, G., Benson, P. and Chik, A. (2014) *Narrative Inquiry in Language Teaching and Learning Research*. New York: Routledge.
Bazeley, P. (2018) *Integrating Analyses in Mixed Methods Research*. London: Sage.
Benson, P. and Reinders, H. (eds) (2011) *Beyond the Language Classroom*. Basingstoke: Palgrave Macmillan.
Benson, P., Barkhuizen, G., Bodycott, P. and Brown, J. (2013) *Second Language Identity in Narratives of Study Abroad*. Basingstoke: Palgrave Macmillan.
Blunden, A. (2016) Translating *Perezhivanie* into English. *Mind, Culture, and Activity: An International Journal* 23, 274–283.
Brecht, R. and Robinson, J. (1995) The value of formal instruction in study abroad: Student reactions in context. In B. Freed (ed.) *Second Language Acquisition in a Study Abroad Context* (pp. 317–334). Amsterdam: John Benjamins.
Brecht, R., Davidson, D. and Ginsberg, R.B. (1995) Predictors of foreign language gain during study abroad. In B. Freed (ed.) *Second Language Acquisition in a Study Abroad Context* (pp. 37–66). Amsterdam: John Benjamins.
Brown, L. (2013) Identity and honorifics use in Korean study abroad. In C. Kinginger (ed.) *Social and Cultural Aspects of Language Learning in Study Abroad* (pp. 268–298). Amsterdam: John Benjamins.
Bruner, J. (1986) *Actual Minds, Possible Worlds*. Cambridge, MA: Harvard University Press.
Bruner, J. (1987) Life as narrative. *Social Research* 54, 11–32.
Canagarajah, S. (2007) Lingua franca English, multilingual communities, and language acquisition. *Modern Language Journal* 91, 923–939.
Canagarajah, S. (2013) *Translingual Practice: Global English and Cosmopolitan Relations*. New York: Routledge.
Charles, M. and Marschan-Piekkari, R. (2002) Language training for enhanced horizontal communication: A challenge for MNCs. *Business Communication Quarterly* 65, 9–29.
Coffey, S. and Street, B. (2008) Narrative and identity in the 'Language Learning Project'. *Modern Language Journal* 92, 452–464.
Cogo, A. (2016) 'They all take the risk and make the effort': Intercultural accommodation and multilingualism in a BELF community of practice. In L. Lopriore and E. Grazzi

(eds) *Intercultural Communication: New Perspectives from ELF* (pp. 365–383). Rome: Tre Press.
Cogo, A. and House, J. (2018) The pragmatics of ELF. In J. Jenkins, W. Baker and M. Dewey (eds) *The Routledge Handbook of English as a Lingua Franca* (pp. 210–223). Abingdon: Routledge.
Coleman, J. (2013) Researching whole people and whole lives. In C. Kinginger (ed.) *Social and Cultural Aspects of Language Learning in Study Abroad* (pp. 17–44). Amsterdam: John Benjamins.
Coleman, J. and Chafer, T. (2011) The experience and long-term impact of study abroad by Europeans in an African context. In F. Dervin (ed.) *Analysing the Consequences of Academic Mobility and Migration* (pp. 67–96). Newcastle: Cambridge Scholars Publishing.
Cressey, W. and Stubbs, N. (2010) The economics of study abroad. In W. Hoffa and S. DePaul (eds) *A History of U.S. Study Abroad: 1965–Present* (pp. 253–294). Carlisle, PA: Forum on Education Abroad.
Creswell, J.W. (2015) *A Concise Introduction to Mixed Methods Research*. Thousand Oaks, CA: Sage.
Crystal, D. (2003) *English as a Global Language*. Cambridge: Cambridge University Press.
Cubillos, J. and Ilvento, T. (2013) The impact of study abroad on students' self-efficacy perceptions. *Foreign Language Annals* 45, 494–511.
Cubillos, J., Chieffo, L. and Fan, C. (2008) The impact of short-term study abroad programs on L2 listening comprehension skills. *Foreign Language Annals* 41, 157–185.
Davidson, D. and Lehmann, S. (2001–2005) A longitudinal survey of the language learning careers of ACTR advanced students of Russian: 1976–2000. *Russian Language Journal* 55, 193–221.
DeGraaf, D., Slagter, C., Larsen, K. and Ditta, E. (2013) The long-term personal and professional impacts of participating in a study abroad program. *Frontiers: The Interdisciplinary Journal of Study Abroad* 23, 42–59.
DeKeyser, R. (2010) Monitoring processes in Spanish as a second language during a study abroad program. *Foreign Language Annals* 43, 80–92.
Dewaele, J.-M. (2008) 'Appropriateness' in foreign language acquisition and use: Some theoretical, methodological and ethical considerations. *International Review of Applied Linguistics in Language Teaching* 4, 245–265.
Dewaele, J.-M. and MacIntyre, P.D. (2014) The two faces of Janus? Anxiety and enjoyment in the foreign language classroom. *Studies in Second Language Learning and Teaching* 4, 237–274.
Diao, W. (2014) Peer socialization into gendered L2 Mandarin practices in a study abroad context: Talk in the dorm. *Applied Linguistics* 37, 599–620.
Diao, W. and Trentman, E. (eds) (2021) *Language Learning in Study Abroad: The Multilingual Turn*. Bristol: Multilingual Matters.
Dietrich, A. (2018) History and current trends in U.S. study abroad. In C. Sanz and A. Morales-Front (eds) *The Routledge Handbook of Study Abroad Research and Practice* (pp. 545–558). New York: Routledge.
DiSilvio, F., Donovan, A. and Malone, M. (2014) The effect of study abroad homestay placements: Participant perspectives and oral proficiency gains. *Foreign Language Annals* 47, 168–188.
Doerr, N.M. (2012) Study abroad as 'adventure': Globalist construction of host-home hierarchy and governed adventurer subjects. *Critical Discourse Studies* 9, 257–268.
Donatelli, L. (2010) The impact of technology on study abroad. In W. Hoffa and S. DePaul (eds) *A History of U.S. Study Abroad: 1965–Present* (pp. 295–324). Carlisle, PA: Forum on Education Abroad.
Dörnyei, Z. and Taguchi, T. (2010) *Questionnaires in Second Language Research: Construction, Administration and Processing* (2nd edn). New York: Routledge.

Duperron, L. and Overstreet, M. (2009) Preparedness for study abroad: Comparing the linguistic outcomes of short-term Spanish programs by third, fourth and sixth semester L2 learners. *Frontiers: The Interdisciplinary Journal of Study Abroad* 18, 157–179.

Durbidge, L. (2020) Study abroad in multilingual contexts: The linguistic investment and development of Japanese adolescents in and beyond year-long exchange programs. Unpublished PhD thesis, Monash University.

Dwyer, M.M. (2004) Charting the impact of studying abroad. *International Educator* 13, 14–17 and 19–20.

Engels, F. (1940) *The Dialectics of Nature*. London: Lawrence & Wishart.

Fantini, A. (2019) *Intercultural Competence in Educational Exchange*. New York: Routledge.

Fischler, C. and Masson, E. (2008) *Manger: Français, Européens et Américains face à l'alimentation [Eating: French, European and American Approaches to Food]*. Paris: Odile Jacob.

Forum on Education Abroad (2018) State of the field 2017. https://forumea.org/wp-content/uploads/2018/03/ForumEA-State-of-the-Field-18-web-version.pdf.

Franklin, K. (2010) Long-term career impact and professional applicability of the study abroad experience. *Frontiers: The Interdisciplinary Journal of Study Abroad* 19, 169–190.

Freed, B. (1995) *Second Language Acquisition in a Study Abroad Context*. Amsterdam: John Benjamins.

Geyer, A., Putz, J. and Misra, K. (2017) The effect of short-term study abroad experience on American students' leadership skills and career aspirations. *International Journal of Education Management* 31, 1042–1053.

Gill, R. and Scharff, C. (eds) (2011) *New Femininities: Postfeminism, Neoliberalism and Subjectivity*. Basingstoke: Palgrave Macmillan.

Gore, J. (2005) *Dominant Beliefs and Alternative Voices: Discourse, Belief, and Gender in Study Abroad*. New York: Routledge.

Greenacre, M. (1992) Correspondence analysis in medical research. *Statistical Methods in Medical Research* 1, 97–117.

Greenacre, M. (1994) Correspondence analysis and its interpretation. In M. Greenacre and J. Blasius (eds) *Correspondence Analysis in the Social Sciences* (pp. 3–22). London: Academic Press.

Greenacre, M. (2017) *Correspondence Analysis in Practice* (3rd edn). London: Chapman & Hall/CRC.

Greenacre, M. and Blasius, J. (eds) (2006) *Multiple Correspondence Analysis and Related Methods*. London: Chapman & Hall/CRC.

Güney, O. and Tracy-Ventura, N. (2021) Residence abroad as social investment: Challenges and gains revealed through a longitudinal study. Paper presented at the Association Internationale de Linguistique Appliquée World Congress of Applied Linguistics, Groningen, August.

Hadis, B.F. (2005) Why are they better students when they come back? Determinants of academic focusing gains in the study abroad experience. *Frontiers: The Interdisciplinary Journal of Study Abroad* 11, 57–70.

Hartman, E., Reynolds, N., Ferrarini, C., Messmore, N., Evans, S., Al-Ebrahim, B. and Brown, J. (2020) Coloniality–decoloniality and critical global citizenship: Identity, belonging and education abroad. *Frontiers: The Interdisciplinary Journal of Study Abroad* 32, 33–59.

Hashemi, M.R. (2019) Expanding the scope of mixed methods research in applied linguistics. In J. McKinley and H. Rose (eds) *The Routledge Handbook of Research Methods in Applied Linguistics* (pp. 39–51). New York: Routledge.

Hashemi, M.R. and Babaii, E. (2013) Mixed methods research: Toward new research designs in applied linguistics. *Modern Language Journal* 97 (4), 828–852.

Hubler, S. (2020) Colleges slash budgets in the pandemic, with 'nothing off limits'. *The New York Times*, October 26. https://www.nytimes.com/2020/10/26/us/colleges-coronavirus-budget-cuts.html.

Huensch, A., Tracy-Ventura, N., Bridges, J. and Cuesta Medina, J. (2019) Variables affecting the maintenance of L2 proficiency and fluency four years post-study abroad. *Study Abroad Research in Second Language Acquisition and International Education* 4, 96–125.
Iino, M. (2006) Norms of interaction in a Japanese homestay setting: Toward a two-way flow of linguistic and cultural resources. In M.A. DuFon and E. Churchill (eds) *Language Learners in Study Abroad Contexts* (pp. 151–173). Clevedon: Multilingual Matters.
Institute of International Education (IIE) (2004) Open doors 2004 fast facts. https://www.iie.org/Research-and-Publications/Open-Doors/Data/~/media/Files/Corporate/Open-Doors/Fast-Facts/Fast%20Facts%202004.ashx.
Institute of International Education (IIE) (2007) Open doors online: Report on international educational exchange. http://www.opendoors.iienetwork.org/.
Institute of International Education (IIE) (2021a) Detailed duration of U.S. study abroad, 2005/06–2019/20. https://opendoorsdata.org/data/us-study-abroad/duration-of-study-abroad/.
Institute of International Education (IIE) (2021b) Fields of study of U.S. study abroad students, 2000/01–2019/20. https://opendoorsdata.org/data/us-study-abroad/fields-of-study/.
Institute of International Education (IIE) (2021c) Profile of U.S. study abroad students, 2000/01–2019/20. https://opendoorsdata.org/data/us-study-abroad/student-profile/.
Irvine, J. (1974) Strategies of manipulation in the Wolof greeting. In R. Bauman and J. Sherzer (eds) *Explorations in the Ethnography of Speaking* (pp. 167–191). Cambridge: Cambridge University Press.
Isabelli, C.A. (2007) Development of the Spanish subjunctive by advanced learners: Study abroad followed by at-home instruction. *Foreign Language Annals* 40, 330–41.
Isabelli-García, C. (2006) Study abroad social networks, motivation and attitudes: Implications for second language acquisition. In M.A. DuFon and E. Churchill (eds) *Language Learners in Study Abroad Contexts* (pp. 231–258). Clevedon: Multilingual Matters.
Isabelli-García, C., Brown, J., Plews, J. and Dewey, C. (2018) Language learning and study abroad. *Language Teaching* 51 (4), 439–484.
Issa, B., Faretta-Stutenburg, M. and Bowden, H. (2020) Grammatical and lexical development during short-term study abroad: Exploring L2 contact and initial proficiency. *Modern Language Journal* 104, 860–879.
Jackson, J. (2006) Ethnographic preparation for short-term study and residence in the target culture. *The International Journal of Intercultural Relations* 30, 77–98.
Jackson, J. (2018) Intervening in the intercultural learning of L2 study abroad students: From research to practice. *Language Teaching* 51, 365–382.
Jenkins, J. (2011) Accommodating (to) ELF in the international university. *Journal of Pragmatics* 43, 926–936.
Keller, J. and Frain, M. (2010) The impact of geo-political events, globalization, and national policies on study abroad programming and participation. In W. Hoffa and S. DePaul (eds) *A History of U.S. Study Abroad: 1965–Present* (pp. 15–53). Carlisle, PA: Forum on Education Abroad.
Khan, S. (2012) *Privilege: The Making of an Adolescent Elite at St. Paul's School*. Princeton, NJ: Princeton University Press.
King, K. and Mackey, A. (2016) Research methodology in second language studies: Trends, concerns and new directions. *Modern Language Journal* 100, 209–227.
Kinginger, C. (2004) Alice doesn't live here anymore: Foreign language learning and identity reconstruction. In A. Pavlenko and A. Blackledge (eds) *Negotiation of Identities in Multilingual Contexts* (pp. 219–242). Clevedon: Multilingual Matters.
Kinginger, C. (2008) Language learning in study abroad: Case studies of Americans in France. *Modern Language Journal* 92, 1–124, monograph.

Kinginger, C. (2009) *Language Learning and Study Abroad: A Critical Reading of Research*. Basingstoke: Palgrave Macmillan.

Kinginger, C. (2016) Echoes of postfeminism in American students' narratives of study abroad in France. *L2 Journal* 8, 76–91.

Kinginger, C. (2019a) Four questions for the next generation of study abroad researchers. In M. Howard (ed.) *Study Abroad, Second Language Acquisition and Interculturality* (pp. 263–278). Bristol: Multilingual Matters.

Kinginger, C. (2019b) Overcoming ethnocentrism in research on language learning abroad. In M. Fuchs, S. Rai and Y. Loiseau (eds) *Study Abroad: Traditions and New Directions* (pp. 15–28). New York: Modern Language Association of America.

Kinginger, C. (2021) Eureka! Or, how I learned to stop worrying and love the survey. *Language Teaching* 54, 38–46.

Kinginger, C. and Carnine, J. (2019) Language learning at the dinner table: Two case studies of French homestays. *Foreign Language Annals* 52, 850–872.

Kinginger, C. and Wu, Q. (2018) Learning Chinese though contextualized language practices in study abroad residence halls: Two case studies. *Annual Review of Applied Linguistics* 38, 102–121.

Kinginger, C. and Schrauf, R. (2023) Mixed-methods research on language learning in study abroad. In C. Pérez-Vidal and C. Sanz (eds) *Methods in Study Abroad Research: Past, Present and Future* (pp. 85–106). Amsterdam: John Benjamins.

Kinginger, C., Wu, Q., Lee, S.-H. and Tan, D. (2016) The short-term homestay as a context for language learning. *Study Abroad Research in Second Language Acquisition and International Education* 1, 34–60.

Konstantinovskii, D. and Voznesenskaia, E. (2009) The sociocultural aspects of education abroad. *Russian Education & Society* 51 (4), 3–28.

Kozulin, A. (1998) *Psychological Tools: A Sociocultural Approach to Education*. Cambridge, MA: Harvard University Press.

Kramsch, C. (2003) The privilege of the non-native speaker. In C. Blyth (ed.) *The Sociolinguistics of Foreign-Language Classrooms: Contributions of the Native, the Near-Native, and the Non-Native Speaker* (pp. 359–369). Boston, MA: Thomson Heinle.

Kramsch, C. (2006) Preview article: The multilingual subject. *International Journal of Applied Linguistics* 16, 97–110.

Kroll, J. and Dussias, P. (2017) The benefits of multilingualism to the personal and professional development of residents of the US. *Foreign Language Annals* 50, 248–259.

Kubota, R. (2016) The social imaginary of study abroad: Complexities and contradictions. *The Language Learning Journal* 44, 347–357.

Landau, J. and Chioni-Moore, D. (2001) Towards reconciliation in the Motherland: Race, class, nationality, gender and the complexities of the American student presence at the University of Ghana, Legon. *Frontiers: The International Journal of Study Abroad* 7, 25–59.

Lantolf, J.P. and Swain, M. (2020) *Perezhivanie*: The cognitive-emotional dialectic within the social situation of development. In A.H. Al-Hoorie and P.D. MacIntyre (eds) *Contemporary Language Motivation Theory: 60 Years Since Gardner and Lambert (1959)* (pp. 80–105). Bristol: Multilingual Matters.

Lanvers, K., Thompson, A. and East, M. (2021) Introduction: Is language learning in Anglophone countries in crisis? In K. Lanvers, A. Thompson and M. East (eds) *Language Learning in Anglophone Countries: Challenges, Practices, Ways Forward* (pp. 1–15). Cham: Palgrave Macmillan.

Lee, C. (2021) *My Year Abroad*. New York: Riverhead Books.

Lee, S.-H. and Kinginger, C. (2018) Narrative remembering of intercultural encounters: An activity-theoretic study of language program reintegration after study abroad. *Modern Language Journal* 102, 578–593.

Lee, S.-H., Wu, Q., Di, C. and Kinginger, C. (2017) Learning to eat politely at the Chinese homestay dinner table: Two contrasting case studies. *Foreign Language Annals* 50, 135–158.

Levenstein, H. (2004) *We'll Always Have Paris: American Tourists in France Since 1930.* Chicago, IL: University of Chicago Press.

Linde, C. (1993) *Life Stories: The Creation of Coherence.* New York: Oxford University Press.

Liu, S. and Kinginger, C. (2021) The sociocultural ontogenesis of international students' use of pragmatic strategies in ELF academic communication: Two contrasting case studies. *Journal of Pragmatics* 186, 364–381.

Looney, D. and Lusin, N. (2019) *Enrollments in Languages Other than English in United States Institutions of Higher Education, Summer 2016 and Fall 2016: Final Report.* Modern Language Association of America. https://www.mla.org/content/download/110154/2406932/2016-Enrollments-Final-Report.pdf.

Macaro, E., Curle, S., Pun, J., An, J. and Dearden, J. (2018) A systematic review of English medium instruction in higher education. *Language Teaching* 51, 36–76.

Magnan, S. and Back, M. (2007) Social interaction and linguistic gain during study abroad. *Foreign Language Annals* 40, 43–61.

Marijuan, S. and Sanz, C. (2018) Expanding boundaries: Current and new directions in study abroad research and practice. *Foreign Language Annals* 51, 185–204.

Mauranen, A. (2018) Conceptualising ELF. In J. Jenkins, W. Baker and M. Dewey (eds) *The Routledge Handbook of English as a Lingua Franca* (pp. 7–24). Abingdon: Routledge.

McAdams, D. (2006) The role of narrative in personality psychology today. *Narrative Inquiry* 16, 11–18.

McGregor, J. and Fernández, J. (2019) Theorizing qualitative interviews: Two autoethnographic reconstructions. *Modern Language Journal* 103 (1), 227–247.

McManus, K., Mitchell, R. and Tracy-Ventura, N. (2014) Understanding insertion and integration in a study abroad context: The case of English-speaking sojourners in France. *Revue Française de Linguistique Appliquée* 14 (2), 97–116.

McManus, K., Mitchell, R. and Tracy-Ventura, N. (2021) A longitudinal study of advanced learners' linguistic development before, during, and after study abroad. *Applied Linguistics* 42 (1), 136–163.

Menard-Warwick, J. (2019) Bocadillos and the karate club: Translingual identity narratives from study abroad participants. *Linguistics and Education* 50, 84–93.

Miller, L. and Ginsberg, R. (1995) Folklinguistic theories of language learning. In B. Freed (ed.) *Second Language Acquisition in a Study Abroad Context* (pp. 293–315). Amsterdam: John Benjamins.

Mitchell, R., Tracy-Ventura, N. and McManus, K. (2017) *Anglophone Students Abroad: Identity, Social Relationships and Language Learning.* New York: Routledge.

Mitchell, R., Tracy-Ventura, N. and Huensch, A. (2020) After study abroad: The maintenance of multilingual identity among Anglophone language graduates. *Modern Language Journal* 104, 327–344.

Mitic, R. (2020) Global learning for local serving: Establishing the links between study abroad and post-college volunteering. *Research in Higher Education* 61, 603–627.

Mok, N. (2015) Toward an understanding of perezhivanie for sociocultural SLA research. *Language and Sociocultural Theory* 2, 139–159.

Morton, J. (2019) *Moving Up Without Losing Your Way: The Ethical Costs of Upward Mobility.* Princeton, NJ: Princeton University Press.

Murphy, D., Sahakyan, N., Yong-Yi, D. and Magnan, S. (2014) The impact of study abroad on the global engagement of university graduates. *Frontiers: The Interdisciplinary Journal of Study Abroad* 24, 1–23.

National Center for Education Statistics (2007) Digest of education statistics. https://nces.ed.gov/pubs2007/2007017.pdf.

Norris, E. and Gillespie, J. (2009) How study abroad shapes global careers: Evidence from the United States. *Journal of Studies in International Education* 13, 382–397.

O'Dowd, R. and Lewis, T. (eds) (2016) *Online Intercultural Exchange: Policy, Pedagogy, Practice.* New York: Routledge.

Ollman, B. (2003) *Dance of the Dialectic: Steps in Marx's Method*. Urbana, IL: University of Illinois Press.

Orahood, T., Kruze, L. and Pearson, D. (2004) The impact of study abroad on business students' career goals. *Frontiers: The Interdisciplinary Journal of Study Abroad* 10, 117–130.

Packer, M. (2018) *The Science of Qualitative Research*. New York: Cambridge University Press.

Paige, R.M., Fry, G.W., Stallman, E.M., Josic, J. and Jon, J. (2009) Study abroad for global engagement: The long-term impact of mobility experiences. *Intercultural Education* 20, S29–S44.

Pavlenko, A. (2003) 'Language of the enemy': Foreign language education and national identity. *International Journal of Bilingual Education and Bilingualism* 6, 313–331.

Pavlenko, A. (2007) Autobiographic narratives as data in applied linguistics. *Applied Linguistics* 28, 163–188.

Plews, J. (2016) The post-sojourn in study abroad research – Another frontier. *Comparative and International Education/Education Comparée et Internationale* 45, 1–13.

Polanyi, L. (1995) Language learning and living abroad: Stories from the field. In B. Freed (ed.) *Second Language Acquisition in a Study Abroad Context* (pp. 271–291). Amsterdam: John Benjamins.

Prior, M. (2011) Self-presentation in L2 interview talk: Narrative versions, accountability, and emotionality. *Applied Linguistics* 32 (1), 60–76.

Pryde, M. (2014) Conversational patterns of homestay hosts and study abroad students. *Foreign Language Annals* 47, 492–500.

Purhonen, S. and Wright, D. (2013) Methodological issues in national-comparative research on cultural tastes: The case of cultural capital in the UK and Finland. *Cultural Sociology* 7 (2), 257–273.

Reddy, M.J. (1979) The conduit metaphor: A case of frame conflict in our language about language. In A. Ortony (ed.) *Metaphor and Thought* (pp. 284–310). Cambridge: Cambridge University Press.

Reinders, H., Lai, C. and Sundqvist, P. (eds) (2022) *The Routledge Handbook of Language Learning and Teaching Beyond the Classroom*. New York: Routledge.

Rexeisen, R.J., Anderson, P.H., Lawton, L. and Hubbard, A.C. (2008) Study abroad and intercultural development: A longitudinal study. *Frontiers: The Interdisciplinary Journal of Study Abroad* 17, 1–20.

Riazi, A. (2017) *Mixed Methods Research in Language Teaching and Learning*. Sheffield: Equinox.

Riazi, A. and Candlin C. (2014) Mixed methods research in language teaching and learning: Opportunities, issues and challenges. *Language Teaching* 47 (2), 135–173.

Riegelhaupt, F. and Carrasco, R. (2000) Mexico host family reactions to a bilingual Chicana teacher in Mexico: A case study of language and culture clash. *Bilingual Research Journal* 24, 405–421.

Riessman, C. (1993) *Narrative Research*. London: Sage.

Ross, K. (1995) *Fast Cars, Clean Bodies: Decolonization and the Reordering of French Culture*. Cambridge, MA: MIT Press.

Salisbury, M.H., An, B.P. and Pascarella, E.T. (2013) The effect of study abroad on intercultural competence among undergraduate college students. *Journal of Student Affairs Research and Practice* 50, 1–20.

Sanz, C. and Morales-Front, A. (eds) (2018) *The Routledge Handbook of Study Abroad Research and Practice*. New York: Routledge.

Savignon, S. (1997) *Communicative Competence: Theory and Classroom Practice*. New York: McGraw-Hill.

Schmidt, R. (1990) The role of consciousness in second language learning. *Applied Linguistics* 11, 129–158.

Schmidt, R. and Frota, S. (1986) Developing basic conversational ability in a second language: A case study of an adult learner of Portuguese. In R. Day (ed.) *Talking to Learn* (pp. 237–326). Rowley, MA: Newbury House.

Schrauf, R.W. (2013) Using correspondence analysis to model immigrant multilingualism over time. In J. Duarte and I. Gogolin (eds) *Linguistic Super-Diversity in Urban Areas – Research Approaches* (pp. 27–43). Amsterdam: John Benjamins.
Schrauf, R.W. (2016) *Mixed Methods: Interviews, Surveys, and Cross-Cultural Comparisons.* Cambridge: Cambridge University Press.
Seargeant, P. and Swann, J. (2012) *English in the World: History, Diversity, Change.* New York: Routledge.
Seidlhofer, B. (2000) Mind the gap: English as a mother tongue vs. English as a lingua franca. *Vienna English Working Papers* 9, 51–69.
Seidlhofer, B. (2011) *Understanding English as a Lingua Franca.* Oxford: Oxford University Press.
Shiri, S. (2015) The homestay in intensive language study abroad: Social networks, language socialization, and developing intercultural competence. *Foreign Language Annals* 48, 5–25.
Sicola, L. (2005) 'Communicative lingerings': Exploring awareness of L2 influence on L1 in American expatriates after re-entry. *Language Awareness* 14, 153–169.
Siegal, M. (1996) The role of learner subjectivity in second language sociolinguistic competency: Western women learning Japanese. *Applied Linguistics* 17, 356–382.
Stallman, E., Woodruff, G., Kasravi, J. and Comp, D. (2010) The diversification of the student profile. In W. Hoffa and S. DePaul (eds) *A History of U.S. Study Abroad: 1965–Present* (pp. 115–160). Carlisle, PA: Forum on Education Abroad.
Sweeney, E. and Hua, Z. (2010) Accommodating toward your audience: Do native speakers of English know how to accommodate their communication strategies toward nonnative speakers of English? *International Journal of Business Communication* 47, 477–504.
Taguchi, N. and Collentine, J. (2018) Language learning in a study-abroad context: Research agenda. *Language Teaching* 51, 553–566.
Talmy, S. (2011) The interview as collaborative achievement: Interaction, identity and ideology in a speech event. *Applied Linguistics* 32 (1), 25–42.
Tashakkori, A. and Teddlie, C. (eds) (2010) *SAGE Handbook of Mixed Methods in Social and Behavioral Research* (2nd edn). Thousand Oaks, CA: Sage.
Terkel, S. (1974) *Working: People Talk About What They Do All Day and How They Feel About What They Do.* New York: Pantheon/Random House.
Toffoli, D. (2020) *Informal Learning and Institution-Wide Language Provision: University Language Learners in the 21st Century.* Basingstoke: Palgrave Macmillan.
Tracy-Ventura, N., Huensch, A. and Mitchell, R. (2020) Understanding the long-term evolution of L2 lexical diversity: The contribution of a longitudinal learner corpus. In B. Le Bruyn and M. Paquot (eds) *Learner Corpus Research and Second Language Acquisition* (pp. 148–171). Cambridge: Cambridge University Press.
Tracy-Ventura, N., Dewaele, J.-M., Köylü, Z. and McManus, K. (2016) Personality changes after the 'year abroad'? *Study Abroad Research in Second Language Acquisition and International Education* 1, 107–127.
Trentman, E. and Diao, W. (2017) The American gaze east: Discourses and destinations of US study abroad. *Study Abroad Research in Second Language Acquisition and International Education* 2, 175–205.
Tullock, B. (2018) Identity and study abroad. In C. Sanz and A. Morales-Front (eds) *The Routledge Handbook of Study Abroad Research and Practice* (pp. 262–274). New York: Routledge.
Van Compernolle, R.A. (2019) The qualitative science of Vygotskian sociocultural psychology and L2 development. In J.W. Schwieter and A. Benati (eds) *The Cambridge Handbook of Language Learning* (pp. 62–83). Cambridge: Cambridge University Press.
Vande Berg, M., Connor-Linton, J. and Paige, R. (2009) The Georgetown Consortium Project: Interventions for student learning abroad. *Frontiers: The Interdisciplinary Journal of Study Abroad* 18, 1–75.

Veresov, N. (2017) The concept of perezhivanie in cultural-historical theory: Content and contexts. In M. Fleer, F. Rey and N. Veresov (eds) *Perezhivanie, Emotions and Subjectivity: Advancing Vygotsky's Legacy* (pp. 47–70). Singapore: Springer Nature.

Veresov, N. and Mok, N. (2018) Understanding development through the *perezhivanie* of learning. In J.P. Lantolf, M. Poehner and M. Swain (eds) *The Routledge Handbook of Sociocultural Theory and Second Language Development* (pp. 89–101). New York: Routledge.

Vygotsky, L.S. (1978) *Mind in Society: The Development of Higher Psychological Processes*. Cambridge, MA: Harvard University Press.

Vygotsky, L.S. (1987) *The Collected Works of L.S. Vygotsky: Volume 1. Problems of General Psychology* (R.W. Rieber and A.S. Carton, eds). Boston, MA: Springer.

Vygotsky, L.S. (1994) The problem of the environment. In R. van der Veer and J. Valsiner (eds) *The Vygotsky Reader* (pp. 338–354). Cambridge: Blackwell.

Whatley, M. (2017) The role of heritage-seeking in the study abroad destination decision-making of minority students. *NAFSA Research Symposium Series* 1, 18–30.

Widdowson, H. (1994) The ownership of English. *TESOL Quarterly* 28, 377–389.

Wieland, M. (1990) Politeness-based misunderstanding in conversations between native speakers of French and American advanced learners of French. Unpublished PhD thesis, Indiana University.

Wilkinson, S. (1998) Study abroad from the participants' perspective: A challenge to common beliefs. *Foreign Language Annals* 31, 23–39.

Winke, P. and Gass, S. (2018) When some study abroad: How returning students realign with the curriculum and impact learning. In C. Sanz and A. Morales-Front (eds) *The Routledge Handbook of Study Abroad Research and Practice* (pp. 526–543). New York: Routledge.

Zemach-Bersin, T. (2007) Global citizenship and study abroad: It's all about U.S. *Critical Literacy: Theories and Practices* 1, 16–28.

Zemach-Bersin, T. (2009) Selling the world: Study abroad marketing and the privatization of global citizenship. In R. Lewin (ed.) *The Handbook of Practice and Research in Study Abroad: Higher Education and the Quest for Global Citizenship* (pp. 303–320). New York: Routledge.

Zhuang, J. and Kinginger, C. (2022) Conceptual metaphors about language and language learning in life history interviews with study abroad alumni. Paper presented at the American Association for Applied Linguistics, Pittsburgh, March.

Index

academic literacy 11, 167
adventure, discourses of 19, 163, 171
Africa 9, 74, 107, 108, 112, 149, 159
American Academy of Arts and Sciences 1, 168
American Councils for International Education xi, 3, 24, 53
Arabic 17, 20, 28, 37, 38, 56, 77, 80, 81, 154, 167
audio-lingual method 127

business 1, 3, 11, 20, 35, 38, 54, 55, 57, 66, 83, 84, 86, 89, 90, 94, 95, 97, 99, 100, 119, 133, 136, 141, 147, 150, 159, 161, 164, 167, 168, 169, 170, 176, 177

Chinese 10, 20, 28, 29, 36, 37, 38, 39, 56, 65, 72, 75, 76, 77, 78, 106, 126, 132, 153, 158, 161
class-related life horizons 132
communicative lingerings 148, 150
creative writing 36, 40, 106, 108
culinary practices 143
Cultural-Historical theory (CHT) 42

Doctors Without Borders 72, 132
drama 3, 44, 49, 54, 85, 106, 112, 123, 132, 133, 135, 139, 166, 169
    cognitive-emotional 44, 45, 48, 57, 88, 89, 106, 112, 116, 123, 132, 133, 135, 139, 152, 166, 169
    developmental 3, 43, 45, 84, 105, 169
desire 1, 10, 17, 21, 63, 89, 92, 94, 97, 102, 104, 115, 120, 123, 131, 133, 140, 141, 148, 164, 167, 169

empathy 9, 20, 52, 59, 86, 92, 122, 123, 158, 162, 164
employment 3, 8, 11, 14, 16, 20, 23, 30, 31, 32, 34, 35, 55, 57, 59, 62, 67, 71, 75, 81, 86, 87, 88, 91, 101, 103, 114, 117, 118, 119, 123, 131, 153, 155, 164, 168, 169, 170, 173, 174, 176

English as a lingua franca (ELF) 18, 153, 155
English-Medium Instruction 2
engineering 3, 54, 57, 71, 83, 97, 115, 117, 118, 164, 169, 177
enjoyment, foreign language 10, 27, 103, 161, 173, 174, 175, 176, 177

Fante/Twi 40
The Forum on Education Abroad xi, 2, 3, 24, 53
Foreign Service 36, 37, 38, 46, 75, 76, 77, 78, 79, 126, 131, 132, 139, 146, 164
French 8, 9, 10, 12, 13, 14, 17, 26, 27, 28, 29, 36, 37, 38, 39, 40, 46, 56, 57, 58, 60, 61, 62, 63, 68, 69, 70, 71, 72, 74, 77, 79, 81, 82, 83, 85, 93, 107, 109, 121, 122, 126, 134, 138, 139, 141, 142, 143, 146, 147, 154, 159, 164

German 12, 28, 29, 36, 37, 38, 40, 56, 60, 63, 64, 77, 89, 90, 117, 126, 138, 153, 160, 164
Global engagement 6, 7, 21, 169
government service 3, 20, 54, 57, 76, 86, 131, 132, 164, 167, 169, 170
Grand Tour 16, 18, 20, 146

healthcare 3, 52, 54, 55, 57, 72, 73, 75, 86, 93, 122, 164, 169, 170
homestay 5, 8, 10, 13, 36, 37, 38, 39, 40, 57, 60, 61, 66, 78, 99, 107, 124, 131, 134, 135, 136, 138, 139, 140, 141, 142, 143, 144, 145, 146, 152, 154, 159, 167, 168
hospitality industry 89
host families 61, 136, 139

identity 6, 13, 35, 51, 58, 62, 69, 101, 102, 104, 105, 106, 110, 111, 114, 115, 123, 126, 150, 166
    development 6, 10, 11, 166
    heritage 4, 89, 93, 99, 103, 105, 107, 114, 123, 173, 174

multilingual 1, 4, 6, 11, 29, 89, 106, 131, 134, 150, 153, 154, 155, 156, 157, 159, 162, 164, 167, 172
queer 106, 117, 123, 150
translingual 13
transnational 6, 21, 131, 152, 166
Institute of International Education (IIE) 1, 26
Insurance 40, 93, 95, 96, 121, 122, 127, 157
Intercultural Communicative Competence (ICC) 7, 21
international development 3, 9, 38, 57, 72, 74, 76, 80, 145, 164
international education administration 113, 139
isiZulu 40, 112
Italian 28, 36, 38, 39, 40, 56, 60, 70, 99, 100, 106, 113, 165

JET (Japan Exchange Teaching) Program 111
Japanese xi, 8, 13, 14, 15, 28, 36, 38, 56, 65, 66, 67, 68, 77, 78, 93, 94, 95, 110, 112, 126, 136, 140, 141, 151, 157, 167

Korean 14, 28, 29, 36, 37, 38, 40, 77, 78, 110, 112, 113, 126, 127, 128, 131, 132

LANGSNAP (Languages and Social Networks Abroad Project) 10
life history typology 23, 30, 53, 163, 164, 171

Major League Baseball 84, 85
marine biology 39, 90, 169
market strategy 36, 89, 93, 141, 157, 169
mixed-methods xi, 2, 4, 5, 14, 15, 22, 23, 30, 53, 152, 165, 171
Modern Language Association of America 1
multiple correspondence analysis 3, 15, 30, 31
multiple sojourns abroad 75, 130, 171

narrative 3, 4, 12, 13, 35, 44, 47, 48, 49, 50, 51, 52, 53, 58, 132, 161, 171
  analysis 12, 47, 48
  coherence 45, 49, 50, 51, 88, 135
  ontological significance 49, 152, 165
  research 49
native speaker problem 156, 157, 162, 168
Navajo 36, 105, 109, 110
neoliberalism 21, 50
nursing 39, 89, 92, 93, 141, 169

online language teaching 40

Perezhivanie 43, 44, 45, 89, 132, 169
politeness xi, 67, 108, 150, 151
Portuguese 14, 26, 28, 56, 60, 96
problem solving 11, 86, 153, 160, 162, 168
psycholinguistics 38, 63, 97, 98, 161

renewable energy 40, 89, 90, 147, 160, 169
residence halls 146, 147
Russian 8, 9, 14, 28, 36, 37, 39, 56, 72, 75, 77, 81, 82, 117, 147, 150, 153, 164, 166

short-term programs 124, 128, 129, 130
Spanish 10, 12, 13, 26, 27, 28, 29, 36, 37, 38, 39, 40, 56, 57, 59, 60, 70, 72, 73, 74, 83, 84, 91, 97, 98, 105, 106, 107, 109, 113, 114, 115, 116, 117, 118, 126, 127, 128, 133, 134, 144, 145, 146, 149, 153, 154, 155, 157, 158, 159, 160, 161

technology 2, 4, 16, 17, 21, 22, 37, 55, 56, 83, 94, 99, 119, 124, 125, 126, 128, 147, 153, 154, 161, 164, 176
text reality 45, 51
theater arts 57, 83, 85, 86, 93

whole lives approach 165
Wolof 8, 39, 93, 141, 142

For Product Safety Concerns and Information please contact our EU Authorised Representative:

Easy Access System Europe

Mustamäe tee 50

10621 Tallinn

Estonia

gpsr.requests@easproject.com